HISTORICAL
GERMAN PHONOLOGY
AND MORPHOLOGY

HISTORICAL
GERMAN PHONOLOGY
AND MORPHOLOGY

CHARLES V. J. RUSS
M.A., M.LITT., PH.D.
LECTURER IN GERMAN AND LINGUISTICS,
DEPARTMENT OF LANGUAGE
UNIVERSITY OF YORK

CLARENDON PRESS · OXFORD
1978

Oxford University Press, Walton Street, Oxford OX2 6DP

OXFORD LONDON GLASGOW
NEW YORK TORONTO MELBOURNE WELLINGTON
IBADAN NAIROBI DAR ES SALAAM LUSAKA CAPE TOWN
KUALA LUMPUR SINGAPORE JAKARTA HONG KONG TOKYO
DELHI BOMBAY CALCUTTA MADRAS KARACHI

© *Charles V. J. Russ 1978*

All rights reserved. No part of this publication may be reproduced, stored in a retrieval system, or transmitted, in any form or by any means, electronic, mechanical, photocopying, recording, or otherwise, without the prior permission of Oxford University Press

British Library Cataloguing in Publication Data

Russ, Charles J V
   Historical German phonology and morphology.
   – (Oxford history of the German language; vol. 2).
   1. German language – Phonology 2. German language –
   Morphology 3. German language – History
   I. Title II. Series
   431′.5′09   PF3131   78–40248
   ISBN 0-19-815727-4

*Printed in Great Britain by
Richard Clay (The Chaucer Press) Ltd.,
Bungay, Suffolk*

to
Jenny and Jamie

PREFACE

IN 1968 Historical German Syntax by W. B. Lockwood was published and this was to be the first of a three volume Oxford History of German under the general editorship of the late Professor C. T. Carr of St. Andrews. Due to considerable delays this volume on phonology and morphology has appeared a decade later. It is intended both to replace J. Wright's Historical German Grammar, of which only the first volume appeared, and to augment it with a volume on syntax. This volume is intended primarily for those students beginning the subject. For this reason no recourse is made (at any stage) to a detailed analysis of any specific texts or author. It is, however, hoped that beginners will be bold enough to fight their way through the section on Primitive Indo-European. This volume may also be used by more advanced students since ample opportunity is given to provide further reading. Professor Carr felt that some mention should be made of how German developed and also of its relationship with other Germanic languages. This has been catered for in the brief introduction, which aims to do no more than point the way to weightier works. The exposition is largely descriptive and attempts to synthesize traditional philology with the phonemic approach. The main thought has been to provide a textbook which clearly sets out the development of German, thus the problematic nature of Old High German, Middle High German and even New High German is neglected in favour of giving an overall picture.

I am very grateful to the late Professor Carr for editorial help and to the Oxford University Press for their expertise in providing the many different symbols I asked for. Last, but not least, I am very indebted to my wife who has supported me throughout this work. She will be very relieved to see its completion.

York
19 June 1978

C. V. J. RUSS

CONTENTS

CONTENTS

ABBREVIATIONS

Gmc.	Germanic
PIE	Proto-Indo-European
PG	Primitive Germanic
OE	Old English
OLG	Old Low German
ON	Old Norse
OHG	Old High German
MHG	Middle High German
NHG	New High German
UG	Upper German
CG	Central German
LG	Low German
ECG	East Central German
WCG	West Central German
sg.	singular
pl.	plural
nom.	nominative
acc.	accusative
gen.	genitive
dat.	dative

PHONETIC AND OTHER SYMBOLS

p   voiceless bilabial stop as in German *packen*, English *pack*.
b   voiced bilabial stop as in German *Bein*, English *bone*.
t   voiceless alveolar stop as in German *tun*, English *tin*.
d   voiced alveolar stop as in German *du*, English *do*.
k   voiceless palato-velar stop as in German *kann*, English *can*.
g   voiced palato-velar stop as in German *gehen*, English *go*.
ʔ   glottal stop as in German *Theater* [theː ʔatər].
w   voiced bilabial fricative or semi-vowel as in English *win*.
v   voiced labio-dental fricative as in German *Wein*, English *vine*.
f   voiceless labio-dental fricative as in German *fein*, English *fine*.
θ   voiceless dental fricative as in English *thin*.
ð   voiced dental fricative as in English *then*.
s   voiceless alveolar fricative as in German *Wasser*, English *save, race*.
z   voiced alveolar fricative as in German *sein*, English *zeal, raise*.
ʃ   voiceless palato-alveolar fricative as in German *schön*, English *shone*.
ʒ   voiced palato-alveolar fricative as in German *Genie*, English *rouge*.
ç   voiceless palatal fricative as in German *ich*.
j   voiced palatal fricative or semi-vowel as in German *ja*, English *yes*.
h   glottal fricative as in German *Hahn*, English *hen*.
m   bilabial nasal as in German *mein*, English *mine*.
n   alveolar nasal as in German *nein*, English *nine*.
ŋ   velar nasal as in German *sang*, English *song*.
l   palatal lateral as in German *lachen*, English *laugh*.
ł   velarized lateral as in English *fall*.
r   dental trill as in prescribed pronunciation of German *reiten*.
R   uvular trill most common pronunciation of German *reiten*.
ɹ   dental frictionless continuant as in English *ready*.
ɾ   dental flap as in English *very*.
ʁ   uvular frictionless continuant as in German *breit*.
pf   voiceless labial affricate as in German *Pfad*.

ts   voiceless alveolar affricate as in German *Zaun.*

tʃ   voiceless palato-alveolar affricate as in German *lutschen,* English *church.*

dʒ   voiced palato-alveolar affricate as in English *judge.*

m̩,n̩,l̩, syllabic nasals and liquid as in German colloquial pronunciation of *leben,* e.g. [leːbm̩], *reden,* [reːdn̩], *Mantel* [mantl̩], and English *ridden, little.*

a   short unrounded open central vowel as in German *Mann.*

ɛ   short unrounded half-open front vowel as in German *Bett,* English *bet.*

æ   short unrounded vowel as in English *hat,* more open than [ɛ].

ɔ   short rounded half-open back vowel as in German *Gott,* English *got.*

I   short unrounded close front vowel as in German *mit,* English *wit.*

e   short unrounded half-close vowel as in MHG *bezzer.*

U   short rounded close back vowel as in German *Fuchs,* English *looks.*

Y   short rounded close front vowel as in German *Hütte.*

œ   short rounded half-open front vowel as in German *können.*

ʌ   short unrounded back, slightly centralized, vowel as in English *but.*

ə   short unstressed half-open central vowel as in German *bitte,* English *bitter.*

iː   long unrounded close front vowel as in German *Biene.*

uː long rounded close back vowel as in German *Blut.*

yː long rounded close front vowel as in German *Bühne.*

eː long unrounded half-close front vowel as in German *leben.*

ɛː long unrounded half-open front vowel as in the prescribed pronunciation of *Bären.*

oː long rounded half-close back vowel as in German *loben.*

ɔː long rounded half-open back vowel as in English *law.*

øː long rounded half-close front vowel as in German *Söhne.*

aː long unrounded open central vowel as in German *Vater,* English *father.*

ɜː long unrounded half-open central vowel as in English *bird.*

ai diphthong as in German *mein,* English *mine.*

au diphthong as in German *Haus,* English *house.*

øy diphthong as in the prescribed pronunciation of German *euch.*

oi diphthong as in some pronunciations of German *euch,* English *boy.*

ei diphthong as in English *name*.

ɔu diphthong as in English *stone*.

ɐ short unstressed central vowel more open than [ə], as in colloquial German pronunciation of -*er*

[ ] encloses phonetic symbols.

/ / encloses phonemic symbols.

* signifies a reconstructed form.

¯, ^ signifies that a vowel is long.

~ signifies that a vowel is nasalized.

The following phonetic signs not belonging to the International Phonetic Alphabet are used:

ƀ voiced labio-dental fricative as in German *Löwe*, English *give* (IPA v).

g̣ voiced palato-velar fricative as in Dutch *dagen*, or North German *Tage* (IPA ɣ).

þ voiceless dental fricative as in English *thing* (IPA θ).

ṣ voiceless apico-alveolar fricative as in MHG *was*.

ş voiceless pre-dorsal alveolar fricative as in MHG *waz*.

ǭ long half-open back rounded vowel as in ON *nǭmum* (IPA ɔ:).

MAP OF MODERN GERMAN DIALECT AREAS

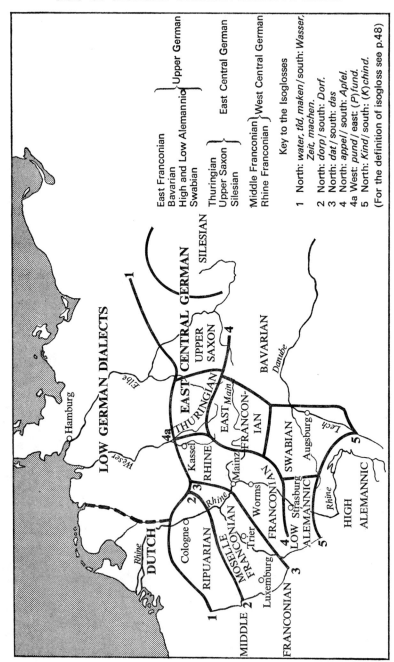

Upper German
{ East Franconian
  Bavarian
  High and Low Alemannic
  Swabian

East Central German
{ Thuringian
  Upper Saxon
  Silesian

West Central German
{ Middle Franconian
  Rhine Franconian

Key to the Isoglosses

1 North: *water, tîd, maken* / south: *Wasser, Zeit, machen.*
2 North: *dorp* / south: *Dorf.*
3 North: *dat* / south: *das*
4 North: *appel* / south: *Apfel.*
4a West: *pund* / east: (*P*)*fund.*
5 North: *Kind* / south: (*K*)*chind.*
(For the definition of isogloss see p.48)

THE ORGANS OF SPEECH

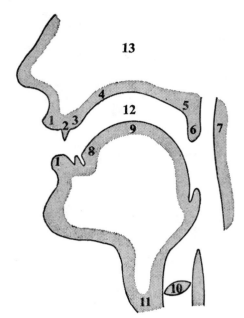

1 Lips
2 Upper teeth
3 Alveolar ridge
4 Hard palate
5 Soft palate or velum
6 Uvula
7 Pharynx
8 Apex of tongue
9 Dorsum or back of tongue
10 Vocal cords
11 Larynx
12 Oral cavity
13 Nasal cavity

POSITIONS OF VOCAL CORDS

1 Closed as for glottal stop

2 Open as for breath. The space between the vocal cords is called the glottis

3 Vibrating as for voiced sounds

GENERAL INTRODUCTION

GERMAN AND THE GERMANIC LANGUAGES

A COMPARISON of words such as German *Tag*, English *day*, Dutch *dag* [dax], Swedish *dag* shows how similar these forms are in the various languages. The reason for this similarity is that these languages are genetically related, that is proto-forms can be reconstructed by comparing cognates from different languages (words which are similar in form and meaning). For instance, from Gothic *dags*, Old Norse *dagr*, OHG *tag*, OE *dæg*, the Primitive Germanic form **dagaz* can be reconstructed. (For the use of * see p. 28, and for the origin of the second *a* see pp. 99 f.) If languages are related there will be sufficient cognates to allow a reconstruction of a large part of the vocabulary common to the parent or proto-language and it is usual to call languages related in this way a language family. German belongs to the Germanic language family.

The ancestor of the Germanic languages is called Primitive Germanic or sometimes Proto-Germanic. Primitive Germanic is reconstructed by comparing the records of the oldest Germanic languages. Gothic is the Germanic language of which the earliest literary records are extant; it is in fact the language of the Goths who migrated from Scandinavia to the Vistula delta and moved to the shores of the Black Sea after A.D. 200. The Goths were converted to Arian Christianity and the most important linguistic record they have left to posterity is a Gothic version of the Bible by Bishop Wulfila (311–83). In the sixteenth century Busbecq, a Flemish envoy to Constantinople, drew up a list of Gothic words which he had heard in the Crimea, but Gothic seems to have died out soon after this.

Another Germanic language with old records is Old Norse, of which Runic inscriptions exist from the third century A.D. The language in these inscriptions is very archaic and similar to

Primitive Germanic. Since most of the records of this language from about 700 to 1200 were written in Iceland the language of this period is sometimes known as Old Icelandic. Written records from this time are also to be found in Old Norwegian. Old Icelandic and Old Norwegian are together referred to as West Norse. Their modern descendants are Icelandic and Faroese, the latter having had a standard form only since the last century, as well as the two Norwegian languages, Bokmål and Nynorsk. Old Danish and Old Swedish have written records from the twelfth century and Runic inscriptions from a century earlier. Together they are known as East Norse; they are the ancestors of modern Danish and Swedish.

Old English has copious records, works of literature as well as glosses and translations, the earliest of which go back as far as the eighth century. Middle English dates from 1100 to 1500; the period after 1500 is called Modern English.

Old Frisian, which has some similarity to Old English, was spoken in modern Friesland, in the Netherlands province of North Holland, and also in some areas of Germany bordering on Friesland. Originally it may have been spoken all along the North German coast as far as Denmark. To this only the relics of North Frisian speech on the North Frisian Islands and part of the mainland of Schleswig-Holstein bear witness. Old Frisian dates from the thirteenth century and most of the texts are legal documents. The descendant of Old Frisian is modern Frisian which is now spoken in the province of Friesland.

Old High German, like Old English, has records dating from the eighth century. The oldest German book is usually considered to be the *Abrogans*, a Latin–German glossary, probably produced in 756 in Freising, so-called because the first word is *abrogans*. The Upper German dialects of OHG were: Alemannic, Bavarian, and East Franconian. Alemannic was spoken in the area from Switzerland northwards up the Rhine to Worms; in the east its domain probably stretched as far as the River Lech. Bavarian was that part of the OHG speech area south of the Main and east of the Lech. East Franconian had as its centre the monastery of Fulda and probably stretched from the River Fulda and Rhön massif in the east to the Westerwald in the west. The Central German dialects of OHG were Middle and Rhine Franconian, Middle Franconian covering an area from north of Cologne to just north of

Mainz. This latter may be divided into Ripuarian, spoken in the
area around Cologne, and Moselle Franconian, the area with
Trier as its main town. Rhine Franconian was the dialect of the
area from Mainz to Strasburg. The southernmost part of Rhine
Franconian, from Worms southwards, is often referred to separately as South Rhine Franconian. The monk Otfrid produced his
Evangelienbuch (*c.* 863–71) in this variety of OHG, which was
slightly different from normal Rhine Franconian.

Old Low German is the collective name for Old Low Franconian, which was spoken in the southern part of the present-day
Netherlands and the eastern part of Belgium, together with old
Saxon, which was spoken from the eastern frontier of the Netherlands to the Elbe and in the western part of Schleswig-Holstein.
Old Low Franconian has only sparse written records from about
the tenth century, the most complete of these being a translation
of the Psalms. The most famous of the Old Saxon works is the
Heliand, an epic poem in alliterative verse on the life of Christ,
believed to have been written about 830. The descendants of
Old Low Franconian and Old Saxon are Middle Dutch (1170–
1500), which has an extensive literature, and Middle Low German
(1100–1500), respectively. In the modern period these have developed into modern Dutch and the present-day Low German
dialects.

THE RELATIONSHIP
BETWEEN THE GERMANIC LANGUAGES

The Germanic languages are not a homogeneous group, but certain languages are obviously more alike than others. It has been
usual to suppose that at one time the Germanic languages consisted of three groups: East Germanic, comprising Gothic,
Burgundian, and Vandalic, the latter two being known only
through proper names; North Germanic, consisting of East and
West Norse; and West Germanic, comprising Old High German,
Old Low German, Old English, and Old Frisian. This division
has been made on the basis of common innovations and retentions
of old forms between the languages. The only real problem is the
West Germanic group which contains the largest number of
languages. The linguistic features which have been adduced to

support a West Germanic unity are not very numerous, the most important being the West Germanic consonant gemination: a consonant other than *r* when followed by a *j*, *r*, or *l* was doubled, Gothic *wilja*, English *will*, (OE *willa*), German *Wille* (see pp. 44 f). Because the innovations by the West Germanic group are by no means numerous some scholars have denied the existence of a West Germanic group and have postulated other groups as stages between Primitive Germanic and the individual Germanic languages, based on the geographical position of certain tribal groups. West Germanic is replaced by three groups: *Elbgermanisch*, taken to be the UG dialects of OHG; *Weser-Rheingermanisch*, the CG Franconian dialects of OHG, and *Nordseegermanisch*, OE, OLG, and probably Old Frisian. The most reasonable explanation seems to be that if there was a West Germanic unity then it was of such short duration that it did not leave many linguistic traits behind.

East and North Germanic share the following innovations. Germanic *w* or *ww* after a short vowel became *ggw* in Gothic and *gg* or *ggv* in ON, whereas in West Germanic a *u* developed in front of it, e.g. Gothic *triggws*, ON *tryggr*, OHG *triuwi*. Germanic *j* or *jj* after a short vowel became *ddj* in Gothic and *ggi* or *gg* in ON whereas in West Germanic an *i* developed in front of it, e.g. Gothic *twaddjē*, ON *tueggia*, OHG *zweiio*. East and North Germanic agree furthermore in retaining the IE perfect ending *-*tha* for the second person sg. past tense of strong verbs, Gothic *namt*, ON *gaft*; West Germanic has -*i*, OE -*e*, which is the IE aorist ending *-*es*, e.g. OHG *nāmi*, *gābi*.

These correspondences have been used to show that at one time there was probably a close relationship between East and North Germanic. In fact the connection may be very old as place-names such as that of the island of Gotland or the Swedish province Götaland may well point to the fact that the Goths originated on the mainland of Scandinavia.

The following innovations are shared by West and North Germanic. Both groups have a long *ā* as the reflex of Germanic *ē¹* (i.e. Germanic *ē¹* corresponds to, or has become, OHG *ā*), whereas in Gothic it is represented by a long *ē*: Gothic *nēmum*, OHG *nāmun* (ninth-century form, see p. 115), ON *nǫmum* (in this form the stem vowel *ā* has become *ǫ* by the influence of the unstressed -*u*, a special development in ON). West and North Germanic have separate reflexes for Germanic *ē¹* and *ē²* (for the origin of these sounds see pp. 42 f.), whereas in Gothic they have merged and are both represented by a long $\bar{e}$: *nēmum* ($\bar{e}^1$), *hēr* ($\bar{e}^2$); OHG *nāmun*, ON *nǫmum* ($\bar{e}^1$), OHG *hier*, *hear*, *hiar* (for the distribution of the different forms in OHG, see p. 55), ON *hēr* ($\bar{e}^2$). Where Gothic has *z* as the reflex of PIE *s*, West and North Germanic have *r*: Gothic *máiza*, OHG *mēro*, ON *meirr*. West and North Germanic show mutation, or umlaut, of back vowels by a following *i* or *j* (this happens at various stages and with various results in the languages concerned), whereas Gothic shows no trace of it: Gothic *harjis*, OHG *heri*, ON *herr*; Gothic *sōkjan*, ON *sœkia*, OE *sēcan* (OHG *suohhen* is a special case); Gothic *þugkjan*, MHG *dünken*, ON *þykkia*, OE *þyncan*.

There are also features common to Gothic and the UG dialects of OHG, e.g. Gothic *is* and OHG *er* can be contrasted with forms in the other West Germanic languages with an initial *h*, e.g. English *he*. Gothic and UG have retained the nasals before the voiceless fricatives: Gothic *fimf*, OHG *finf*, English *five* (with later voicing and diphthongization); Gothic *uns*, English *us*; Gothic *anþar*, English *other*.

Primitive Germanic may have split up into the individual Germanic languages in the following stages.

1. Primitive Germanic, spread over a wide area from Scandinavia to the Elbe, showed dialect features. Possibly Gothic and North Germanic were adjacent to each other and this would account for the similarities between them.
2. The Goths left Scandinavia for the Vistula delta where they may have lived in an area adjacent to the tribes which were later to settle in the south of Germany, thus accounting for the similarities between Gothic and the UG dialects of OHG.
3. The Goths migrated to the Black Sea and the other Germanic languages remained together and developed common innovations which Gothic does not have. This would account for the large number of similarities between West and North Germanic.
4. This North and West Germanic unity split into separate North and West Germanic groups, the latter only remaining together for a short time, leaving very few common linguistic traits. Probably before developing into the individual Germanic languages the West Germanic group split into the three groups: *Elbgermanisch*, *Weser-Rheingermanisch*, and *Nordseegermanisch*.

A SURVEY OF THE PERIODS
OF THE HISTORY OF GERMAN

Old High German and Middle High German

It is usual to divide the historical development of German into four periods: Old High German, Middle High German, Early New High German, and New High German. This division into periods is for the most part arbitrary; it must not be supposed that the periods are separated from each other by rigid boundaries. In this book we will not treat Early NHG as a section in its own right but as a subsection of NHG.

Today it is easy to talk about German knowing we can describe this language and can teach a body of agreed facts. This is characteristic of the modern age in which we are dealing with standard languages which are spoken and understood in most parts of all European countries. When we go back to Old High German we find that this was not the case. OHG can be taken as extending in time from 750 to 1050. It is more realistic to speak of several kinds of OHG than of one particular kind, since all the literary monuments from OHG times show quite a marked difference in spelling and form according to where they come from. The writers of most of the OHG literary monuments were clerics and the centres which produced them were monasteries. It is normally assumed that the differences in writing reflected dialectal differences in pronunciation, each dialect region having one or more centres which produced literary works. For example, St. Gall and Reichenau were the centres of the Alemannic dialect. The most famous works written in Alemannic are: the *Reichenau Glosses* (c. 775–800), the *Benedictine Rule* (c. 800), the *St. Gall Vocabulary* (c. 790), and Notker's translation of the works of Boethius, Aristotle, and the Psalms (c. 1000), referred to as *Notker*. Among the centres of the Bavarian dialect were Mondsee and Freising. Works written in Bavarian are: the *Wessobrunn Prayer* (c. 770–90), the *Muspilli* (c. 800), a fragment of a poem about the end of the world, and the *Exhortatio ad plebem christianam* (c. 815). The centre of the East Franconian dialect in OHG was the famous monastery at Fulda founded by Boniface and the most famous work written in East Franconian is the translation from the Latin version of the Gospel Harmony by Tatian (this work will be referred to as

Tatian). The so-called *Isidor* (*c.* 790–800), which is a translation of the *Tractatus de fide catholica contra Judaeos* by Isidore of Seville, is a most important work. It probably came from the West Franconian region west of Cologne but its exact provenance is uncertain. Another important work claimed to have been written in the same dialect is the *Lay of Ludwig* (*Ludwigslied*), which celebrates the victory of Louis the Pious over the Norsemen in 881. Otfrid, who was a monk at Weissenburg (now Wissembourg), wrote his *Evangelienbuch* (*c.* 863–71) in South Rhine Franconian (this will be referred to as *Otfrid*).

The details of the linguistic features of each dialect are best shown by a map which should be studied in conjunction with the section on the High German sound shift (see pp. xvi and 45 f.).

Middle High German is usually regarded as extending from 1050 to 1350 and was widely used for works of literature. During the thirteenth century legal documents in many towns were also written in German: in Strasburg in 1270, Freiburg in 1275, Augsburg in 1276, Schaffhausen in 1290, and Vienna in 1296. The language of these legal documents varied from town to town. In non-literary texts there was thus a great deal of regional variation. The language of the MHG poets was also not completely uniform although poets tended to avoid rhymes which were too obviously characteristic of their particular region. The exact nature of the MHG literary language, often referred to as 'classical' Middle High German, has been hotly debated.

One important difference between OHG and MHG is that in MHG times the German-speaking area increased in size. Previously it had extended in the east as far as the River Elbe, but in the Middle Ages colonists pushed into Slavic territories and founded villages and towns which soon grew into areas of German settlement; some groups even travelled as far as present-day Hungary and Romania. All the German territory east of the Elbe was colonized in the thirteenth century; East Prussia was invaded by the knights of the Teutonic Order for the first time in 1230 and German farmers established themselves in that territory after 1280. The settlers came from many parts of Germany and were of three main kinds: the nobles and military who built castles to subdue the land; craftsmen and artisans who worked in the towns which had grown up around the castles; and the farmers who came later when it was safe to set up farms and till the land. The main reasons for this expansion were overcrowding and the lack of land for farms in the west. Settlers from Low Germany, or in some cases from the Netherlands, settled in Mecklenburg, Pomerania, and Brandenburg. As they were Low German speakers the dialect of these newly settled areas became Low German. The settlers in the area along the axis Leipzig–Dresden–Breslau came from various parts of Germany: the Rhineland, Hesse, East Franconia, and Bavaria, and the language which arose in this East Central German basin from the mixing of the different dialects of the colonists formed the linguistic basis for New High German.

New High German

New High German is normally regarded as extending from 1650 to the present-day with Early New High German from 1350 to 1650. NHG is a standard language and is not to be equated solely with any particular dialect; it is in fact a mixture of several features from several dialects. In the East Central German basin it has been shown that there developed a lingua franca (called by Frings *die koloniale Ausgleichssprache*) which was formed from the dialects used by the settlers. The similarities between the scribal traditions of Meissen, Dresden, and Prague are due to uniformity of the ECG dialects and not, as was previously assumed, to the influence of the Prague Chancery on the others. This ECG written language differed in a number of ways from other regional written languages such as *das gemeine Deutsch* which was used in Upper Germany, or the standard form of Middle Low German which was current in North Germany and was used as a lingua franca among the towns of the Hanseatic league. It was intelligible to both North and South Germans. The following phonological and grammatical features are usually cited as being the most important in distinguishing it from UG and Low German: diphthongs in the words *Zeit*, *Haus* (MHG *zît*, *hûs*); monophthongs in words like *lieb* [liːp], *Bruder* (MHG *liep*, *bruoder*); the retention of the unstressed *e* in some endings and prefixes, e.g. dat. *zu Hause*, past participle *gestellt*, prefix *be-*, *bestellt*; the pronunciation [k] for *ch* before *s* in *sechs*, *Ochsen*; a long *ē* in the words *gehen*, *stehen*; *-chen* as the main diminutive ending, *Stückchen*; attributive adjectives with a pronominal ending in the nom. sg. neuter, e.g. *mein liebes Kind*; and personal pronoun forms

for the first and second person sg. with the accusative ending in
-*ch*, *mich*, *dich*, and the dative in -*r*, *mir*, *dir*.

It was this variety of German which Martin Luther (1483–
1546) used for his works, including his translation of the Bible,
and it quickly spread to most Protestant areas of German-speaking
Europe; by the beginning of the seventeenth century it had ousted
Low German as a written language and by the latter half of the
seventeenth century it was the main basis of the written language
used in Switzerland. Its progress was not so quick in the Roman
Catholic south-east but by the middle of the eighteenth century it
had found acceptance even there. This ECG written variety of
German underwent changes in orthography, grammar, and
vocabulary in the seventeenth century. Luther, however, had laid
the foundations for the acceptance of one variety of written German as a standard. During the late fifteenth and the sixteenth
centuries the question of what was the best type of German was
the subject of heated debate.

In the seventeenth century many language societies (*Sprachgesellschaften*) were founded, having as their chief aims the cultiva-
tion of the German language and its literature, its protection from
Latin, and the preservation of its purity from the influx of foreign
words. The first of these societies, the Fruchtbringende Gesellschaft, was founded at Weimar in 1617 and it continued its ac-
tivities until 1680. The *Sprachgesellschaften* had only a limited
sphere of influence themselves but some of their members made
lasting contributions in the search for a German standard. Martin
Opitz (1597–1639), whose *Buch von der deutschen Poeterey* (1624)
had an important influence on the use of German as a literary
medium, was a member of the Fruchtbringende Gesellschaft.
Another member of this society was the grammarian Justus Georg
Schottel (1612–76), who regarded the written language of the
greatest and wisest men as the best German and described the
same in *Teutsche Sprachkunst* (1641) and *Ausführliche Arbeit von
der Teutschen Haubt-Sprache* (1663).

In the eighteenth century the task of establishing a written standard for German was carried on by Johann Christoph Gottsched
(1700–66) in *Deutsche Sprachkunst* (1748) and by Johann Christoph
Adelung (1732–1806) in *Umständliches Lehrgebäude der deutschen
Sprache* (1782) and *Vollständige Anweisung zur deutschen Orthographie* (1788). Both Gottsched and Adelung emphasized the

importance of usage in establishing a standard. In their opinion the best German was the language of the educated classes of Upper Saxony, *das Meißnische*. Adelung also produced a dictionary, *Versuch eines grammatisch-kritischen Wörterbuches der hochdeutschen Mundart* (1774–86), which was intended to be a definitive dictionary of German in the same way as the one produced by the Académie française (1694) was for French.

During the nineteenth and early twentieth centuries the final steps were taken towards a standardization of German, chiefly in the realms of orthography and pronunciation. In 1880 the first edition of the *Vollständiges Orthographisches Wörterbuch der deutschen Sprache* was published by Konrad Duden (1829–1911). This was primarily intended for the German Empire, but in 1901 a conference was held in Berlin which was attended by delegates from Austria and Switzerland who proposed reforms to make the spelling proposals of 1880 and other reforms more widely acceptable. The results of the conference were incorporated into the second edition of the *Orthographisches Wörterbuch* in 1902. The *Duden Rechtschreibung der deutschen Sprache und der Fremdwörter* (17th edn. 1973) is still regarded as the ultimate authority on spelling matters in German. Since 1954, however, separate *Duden Rechtschreibung* volumes have been published in Mannheim and Leipzig.

A standardization of pronunciation was also agreed upon at the end of the nineteenth century. In 1898 Theodor Siebs published his *Deutsche Bühnenaussprache* which was the result of a conference held in the same year at Berlin attended by phoneticians, theatre managers, and educationalists. The pronunciation recommended by Siebs was set up as a standard, not only for the stage, but for public speaking in general, later being applied to broadcasting. Because of its wide application the title was amended in 1922 to *Deutsche Bühnenaussprache-Hochsprache*; in 1958 it became simply *Deutsche Hochsprache*. This norm allowed no alternatives in pronunciation, but in the latest edition, the nineteenth, with the title *Deutsche Aussprache, Reine und gemäßigte Hochlautung* (1969), alternatives are allowed. The Siebs model reflects North German pronunciation. In Leipzig a rival pronouncing dictionary has been published, *Wörterbuch der deutschen Aussprache* (2nd edn. 1967), based on pronunciation in radio, films, and television.

Further reading

1. Germanic languages

ANTONSEN, E. H., 'On defining stages in prehistoric Germanic', *Language*, 41 (1965), 19–36.

CAMPBELL, A., *Old English Grammar* (Clarendon Press, Oxford, 1959).

CORDES, G., *Altniederdeutsches Elementarbuch*, mit einem Kapitel 'Syntaktisches' von F. Holthausen (Winter, Heidelberg, 1973).

GOOSSENS, J. (ed.), *Niederdeutsch: Sprache und Literatur*, vol. i: *Sprache*, (Wachholtz, Neumünster, 1973).

GORDON, E. V., *An introduction to Old Norse*, 2nd edn., A. R. Taylor (Clarendon Press, Oxford, 1954).

HAUGEN, E., *The Scandinavian languages* (Faber, London, 1976).

HOLTHAUSEN, H., *Altsächsisches Elementarbuch* (Winter, Heidelberg, 1921).

HUTTERER, C. J., *Die germanischen Sprachen* (Akadémemiai Kiadó, Budapest, 1975).

KRAHE, H., *Germanische Sprachwissenschaft*, 2 vols., 7th edn., ed. W. Meid (Sammlung Göschen 238, 780, De Gruyter, Berlin, 1969).

KUHN, H., 'Zur Gliederung der germanischen Sprachen', *Zeitschrift für deutsches Altertum*, 86 (1955–6), 1–47.

MAURER, F., *Nordgermanen und Alemannen*, 3rd ed. (Francke, Berne, 1952).

MOSER, H., 'Deutsche Sprachgeschichte der älteren Zeit', *Deutsche Philologie im Aufriß*, vol. i, hrsg. von W. Stammler (Schmidt, Berlin, 1966), 621–854.

PROKOSCH, E., *A comparative Germanic grammar* (Linguistic Society of America, Philadelphia, 1939).

SCHWARZ, E., *Goten, Nordgermanen und Angelsachsen* (Francke, Berne, 1951).

STELLER, W., *Abriß der altfriesischen Grammatik* (Niemeyer, Halle, 1928).

WRIGHT, J., *Grammar of the Gothic language*, with supplement by O. L. Sayce (Clarendon Press, Oxford, 1954).

2. Historical development of German

BACH, A., *Geschichte der deutschen Sprache*, 9th edn. (Quelle & Meyer, Heidelberg, 1970).

BLACKALL, E. A., *The emergence of German as a literary language* (Cambridge Univ. Press, 1959).

CHAMBERS, W. W. and WILKIE, J. R., *A short history of the German language* Methuen, London, 1970).

FRINGS, T., *Sprache und Geschichte*, iii (Niemeyer, Halle, 1956).

GUCHMANN, M. M., *Der Weg zur deutschen Nationalsprache*, 2 vols., trans. G. Feudel (Akademie, Berlin, 1964 and 1969).

LOCKWOOD, W. B., *An informal history of the German language*, 2nd edn. (Heffers, Cambridge, 1975).

MOSER, H., *Deutsche Sprachgeschichte*, 6th edn. (Niemeyer, Tübingen, 1969).

OTTO, K. F., *Die Sprachgesellschaften des 17. Jahrhunderts* (Sammlung Metzler 109, Stuttgart, 1972).

PENZL, H., *Vom Urgermanischen zum Neuhochdeutschen* (Schmidt, Berlin, 1975).

POLENZ, P. von, *Geschichte der deutschen Sprache*, 8th edn. (Sammlung Göschen 4015, De Gruyter, Berlin, 1972).

PRIEBSCH, R. and W. E. COLLINSON, *The German Language*, 6th edn. (Faber, London, 1966).

SCHMIDT, W., *Geschichte der deutschen Sprache*, 2nd edn. (Volk und Wissen, Berlin, 1970).

TSCHIRCH, F., *Geschichte der deutschen Sprache*, 2 vols. (Schmidt, Berlin, 1969 and 1971).

WATERMAN, J., *History of the German language*, 2nd edn. (Univ. of Washington Press, Seattle, 1975).

I · PHONOLOGY

THE word 'phonology' can be used in several different senses. For example, it is sometimes used to refer exclusively to the historical development of sounds, e.g. historical phonology (German *Lautlehre*), but other linguists have also used it to refer to the study of the distinctive differences between sounds (German *Phonologie*), either on its own, or prefaced by an adjective describing a particular linguistic approach, e.g. prosodic phonology, generative phonology. In this work 'phonology' will be used to refer to the general study of sounds, both historically and descriptively. It will be regarded as having two divisions: phonetics and phonemics.

PHONETICS
(The diagram on p. xvii should be consulted in connection with this section)

Phonetics is the science of the description and classification of sounds regardless of their function. It has three branches: articulatory, acoustic, and auditory phonetics. The last one, how the ear registers sound, has not been widely developed. Acoustic phonetics consists of recording sounds and registering their pitch (frequency), amplitude (strength of articulation), and their duration. The branch of phonetics which concerns us here is the articulatory branch, that is how sounds are produced or articulated.

Sounds are produced by a stream of air which is usually set in motion by the lungs. In most languages the air-stream is forced outwards and is called egressive. The air-stream from the lungs passes outwards through the throat and oral cavity and is subject to modification by the organs of speech. The hard palate and teeth are static organs of speech, whereas the soft palate, or velum, the tongue, and lips are active. Before reaching the throat or oral cavity the air-stream may be modified by the vocal cords (muscles at the top of the larynx), which can either vibrate or not vibrate. If the vocal cords vibrate then the sound is voiced, if they do not vibrate then the sound is voiceless.

The biggest division of sounds is into vowels and consonants. In the articulation of vowels the air-stream from the lungs passes unhindered over the centre of the tongue through the mouth, whereas in the case of consonants the air-stream is either completely stopped, or narrowed so that audible friction is produced. Vowels usually form the nucleus of a syllable. In English and German vowels are always voiced.

The nasal cavity through which air from the lungs is expelled through the nose also plays an important role. The entrance to the nasal cavity can be controlled by the soft palate, or velum, which can either seal it off by making a closure with the back wall of the mouth (the pharynx), only allowing the air-stream to pass through the mouth, or it can hang loose and allow the air-stream to be expelled through both the mouth and the nose. Sounds in the production of which the air-stream is expelled only through the mouth are called oral sounds, and those in the production of which the air-stream is expelled through both the mouth and nose are called nasal sounds. In English both oral and nasal consonants exist, for instance the initial consonant in *mad* is nasal and the initial consonant in *bad* is oral. However, vowels in English are only oral. In languages such as French and Portuguese both nasal and oral vowels exist: contrast the vowels in the two French words spelt *pas* and *pain*. The former is an oral vowel and the latter a nasal vowel.

It is evident that spelling in many languages does not accurately reflect pronunciation. For this reason various phonetic alphabets have been invented in order to record the pronunciation of words as accurately as possible. The symbols of the International Phonetic Alphabet (I.P.A.) will be used for the sounds described in this introduction. They will be enclosed in square brackets [ ]. Some of the symbols are the same as letters in the English and German alphabets but others are different.

During the production of vowels by the air-stream from the lungs passing unhindered over the centre of the tongue, the height of the tongue may vary, making the oral cavity large or small. In the pronunciation of the vowel of the English word *bit* the tongue is high in the mouth and narrows the oral cavity considerably, whereas in the pronunciation of the German word *das* the tongue is low in the mouth and the oral cavity is very open. In the pronunciation of the vowel of the English word *foot* the oral cavity is very closed and the tongue is high in the mouth. Phoneticians class vowels according to whether they change the shape of the oral cavity, saying that vowels such as [i] and [u] are close vowels and that [a] is an open vowel.

The vowels [i] and [u] differ from one another in that the tongue is positioned in a different part of the mouth. Whereas [u] is produced by the tongue being at the back of the mouth, [i] is produced by the tongue being at the front of the mouth. The vowel [a] can also be produced at the front or back of the mouth, but this difference does not concern us in English and German. Vowels produced at the front of the mouth are called front vowels and those produced at the back of the mouth are called back vowels. The vowel [i] is therefore a close front vowel and [u] is a close back vowel.

In the pronunciation of [i] and [u] yet another dimension can be seen, i.e. the shape of the lips. In the articulation of [u] the lips are rounded and in the articulation of [i] the lips are spread, or neutral, and not rounded.

Before dealing with the shape of the lips in more detail, the articulation of other vowels must first be described. Between the two extremes of close [i] and [u] and open [a] there are intermediate stages. These are represented by the vowels in the English words *bed* and *odd* and the German words *Bett* and *Gott*. The vowels in *bed* and *Bett* are written [ɛ]. They are usually classed as half-open front vowels. The vowels in *odd* and *Gott* are written [ɔ] and are usually classed as half-open back vowels. The vowel in English *bad* is not the same as the vowel in German *das*. It is a vowel which is more open than [ɛ], but not as open as [a]. It is symbolized [æ]. A diagram can be drawn which shows the position of the tongue in the mouth and the degree of closeness and openness of vowels in relationship to each other:

	Front unrounded	Front rounded	Central	Back rounded
Close (high)	i	y		u
Half-close (mid-high)	e	ø		o
Half-open (mid-low)	ɛ	œ	ə	ɔ
Open (low)			a	

The vowels written [e] and [o] and classified as half-close do not appear in English or German as short vowels but only as long vowels. The vowels in German *leben* and *loben* are long half-close vowels. In phonetic transcription long vowels are usually written with a following [ɪ], [eɪ], [oɪ]. Potentially any vowel may be short or long. The half-open short [ɔ] does not appear long in German but it does in English, where it represents the vowel in *law* [ɔɪ]. the half-open short [ɛ] appears long only in some varieties of German: some speakers distinguish between the stressed vowels in *Beeren* and *Bären* by pronouncing the first as a long half-close vowel [eɪ] and the second as a long half-open vowel [ɛɪ]. The short vowels [i] and [u] have long counterparts in English and German; compare the pairs *binnen* and *Bienen*, *Bucht*, and *Buch*. It has become usual to consider the short close vowels as being slightly more open than the long close vowels and to write the former [I] and [U] and the latter [iɪ] and [uɪ]. The long vowels in English *beat* and *boot* are diphthongs in southern England, that is the tongue position is not constant in the articulation of the sounds, whereas the vowels in German *Bienen, Bude* are 'pure' or steady-state long vowels.

Diphthongs, i.e. vowel sounds in the production of which the position of the tongue changes during their articulation, are, for purposes of transcription, considered as having two components. They can be described in the same way as ordinary vowels. German has three diphthongs, all falling, that is having the stress on the first component. These are the sounds in the words: *mein, Haus, euch*. Phonetically they may be written [ai] [au], and [oi] respectively. There is also the rising diphthong in the interjection *pfui* in German. English has falling diphthongs in *name, boy, my*, and *stone* which are transcribed [ei], [oi], [ai], and [ou].

The front vowels so far mentioned are pronounced with no lip-rounding, all the back vowels having had lip-rounding. The open vowel [a] is neutral with respect to lip-rounding. This is quite sufficient for the description of English vowels, but not for German. In the vowel diagram (p. 15) all the examples of front-rounded vowels were from German. The German vowel sounds in *Bühne, schön*, and *können* are examples of front vowels with lip-rounding. In western European languages back vowels without lip-rounding do not occur, but they are found in Turkish, for example. The German front-rounded vowels are also distinguished according to whether they are close or open. The vowel in *Bühne* is close, the vowel in *schön* is half-close, and the vowel in *können* is half-open. They are transcribed [yɪ], [øɪ], and [œ] respectively.

The short counterpart of [yɪ] appears in *müssen* and is slightly more open. It is written [Y] in phonetic script.

One other vowel must be added, written phonetically [ə], which is the vowel occurring in the unstressed syllables of English *bitter* and German *bitte*. The vowel in English *bird* is a long, central, half-open, unrounded vowel symbolized [ɜɪ] and the vowel in English *but* is a back, slightly centralized, half-open, unrounded vowel symbolized [ʌ].

Three things must be looked for in classifying vowels:

1. Whether the oral cavity is close, open, half-close, or half-open.
2. Whether the tongue is at the front or the back of the mouth.
3. Whether the lips are rounded or not.

In the production of consonants the air-stream from the lungs is modified by the organs of speech in the mouth. They are usually described according to the manner of articulation (how the air-stream is modified as it passes through the oral cavity), and then according to the place of articulation (where this modification takes place). The term modification has been used as a neutral term. Either the air is completely blocked at some point in the mouth or the oral cavity is narrowed so much that audible friction is produced at some point. When the air-stream is completely blocked the consonants are called stops, or plosives. When the air-stream is forced out with friction but there is no stoppage the sound is termed a fricative, or spirant. The initial consonants in English and German *Pein, pine, tin, tun, coke, Koch* are stops and the initial consonants in *fein, vine, sign, thine, scheinen* are fricatives. If there is a complete sealing off of the nasal cavity by the soft palate then the resultant consonants are oral: [p t k b d g] or [ʃ x v z ʒ ɣ], but if there is a stoppage in the oral cavity which is later released and air also escapes through the nose, then the resultant sound is simply called a nasal, since there are not both nasal stops and fricatives. The initial sounds in *mad, Mut, nein, nut* and the final sound in *sang* are nasals. These three groups, distinguished by their manner of articulation, are also divided into several different places, or points, of articulation. These are the same for each manner of articulation, although all possible combinations do not exist. Usually it is enough to mention one point of articulation in describing the stop, fricative, or nasal. The sounds [p b f v m] are labial sounds, that is the stoppage is made by the lips or else the lips coming close together produce the friction. In the case of the stops and nasals in English and German they are bilabial, that is both lips are involved in the articulation of the sound. In the case of the fricatives they are articulated not by the two articulators in the mouth which are exactly opposite to each other vertically but by two which are not exactly opposite to each other. The fricatives [f] and [v] are labio-dental and are produced by the lower lip approaching the upper teeth. The sounds [t d], [s z], [n] are alveolar in English and German, that is the stoppage or friction is made at the teeth ridge or alveoli by the tongue. In languages such as Spanish the sounds are dental, that is made at the teeth themselves and not behind the teeth at the gums, or alveolar ridge. Among the fricatives, however, English does distinguish between alveolar and dental fricatives: [s] and [z] are alveolar fricatives, and [θ] and [ð] are dental. Therefore [t d] are alveolar stops, [s z] alveolar fricatives, and [θ ð] dental fricatives, [n] is an alveolar nasal.

At the next point of articulation there are only fricatives in English and German. This is the region between the alveolar ridge and the beginning of the hard palate; this is where the initial sounds in *shin, scheinen, Genie*, and the final sound in *rouge* are formed. They are known as palato-alveolar fricatives, or sometimes as pre-palatal fricatives. They are symbolized [ʃ], [ʒ]. The alveolar and palato-alveolar fricatives are sometimes known together by the collective name of sibilants, as they have the acoustic effect of a hissing or buzzing.

The hard and soft palates, as far as English and German are concerned, can be taken as one place of articulation. Some languages, such as Arabic, distinguish between palatal and velar consonants. Although the exact point of articulation is determined by the following vowel, compare the initial sounds in *Kind, kann, Kunde*; these stops in English and German may be called velar or palato-velar stops. The same variation occurs with [g] *Gift, gab, Gunst*. English has no velar fricative but German has, e.g. the final sound in *Buch, Loch*. This also varies in articulation according to the preceding vowel; *Dach* has a velar fricative, written phonetically [x], and *dich* has a palatal fricative [ç].

English and German do agree, however, in having a velar nasal, written phonetically [ŋ], which only occurs medially and finally, *hangen, singer, sang*.

Another type of articulation is represented by the initial sounds in *Pferd, Zeit, church, judge*. Phonetically these sounds are written [pf ts tʃ dʒ] and represent a consonant cluster of a stop and a fricative at the same or similar point of articulation. [pf] comprises a labial stop and a labio-dental fricative, [ts] is an alveolar stop plus an alveolar fricative. They are known as affricates.

The next two types of articulation are represented in English and German by only one sound each. In the articulation of the initial sound in *lachen*, the tongue almost touches the teeth and the air-stream flows out past the sides of the tongue. This type of articulation is called lateral. In the articulation of *r* in *reiten*, either the tongue tip is trilled against the teeth, or the uvula against the back of the throat. These articulations are symbolized [r] and [R] respectively. The *r* sounds in English and German vary a great deal in the amount of friction and trill created in their production. Sometimes they are produced with little or no friction and can be called frictionless continuants, symbolized by writing the *r* symbols upside down, [ɹ], [ʁ]. If they are produced with just one flap of the tip of the tongue against the teeth, or of the uvula against the wall of the throat, they are called flaps and are symbolized [ɾ], as in English *very*, and [R]. The alveolar frictionless continuant occurs in English in initial position, e.g. *ride*. The lateral [l] in German is pronounced only in the centre and front of the mouth, whereas in English after vowels the [l] is velarized and pronounced in the back of the mouth, e.g. *ball, soul*. The [r] and [l] sounds are often referred to together as liquids.

Among the stops and fricatives, sometimes classed together as obstruents, there is another fundamental distinction created by the behaviour of the vocal cords. The stops [b d g] and the fricatives [v z ʒ] are voiced, i.e. the vocal cords vibrate, whereas the stops [p t k] and the fricatives [f s ʃ x] are voiceless, i.e. the vocal cords do not vibrate. Affricates may also be voiced, e.g. [dʒ], while [pf ts tʃ] are voiceless.

There are three stages in the articulation of stops: the onset (when the closure or occlusion is made), the hold (the length of the closure), and then the release (when the closure is opened). When an initial voiceless stop is released in English and German a puff of air immediately follows, this being symbolized by writing [h] after the stop, [ph th kh]. These stops are known as aspirated stops. In French, for instance, the initial voiceless stops are not aspirated, but the vocal cords start to vibrate immediately after the closure is released, whereas in the case of the aspirated voiceless stops this vibration does not start immediately. Aspiration is acoustically the absence of voicing between the release of the closure and the beginning of voicing in the following vowel. Unaspirated voiceless stops also occur in some German dialects, particularly in the south, and in these cases the distinction between [p] and [b] is not between a voiceless and a voiced stop, but rather between different strengths of articulation. The stop [p] is described as being fortis, that is more force is used in its articulation, and [b] is described as being lenis, less strength being used in its articulation. The terms 'fortis' and 'lenis' are sometimes used very vaguely and in general they will be avoided here. The terms 'tense' and 'lax' have also been suggested to describe the difference in strength of articulation of consonants.

The initial sound in English and German *yes* and *ja* is often classed as a palatal semi-vowel, and the initial sound in English *win* as a bilabial semi-vowel. The German spelling *w*, however, represents a voiced labio-dental fricative. The amount of friction used to produce these sounds varies a great deal; sometimes they are frictionless continuants and have little or no friction. The term 'approximants' has also been used for sounds such as these which have no friction and in the production of which the organs of speech do nothing more than 'approximate' to an articulation. Phonetically the palatal semi-vowel is written [j] and the bilabial one [w].

The initial sound in English and German *hat* is classed as a glottal fricative, that is the glottis, the space between the vocal cords, is almost closed. It is also called a cavity fricative since most of the friction is produced in the throat cavity. The articulation of [h] is determined by the vowel that follows, and there are as many different positions of the oral cavity for [h] as there are vowels. If the glottis is closed completely a glottal stop results, symbolized [ʔ]. In German it is found initially before a vowel, *ein* [ʔain] (also called *harter Vokaleinsatz*), or between vowels as in *Theater* [teɪʔatər].

The terms vowel and consonant are ambiguous since they are

not only used to describe the articulation of sounds but also their position or function in the syllable. A simple syllable consists of an initial element, a nucleus and a releasing element. Thus the word *bin* can be symbolized CVC (C standing for any consonant and V for any vowel). A word such as *Streit* could be symbolized CCCVVC. Some sounds, often called resonants, function as both vowels and consonants in the syllable. These are the semi-vowels [j w], the nasals [m n ŋ], and the liquids [l] and [r]. In German the ending *-en*, usually pronounced [-ən], is replaced in colloquial speech by a syllabic nasal symbolized [n̩], thus *leben* may be pronounced [leɪbn̩], and in some cases the syllabic nasal is assimilated to the place of articulation of the preceding stop, [leɪbm̩]. The ending *-el* is sometimes replaced by a syllabic [l̩], e.g. *Mantel* [mantl̩].

The articulation of sounds does not merely consist of segments of words, for there are also suprasegmental phenomena such as pitch, stress, and intonation which extend over whole words and also over sentences. In our description of English and German we will concern ourselves only with the segmental sounds, i.e. vowels and consonants.

Further reading

MacCarthy, P., *The Pronunciation of German* (Oxford Univ. Press, 1975).

Martens, C. and P., *Phonetik der deutschen Sprache* (Hueber, Munich, 1961).

Meinhold, G., *Deutsche Standardaussprache: Lautschwächungen und Formstufen* (Friedrich-Schiller–Universität, Jena, 1973).

Moulton, W. G., *The sounds of English and German* (Univ. of Chicago Press, 1962).

O'Connor, J. D., *Phonetics* (Penguin, London, 1973).

Wängler, H-H., *Grundriß einer Phonetik des Deutschen*, 2nd edn. (Elwert, Marburg, 1967).

Isacenko, A. and H.-J. Schädlich, *A model of Standard German intonation* (Mouton, The Hague, 1970).

Von Essen, O., *Grundzüge der hochdeutschen Satzintonation* (Henn, Düsseldorf, 1964).

PHONEMICS

Theoretically the number of sounds that the organs of speech can produce is infinite, but in reality only a limited number is used in each language. The reason for this limitation is that phonetic differences are not all of the same importance. In German the difference between voiced and voiceless stops is normally distinctive, as it is in English; the difference in meaning between *Pein* and *Bein*, *pin* and *bin* is carried solely by the difference between a voiceless stop [p] and a voiced stop [b]. Sound differences which must be made in a language in order to distinguish between the meaning of words are termed phonemic, and the sounds which make this difference are called phonemes. Thus in German and English the stops [p] and [b] are phonemes and the difference between them, the difference of voice, is phonemic. The stops can be written as phonemes between slant lines /p/, /b/. They form a phonemic opposition. There are many pairs of words in German and English which are distinguished solely by a difference of voice: *Wein*: *fein*; *vile*: *file*; *leiden*: *leiten*; *ladder*: *latter*. Words which differ only in one phoneme from each other are known as minimal pairs. The easiest way of establishing the phonemic system of a language is by using minimal pairs, but contrasts in a similar environment, e.g. before vowels, *weil*: *fiel*, are considered to be sufficient if minimal pairs are not available. Phonetic differences which are not phonemic are allophonic. Thus in German the voiceless fricative written *ch* is palatal in *nicht* but velar in *Nacht*. The articulatory difference palatal: velar does not serve to distinguish in meaning between words in German but is conditioned by the preceding vowel: the palatal fricative [ç] occurs after front vowels, e.g. *tüchtig*, *möchte*, *Licht*, *recht*, *reich*, and the velar fricative [x] occurs after back vowels: *Dach*, *doch*, *Bucht*, *Bauch*. The sounds [ç] and [x] are therefore allophones, or positional variants of phonemes, in complementary distribution, i.e. where [ç] occurs [x] does not, and vice versa. (Some linguists, however, consider them to be phonemes on the basis of such alleged contrasts as *Kuchen* /x/ : *Kuhchen* 'cow (diminutive)' /ç/, but this view will not be adopted here.) In German the opposition between voiced and voiceless stops and fricative does not exist in word-final position, only the voiceless sounds occur (the spelling masks this): *Pein* : *Bein*; *rauben* : *Raupen*; but *Raub* [Raup]. The phonemic opposition of voice is said to be neutralized in this position in German.

Phonemic and allophonic differences are set up separately for each language. The difference between aspirated and unaspirated stops in English is allophonic, aspirated stops occur pre-vocalically, *pin*, whereas unaspirated stops appear after initial *s*, *spin*; in Chinese and Hindi, for example, the difference is phonemic. The difference between [s] and [z] in English and German is phonemic: *seal* : *zeal*; *reißen* : *reisen*, but in Spanish the difference is allophonic. A definition of the phoneme has proved very difficult to formulate but there are two suggestions which may be helpful. One such suggestion regards the phoneme as a family of sounds which are never in contrast with each other and which are phonetically similar; the other suggestion regards the phoneme as an abstraction consisting of a bundle of distinctive, or phonemic, features which occur together. The phoneme /p/ in English has certain distinctive features: it is a stop, it contrasts with fricatives, *pin* : *fin*; it is labial, it contrasts with stops at other points of articulation, *pin* : *tin* : *kin*; it is voiceless, it contrasts with voiced stops, *pin* : *bin*. The English phoneme /p/ as an abstract unit consists of three distinctive features: voice, point of articulation, i.e. labial, and manner of articulation, i.e. stop. Its allophones show other non-distinctive, or purely phonetic, features (e.g. aspiration initially before a vowel) in addition to the three distinctive features. This approach regards the phoneme as an abstraction which is realized by its allophones in the speech chain.

A recent approach to phonology, called generative phonology, dispenses with the phoneme altogether and simply deals with phonological, or distinctive, features. Phonology is seen as a system of rules which derive surface forms (words with their full allophonic variation) from the so-called underlying forms which are usually more abstract. For example, the underlying form for German *Raub* [Raup] would be /raub/ with a final voiced stop. The surface form /raup/ is derived from the underlying form by a rule which devoices any underlying voiced obstruent in final position. For those speakers who have a uvular [ʀ], an optional rule is needed which derives a surface uvular [ʀ] from an underlying dental [r]. Similarly the underlying form for *nicht* will be /nixt/ with a velar fricative which is then fronted to [ç] after front

vowels by a rule. This approach will not be adopted in this book
(for greater detail see Schane (1973) and Wurzel (1970)).

Further reading

FUDGE, E. C. (ed.), *Phonology*, Penguin Modern Linguistics Readings
    (London, 1973).
GLEASON, H. A., *Introduction to Descriptive Linguistics* (Holt, Rinehart,
    and Winston, New York 1961), Chs. 16 and 17.
HEIKE, G., *Phonologie* (Sammlung Metzler 104, Stuttgart, 1972).
HYMAN, L. M., *Phonology: Theory and Analysis* (Holt, Rinehart, and
    Winston, New York, 1975).
KOHLER, K. J., *Einführung in die Phonetik des Deutschen*, (Berlin:
    Schmidt, 1977).
SCHANE, S. A., *Generative Phonology* (Prentice-Hall, Englewood Cliffs,
    N.J., 1973).
WERNER, O., *Phonemik des Deutschen* (Sammlung Metzler 108, Stutt-
    gart, 1972).
WURZEL, W. U., *Studien zur deutschen Lautstruktur, Studia Gramma-
    tica*, viii (Akademie, Berlin, 1970).

HISTORICAL PHONOLOGY

Phonetics and phonemics are not only used to describe the sounds
of present-day English and German, but they can also be used to
describe the sound changes that have taken place in the history of
languages. Hitherto it has been traditional to describe the history
of the sound system of a language by simply describing the process
by which each individual sound changes into another sound, but
it is truer to say that the sound system of one stage of a language
changes into the sound system of the next stage in the language.
This is particularly true when sound changes are dealt with according to phonemes and not merely according to sounds. Historical
phonology, conceived in phonemic terms, deals not only with the
changes in the phonetic realization of the phonemes, even though
the number of phonemes remains the same, but also with the
changes in the number of phonemes. This is called phonetic and
phonemic sound change respectively. Changes also occur in the
distribution of the phonemes. Most sound changes that occur are

phonemic sound changes which affect the number or distribution of phonemes.

There are three chief types of phonemic change: merger, split, and shift. In phonemic merger a phonemic opposition is lost and two phonemes merge into one, either in all positions (unconditioned merger) or only in certain positions (conditioned merger). The resulting phoneme may be one of the original members of the opposition or it may be a phoneme with a different phonetic realization. The examples will be given in diagram form followed by examples from German.

$$
\begin{array}{lll}
/A/\searrow & \text{MHG } /\hat{\imath}/ \ \textit{mîn}\searrow & \\
\quad\ \searrow /C/ & & \searrow \text{NHG } /ai/ \ \textit{mein, ein} \\
/B/\nearrow & \text{MHG } /ei/ \ \textit{ein}\nearrow &
\end{array}
$$

Conditioned merger, sometimes called 'split with merger', involves not the number of phonemes but their distribution. In MHG after /l/ and /r/ the phonemes /w/ and /b/ contrasted: MHG *swalwe* : *selbe*; *varwe* : *gestorben*. In NHG they have merged in /b/ in this position: *Schwalbe, selbe*; *Farbe, gestorben*.

In phonemic split, sometimes called 'primary' split, new phonemes are introduced. Where there was an allophonic variation there is now a phonemic contrast. Usully phonemic split comes about through another change which removes the allophonic conditioning factors. A classic case of this is umlaut or *i*-mutation (see pp. 56 f.).

$$
\text{OHG } /\bar{o}/
\begin{array}{l}
[\text{øː}] \ \textit{sköni} \nearrow \\
[\text{oː}] \ \textit{skōno} \searrow
\end{array}
\begin{array}{l}
\nearrow \text{MHG } /\text{œ}/ \ \textit{schœne} \text{ (NHG } \textit{schön}) \\
\searrow \text{MHG } /\hat{o}/ \ \textit{schône} \text{ (NHG } \textit{schon})
\end{array}
$$

The third type of phonemic change is phonemic shift. In this case only the distinctive features of the phonemes change. Germanic *þ* was a voiceless interdental fricative but by late OHG it had become a voiced alveolar stop, *d*. Sometimes phonemic shifts affect series of phonemes, for instance the Germanic sound shift, where the number of the consonants remains the same but they are realized with different distinctive features (pp. 31 ff.). Generative phonology speaks of rule change rather than sound change (King (1969)).

Sound change has been regarded as regular ever since certain linguists, called Neogrammarians (*Junggrammatiker*), maintained in the 1870s that 'sound laws have no exceptions'. Some linguists, notably those working in Romance linguistics such as H. Schuchardt (1842–1927), did not agree with this view; but nowadays most historical linguists regard sound changes, in practice at any rate, as being regular, i.e. any exceptions can be explained as being due to other factors, of which the two most important are analogy and dialect borrowing. The regular reflex of MHG *ei* is *ei* [ai] in NHG, MHG *stein*, NHG *Stein*, but the reflex of *ei* in MHG *er reit* 'he rode' is *i* in NHG, *er ritt*. This is not a regular sound change but has happened only in the strong verbs of MHG Class I (see p. 154). The short *i* in NHG *ritt* has come from the past tense plural, MHG *wir riten*, which has been introduced by analogy into the sg. past tense. Dialect borrowing can be seen in the NHG reflex [oː] for MHG *â* whose normal reflex is [aː], MHG *jâr*, NHG *Jahr*. NHG *ohne*, *Mond*, and several other words go back to MHG forms with *â*, *âne*, *mâne*. These forms with [oː] were borrowed into standard NHG from a dialect where a long [oː] was the regular reflex of MHG *â* (see p. 87). These are not the only factors which are at work in explaining the exceptions to regular sound change; for example, in the case of NHG *Neffe* (MHG *neve*) it was the spelling with *ff* which caused it to retain its short vowel which should have been lengthened, cf. MHG *hove*, NHG *Hofe*. They are, however, the most frequent and the most important.

It is possible to divide historical phonology into the study of reconstructed sound changes and historical sound changes proper. In reconstructed sound changes there are no written records to help describe the process of a sound change. Sound changes from PG to OHG are reconstructed sound changes, whereas changes from MHG to NHG, when written records are available, are historical sound changes proper. When historical records are in existence then another problem presents itself, that of deducing from the orthography the phonetic and phonemic values represented. Several methods have been used to achieve this. Some of the more important are indicated below:

1. Sometimes there are specific statements by the grammarians as to how sounds are pronounced. Normally these are only available in modern times, but statements by grammarians of the ancient world do exist which help to shed light on how such languages as Latin, Greek, and Sanskrit were pronounced.

2. Words either loaned into other languages or borrowed from them often help to show how a sound may have been pronounced. The modern English affricates in *chant, judge* were probably the same as the Old French affricates in these words which have been smoothed to the fricatives [ʃ], [ʒ] in modern French *chant, juge*.

3. The rhymes of poets often tell us which sounds were pronounced the same. In general MHG poets did not rhyme MHG *ë* from Germanic *e* and MHG *e* from Germanic *a* by *i*-mutation, therefore we conclude they were pronounced differently in MHG, even though they are pronounced the same in NHG.

4. The subsequent development of sounds often helps to show us that sounds may have been pronounced differently. The modern English words *root* and *note* were spelt *rote* and *note* in Middle English. However, although the vowels are spelt with the same sign in Middle English we can assume them to have been pronounced differently since they are pronounced differently in modern English, and the difference in pronunciation does not seem to have resulted from a phonemic split.

5. The modern dialects give us good evidence of the phonetic value of the sounds of an older period of a language. The modern Alemannic and Bavarian dialects have diphthongs [iə, iɐ] and [uə, uɐ] as reflexes of the MHG digraphs *ie* and *uo* respectively. The occurrence of diphthongs in these dialects is traditionally assumed to reflect the retention of the original MHG diphthongal pronunciation of *ie* and *uo* which have become monophthongs in the standard language.

Further reading

ANTTILLA, R., *An Introduction to Historical and Comparative Linguistics* (Macmillan, New York, 1972), Ch. 4.

HOENIGSWALD, H. M., *Language Change and Linguistic Reconstruction* (Univ. of Chicago Press, 1960), Ch. 9.

MARTINET, A., *Économie des changements phonétiques* (Francke, Berne, 1955).

KING, R. D., *Historical Linguistics and Generative Grammar* (Prentice-Hall, Englewood Cliffs, N.J., 1969).

MOULTON, W. G., 'Types of phonemic change', in *To honor Roman Jakobson*, 2 (Mouton, The Hague, 1967), 1393–1407.

PENZL, H., 'The evidence for phonemic changes', in *Studies presented to Joshua Whatmough* (Mouton, The Hague, 1957), 193–208; repr. in

R. Lass (ed.), *Approaches to English Historical Linguistics* (Holt, Rinehart, and Winston, New York, 1969), 10–24.
—— *Methoden der germanischen Linguistik* (Niemeyer, Tübingen, 1972).
Russ, C. V. J., 'The data of historical linguistics: sources for the reconstruction of pronunciation from written records', *York Papers in Linguistics*, 6 (1976), 65–73.

THE SOUNDS OF INDO-EUROPEAN AND THEIR DEVELOPMENT TO GERMANIC

Proto-Indo-European (PIE) is a hypothetical construct produced by comparing the written records of the various languages which are assumed to belong to the Indo-European family. The best-known languages which are used for this purpose are Latin, Greek, Sanskrit, and the oldest written records of the Germanic languages, and perhaps Celtic. A proto-language reconstructed by the comparative method cannot be described with the same phonetic detail as a living language, but nevertheless the broad phonemic distinctions can be established. The sound system reconstructed here will largely follow traditional lines (for a more controversial view see Lehmann (1952)). Sometimes the symbol * is used to show that a sound or a form belongs to a reconstructed language. In our account reconstructed sounds will be symbolized by using orthographic symbols without any signs or brackets but reconstructed forms where they are used will be asterisked.

PIE is assumed to have had five short vowels and five long vowels. There were three degrees of tongue height: high, mid, and low, or preferably three degrees of openness of the vocal cavity: close, half-close (or half-open), and open. Wherever possible examples will be taken from Latin or Greek.

	Short vowels	Long vowels				
Close	*i u*	*ī ū* Latin	*piscis*	*custōs*	*vīvus*	*mūs*
Half-close	*e o*	*ē ō*	*medius*	*octō*	*tēgula*	*flōs*
Open	*a*	*ā*	*ager*		*frāter*	

This reconstructed vowel system has the same number of items as that of Latin and Greek.

It has also been traditional to assume diphthongs for PIE: *ai*, Latin *haedus*, *oi*, Latin *poena*, *au*, Latin *augeō*. Also assumed for PIE are the diphthongs *ou*, *ei*, and *eu*, but *ou* and *eu* have become long *ū* in Latin, and *ei* has become long *ī*. It will be noticed that the second part of all these diphthongs is either *i* or *u* which were resonants, that is sounds which could function as both a vowel and a consonant. When they occurred between two consonants they functioned syllabically as vowels, but after a vowel they functioned as semi-vowels. The PIE diphthongs can be regarded as sequences of a vowel plus a resonant. In PIE the resonants comprised not only the two semi-vowels *i* and *u*, phonetically [j w], but the liquids *l* and *r* and the nasals *m* and *n*. In Latin, Greek, and the other IE languages the liquids and nasals when they functioned syllabically have developed vowels, either before or after them; only in Sanskrit and in Slavonic languages is there a syllabic *r*. The analysis of vowel plus the semi-vowels *i* and *u* is not valid for the Germanic languages since these clusters develop as units and each member does not develop independently. Some scholars have also assumed long diphthongs for PIE.

The reconstructed consonant system of PIE is one in which stops predominate. It seems that there was only one fricative, *s*. The stops occur at the following points of articulation: labial, dental, velar, and labio-velar. This last point of articulation (or rather co-articulation, since the closure at the velar point of articulation is accompanied by lip-rounding as in the initial sound in English *quick* or German *Quelle*) is retained in the Germanic languages. Some scholars assume a separate palatal point of articulation but there is no evidence for this in the Germanic languages. The stops are assumed to have been released in a threefold way: as voiced stops, as voiceless stops, and as voiced aspirated stops. There is some slight evidence for a separate row of voiceless aspirated stops, but this will be disregarded here. The voiced aspirated stops can be heard in some modern Indic languages such as Hindi.

	Labial	Dental	Velar	Labio-velar
Voiceless stops	*p*	*t*	*k*	*kw*
Voiced stops	(*b*)	*d*	*g*	*gw*
Voiced aspirated stops	*bh*	*dh*	*gh*	(*ghw*)

There is some doubt about the reconstruction of the sounds in brackets since they only occur in a few words.

Examples of the consonants:

	Initially	Medially
p	*pēs, pater, piscis, primus*	*nepōs, clepō,*
	spuō, Greek *plōtós*	*captus, neptis*
t	*tū, tacēre, tenuis,*	*frāter, māter*, Greek *metá,*
	trēs, stō	*captus, neptis*
k	*centum, canis, cor,*	*pecus, decem, tacēre,*
	clepō, (in)clināre, Greek *skótos*	*octō, noctem*
kw	*quod, quis*	*sequor, (re)linquere, aqua*
b	Sanskrit *balam*	*dē-bilis*
d	*duo, dēns, domāre*, Greek *drûs*	*pedes, sedēre, vidēre*
g	*genū, gustus, grānum*	*iugum, ager*, Greek *mēgas*
gw	*vivus, veniō*	

The voiced labio-velar stop *gw* is represented by the bilabial fricative [w], spelt *v* in Latin, and by the voiced bilabial stop *b* in Greek, *bíos, baínō*, or else by a voiced velar stop, *gunḗ*. In the Germanic languages the labial articulation has been retained, English *quick, queen*, Dutch *kwam*, the past tense of *komen*.

The voiced aspirated stops are the most controversial point in the reconstruction of PIE since they are found only in Sanskrit and the modern Indic languages. Examples to illustrate them will be taken chiefly from Latin where they are represented by voiced fricatives and stops, and from Greek where they are represented by voiceless aspirated stops, written *φ*, *θ*, *χ*, here transcribed *ph, th, ch*.

	Initially	Medially
bh	*ferō, fāgus*, Sanskrit *bhar-,*	Greek *nephélē*
	flōs, frāter	
dh	*fūmus*, Sanskrit *dhuma*, Greek *thúra*	*medius*, Sanskrit *mádhyas*
gh	*haedus, hortus, hostis*	Greek *steíchō, léchos*

Further reading

HUDSON-WILLIAMS, T., *A short introduction to the study of comparative grammar (Indo-European)* (1935; repr. Univ. of Wales Press, Cardiff, 1961), 24–40.

KRAHE, H., *Indogermanische Sprachwissenschaft*, vol. i: *Einleitung und*

Lautlehre, 5th edn. (Sammlung Göschen 59, De Gruyter, Berlin, 1966).

LEHMANN, W. P., *Proto-Indo-European Phonology* (Univ. of Texas Press, Austin, 1952).

SZEMERÉNYI, O., *Einführung in die vergleichende Sprachwissenschaft* (Wissenschaftliche Buchgesellschaft, Darmstadt, 1970), 31–64.

THE DEVELOPMENT OF THE CONSONANTS

The first or Germanic sound shift

On the basis of such correspondences as: Latin *pater,* Gothic *fadar,* Latin *tū,* Gothic *þū,* Latin *cornū,* OHG *horn*; Latin *decem,* Gothic *taíhun,* Latin *grānum,* OHG *korn,* scholars in the nineteenth century presumed that in Germanic the PIE consonant system had undergone a radical change, not in the number of phonemes, but rather in their relationship with each other and in their phonetic value. These regular correspondences, the PIE voiceless stops corresponding to voiceless fricatives in Germanic, the voiced unaspirated stops in PIE corresponding to voiceless stops, and the PIE voiced aspirated stops corresponding in some positions to voiced stops and in other positions to voiced fricatives, were first formulated by the Danish linguist Rasmus Rask (1787–1832) in 1818. However, it was Jakob Grimm (1787–1863) who dealt with them in detail and tried to explain them in the second edition of his *Deutsche Grammatik* of 1822. He it was who gave these correspondences the name of the Germanic sound shift (*germanische Lautverschiebung*), which is sometimes known as Grimm's Law or more commonly as the first or Germanic sound shift. Before discussing how the sound shift came about and what were its possible causes, examples of the correspondences are given.

Voiced stops corresponding to voiceless fricatives

IE		Germanic	
p	*pēs, piscis, pecus*	*f*	Gothic *fōtus, fisks, faíhu*
	primus, precārī		Gothic *frumists,* OHG *frāgēn*
	nepōs		OHG *nefo*
t	*tū, tacēre, tenuis*	*þ*	Gothic *þū, þahan,* Old Norse *þunnr*
	tria, frāter		Gothic *þrija, brōþar*

k	canis, caput, cutis	x	Gothic *hunds*, *háubiþ*, OHG *hūt*
	(*in*)*clīnāre*		OHG *hlinēn*
	decem, dūcere, pecus		Gothic *taíhun, tiuhan, faíhu*
kw	*quod, quis*	xw	Gothic *hwa*, OHG *hwer*
	sequor, (*re*)*linquere, aqua*		Gothic *saíhwan* (OHG *sehan*), *leih-wan* (OHG *līhan*), *ahwa*

The PIE voiceless stops remained as stops when they followed an initial *s*: Latin *spuō*, OHG *spīwan*, Greek *skótos*, Gothic *skadus*, Latin *stō*, Gothic *standan*. PIE *p* and *k* become fricatives before PIE *t*, but the *t* remained a stop: Latin *captus*, Gothic *hafts*, Latin *octō*, Gothic *ahtáu*.

Voiced unaspirated stops corresponding to voiceless stops

d	*dēns, duo, domāre*, Greek	t	Gothic *tunþus, twā, ga-tamjan, triu*
	drûs, pedēs, edere, odium		Gothic *fōtus, itan, hatis*
g	*gustus, genū, gelū,*	k	Gothic *kustus, kniu, kalds,*
	augeō, iugum, Greek *mégas*		Gothic *áukan, juk, mikils*

Voiced aspirated stops corresponding to voiced stops and fricatives

bh	*ferō, fāgus, flōs*, Greek	b/ƀ	Gothic *baíran, bōka, blōma,*
	nephélē		Old Low German *neƀal*, OHG *nebal*
dh	Greek *thugátēr, thúra*	d/đ	Gothic *daúhtar, daúr*
	medius, vidua		Gothic *midjis, widuwō*
gh	*haedus, hortus, hostis*	g/ǥ	Gothic *gáits, gards, gasts*
	Greek *léchos, steíchō*		Gothic *ligan, steigan*

In the Germanic languages the voiced stops were to be found at the beginning of words, after nasals, and when the consonants were doubled. Fricatives were to be found in all other positions. In Gothic the medial fricatives were written *b, d, g* and were positional variants of the voiced stop phonemes. Evidence that *b, d* represent fricative pronunciation is provided by the fact that they alternate with *f* and *þ* in final position, *hláibōs* 'loaves' nom. pl., *hláif* 'loaf' acc. sg., *háubida* 'heads' nom. pl., *háubiþ* 'head' nom. sg. The orthography does not show such an alteration in the case of *g* which is used for both the voiced and voiceless sound, *dagōs* 'days' nom. pl., *dag* 'day' acc. sg. Scholars used to be of the opinion that either the PIE voiced aspirated stops first of all became stops which then in certain positions became fricatives, or that they became fricatives in all positions and then became stops in certain positions. This dilemma can easily be solved by saying that the voiced aspirated stops are represented in Germanic by phonemes which have stop allophones initially, after nasals, and when the consonants were doubled, and fricative allophones else-where, i.e. medially between vowels and finally after vowels. The value of the initial allophone of Germanic *g* is certain. Since modern Dutch and many Central German dialects have a fricative pronunciation for this sound, this may well have been its value in Primitive Germanic.

The exceptions to the first sound shift

Mention has already been made of the fact that PIE *p* and *k* after initial *s* were not shifted and also that PIE *t* was not shifted when it followed *p* or *k*. Further exceptions to the sound shift have also been discovered. The medial voiceless dental stop in the Latin words *fráter* and *pater* is represented in Gothic by two different sounds, a voiceless fricative, *brōþar*, and a voiced fricative, *fadar*. From the rules so far given the voiceless fricative should be the regular development of a voiceless stop. This is true of many other examples where there is a labial, dental, or velar-voiced fricative when a voiceless fricative would have been expected. This so-called 'exception' puzzled scholars for a long time until the Dane Karl Verner (1846–96) explained it in 1876. He noticed that although the first syllable (i.e. the one before the voiceless stop) of Gothic *brōþar*, *fadar* and Latin *fráter*, *pater* was stressed, in Greek *patḗr* and Sanskrit *pitár* the stress fell on the second syllable (i.e. after the voiceless stop). The two words had developed differently in Germanic because they had been stressed on differ-ent syllables in PIE. It is assumed that in PIE word stress, or ac-cent, was movable, i.e. it could potentially fall on any of the syllables of the word. The fixing of the stress on the initial or root syllable of the word, as has happened in Latin and the Germanic languages, is a secondary development. The rules of the sound shift must be reformulated to state that PIE voiceless stops became voiceless fricatives *only* when the PIE stress accent immediately preceded them, e.g. in the pattern VC, where V stands for any stressed vowel and C for a voiceless stop. In other cases the PIE voiceless stops correspond to the voiced fricatives *b̄*, *ð*, *g* in Germanic, where they have in fact fallen together with the reflexes of PIE *bh*, *dh*, *gh*. It is an open question whether PIE *p*, *t*, *k* first became voiceless fricatives and then became voiced, or whether they changed straight from voiceless stops to voiced fricatives. The PIE voiceless fricative *s* was also affected in the same way and is represented in Gothic by a voiced fricative *z*, but it is represented in OHG by *r*, which was either a fricative or a trill, Gothic *máiza*, OHG *mēro*.

Since the alternation in stress which gave rise to this twofold development of PIE *p*, *t*, *k* was principally, but not exclusively, found in a predictable morphological series, namely in the principal parts of the strong verbs, Verner's Law is sometimes known as grammatical change (*grammatischer Wechsel*). The development of a PIE voiceless stop to a voiced fricative is chiefly found in the past tense plural and past participle of the strong verbs, and the development of a PIE voiceless stop to a voiceless fricative is found in the past tense singular, present, and infinitive. Since grammatical change has mostly been removed by analogy in Gothic it must be chiefly illustrated from other Germanic languages:

f alternating with *b*	Gothic *þarf þaúrbum*
þ alternating with *d*	OLG *lithan lidum*
h alternating with *g*	OHG *ziohan gizogan*
s alternating with *r*	OHG *kiosan kurun*

There is yet a further consonantal alternation, concerning consonants before *t*, which is also the result of the first sound shift. In Latin a voiced stop became voiceless before a *t*, *regere*, *rēctum*. In the Germanic languages this has become an alternation between either a voiceless stop and a voiceless fricative, e.g. Gothic *skapjan*, *ga-skafts*, or else between a voiced and a voiceless fricative, Gothic *giban*, *fra-gifts*. This process is sometimes known as the Primitive Germanic Dental Rule, or in German, *germanisches Spirantengesetz*. More frequently it is not referred to by any special name. Relics of this alternation can still be seen in modern English *give*, *gift*, where a voiced fricative alternates with a voiceless fricative before the suffix -*t*. In NHG there are examples of this for labial and velar consonants:

Labial consonants		Velar consonants	
geben	*Gift*	*mögen*	*Macht*
graben	*Gruft*	*schlagen*	*Schlacht*
schreiben	*Schrift*	*tragen*	*Tracht*
klieben	*Kluft*	*taugen*	*tüchtig*

In PIE when two dental stops came together they were assimilated to *ss*, Latin *obsideō*, *obsessus* (**obsed-tos*), thus the dental consonants are not involved in these alternations.

Theories about the first sound shift

Ever since the discovery of the correspondences that make up the first sound shift scholars have tried to formulate theories about them. Jakob Grimm established the following table to show the tendency of the sound shift, but he also included the second or High German sound shift (see pp. 45 ff.).

	Labial			Dental			Velar		
Greek	*P*	*B*	*F*	*T*	*D*	*TH*	*K*	*G*	*CH*
Gothic	*F*	*P*	*B*	*TH*	*T*	*D*	..	*K*	*G*
OHG	*B*	*F*	*P*	*D*	*Z*	*T*	*G*	*CH*	*K*

Grimm arranged his series according to the place of articulation. He did not, however, distinguish between aspirated stops and fricatives: *F* in the third line, in OHG, stands for both the affricate in *pforta* and the fricative in *slāfan*. If we compare each vertical line, for example among the labials, a certain regularity in the sequence of symbols is apparent. Below a *P*, standing for an unaspirated voiceless stop, there is always an *F*, which Grimm regarded as representing an aspirated voiceless stop, an affricate or a fricative, and below an *F* there is always a *B*, standing for a voiced stop. The symbols (Grimm called them *Buchstaben*) are retained, but they change their positions as we move downwards from line one to line three. Grimm recognized this and thought he saw a regular tendency in the shifting of sounds: voiceless unaspirated stops become aspirated stops, or affricates, or fricatives, and fricatives become voiced stops, which in turn become voiceless stops, as can be seen in the first two lines of the second column of each point of articulation. This tendency can also be seen among the velar stops and fricatives and even the dentals show this tendency if we compare the Greek and the Gothic lines. The OHG development will be dealt with under the second sound shift as it results in different sounds for the dentals.

The most widespread theory of the sound shift is that which was put forward by the Neogrammarians, who pressed for extreme rigour in linguistic description. They adopted Grimm's correspondences but instead of arranging them according to the place of articulation they arranged them according to their manner of articulation:

	PIE			Germanic		
Voiceless stops	*p*	*t*	*k*	*f*	*þ*	*x*
Voiced aspirated stops	*bh*	*dh*	*gh*	*b/ƀ*	*d/đ*	*g/ǥ*
Voiced stops	*b*	*d*	*g*	*p*	*t*	*k*

They were more interested in the fate of each sound; *p* becoming *f*, *t* becoming *þ*, and so on. This gradually led them to postulate a chronology of the rules of the sound shift. The steps they usually assume are the following:

> first step: *p t k*   becomes *f þ x*
> second step: *bh dh gh* becomes *b/ƀ d/đ g/ǥ*
> third step: *b d g*   becomes *p t k*

One of the most thorough examinations of the whole problem of the sound shift is that of Jean Fourquet. He criticizes the atomism of the Neogrammarians in dividing the sound shift into several stages, 'Das landläufige Bild der "Akte" der ersten Lautverschiebung ist nichts anderes als die Heinstellung der Einheiten, die durch die Vergleichung geliefert werden, als einfache, einheitliche, phonetische Ereignisse . . . ' (1954, p. 15). He suggests that instead of trying to find out when the voiceless stops became voiceless fricatives, and when the voiced unaspirated stops became voiceless stops, one should bear in mind that both might have changed simultaneously or, more accurately, that the distinctive features which connected each row might have changed simultaneously.

The first change in the sound shift was that the distinctive feature of voice that separated *p*, *t*, *k* from *b*, *d*, *g* was replaced by the distinctive feature of aspiration and at the same time the distinctive feature of aspiration which separated *b*, *d*, *g* from *bh*, *dh*, *gh* was replaced by the distinctive feature of voice. This can be shown as follows:

(i) PIE

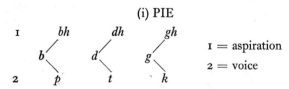

1 = aspiration

2 = voice

(ii) After change in distinctive features

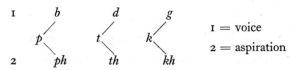

1 = voice

2 = aspiration

There is thus in all probability an intermediate system to be postulated between PIE and Germanic with the following sounds:

Voiceless aspirated stops	*ph*	*th*	*kh*
Voiceless unaspirated stops	*p*	*t*	*k*
Voiced sounds, stops or fricatives	*B*	*D*	*G*

It seems likely that there was an intermediate system similar to the one that has been postulated, since Armenian, an IE language now spoken in parts of Turkey and the U.S.S.R., has a similar consonant system. Meillet speaks of an Armenian sound shift. The final stage of the sound shift was when the whole intermediate system underwent an 'opening' process, that is all the consonants except *p*, *t*, *k* became fricatives; the voiced ones, however, only became fricatives medially between vowels.

Several theories have been advanced to explain why the sound shift took place, for instance that it was because of climatic conditions or that it was the result of 'the maintenance of habits of articulation by the populations which received and adopted the Indo-European dialect, called thereafter Germanic' (Meillet, 1970, p. 22), but we cannot be sure exactly why it happened. It was certainly completed before the Germanic tribes came into contact with the Romans because no early Latin loan-word is shifted. The beginning of the shift may reach back into the second century B.C. It was probably finished by 500 B.C.

Grimm's Law is an example of a phonemic shift; no phonemes have been lost, nor have any new ones arisen, merely the distinctive features which separated the phonemes have changed. Attempts have been made to interpret the first sound shift in terms of the ordered rules of generative phonology. For this see the article by Voyles (1967). Lass (1974) explains the first sound shift as occurring solely to get rid of the 'unnatural' sounds *bh*, *dh*, *gh*, which are not very common in the languages of the world. They are changed into voiced fricatives and both the other changes,

p, *t*, *k* to *f*, *þ*, *x*, and *b*, *d*, *g* to *p*, *t*, *k*, are the direct consequences of
the first change.

Further reading

ESAU, H., 'The Germanic consonant shift. Substratum as an explanation for the first sound shift', *Orbis*, 22 (1973), 454–73.

FOLEY, J., 'Phonological distinctive features', *Folia Linguistica*, 4
(1970), 87–92.

FOURQUET, J., *Les Mutations consonantiques du Germanique* (Klincksieck, Paris, 1948).

—— 'Die Nachwirkungen der ersten und zweiten Lautverschiebung',
Zeitschrift für Mundartforschung, 22 (1954), 1–33.

LASS, R., 'Strategic design as the motivation for a sound shift: the
rationale of Grimm's Law', *Acta Linguistica Hafniensia*, 15 (1974),
51–66.

MEILLET, A., *General characteristics of the Germanic languages*, trans.
W. P. Dismuke (Univ. of Miami Press, Coral Gables, Fla., 1970)
(original title *Caractères généraux des langues germaniques*, 1926).

VOYLES, J. B., 'Simplicity, ordered rules and the first sound shift',
Language, 43 (1967), 636–60.

WEINSTOCK, J. M., 'Grimm's Law in distinctive features', *Language*,
44 (1968), 224–9.

THE DEVELOPMENT OF THE VOWELS

The PIE vowel system did not undergo radical changes like those
of the consonant system. Two mergers took place: among the
short vowels PIE *o* and *a* merged in a short *a*, Latin *hostis*, *octō*,
ager; Gothic *gasts*, *ahtáu*, *akrs*. Among the long vowels PIE *ō* and
ā merged in a long *ō*: Latin *fräter*, *fāgus*, *flōs*; Gothic *brōþar*,
bōka, *blōma*. The merger of short *o* and *a* also meant that the PIE
diphthongs *ai* and *oi* merged in *ai*: Greek *oida*, *oinḗ*, Latin *aes*;
Gothic *wáit*, *áins*, *áiz* and also that the PIE diphthongs *au* and
ou merged in *au*, Latin *augeō*, PIE **roudhos* (Latin *rūfus*); Gothic
áukan, *ráuþs*. These mergers resulted in there being only four
short vowels: *a*, *e*, *i*, and *u*, and four long vowels: *ō*, *ē*, *ī*, and *ū*.

The place in the long vowel system left by the merger of PIE
ō and *ā* in *ō* was soon filled by another long *ā* which came from the
sequence [anx]. The *n* disappeared and the *a* was lengthened,

possibly through an intermediate stage of nasalization. This is the origin of the NHG past tense forms *brachte, dachte* (in MHG these forms had long vowels, *brâhte, dâhte*), while their infinitives have nasal consonants, *bringen, denken*. This new long *ā* which developed in all the Germanic languages is the result of a phonemic split of PIE short *a*. Early Primitive Germanic short *a*, which includes PIE short *o*, must have had two main allophones, an open oral allophone [a] before all consonant groups, except before nasals plus voiceless velar fricatives where the allophone was probably a long nasalized [ãː]. As long as the *n* remained, the allophones [a], [ãː] were in complementary distribution. However, the *n* became lost and the long nasalized allophone lost its nasality and became a new long *ā* phoneme. This can be shown schematically as follows:

Stage 1   short /a/ phoneme has two allophones /a - ãː/
Stage 2   the allophones have become phonemes /a/ : /aː/

This split of short vowels also happened in the case of short *i* and *u* before a nasal plus a voiceless velar fricative. They underwent the same allophonic development as in Stage 1, but when the nasalized allophones lost their nasality they merged with already existing phonemes, long *ī* and *ū*. Relics of this can be found in OHG where the weak verb *dunken* has a past tense *dūhta*, cf. NHG *dünken*, archaic past tense *deuchte* (originally from the subjunctive), which has now been replaced by *dünkte*, and the strong verb *dīhan*, NHG *gedeihen*, which goes back to early Primitive Germanic **þinhan*.

The PIE diphthong *ei* merged with the long *ī* of PIE. As this change also took place in Latin, examples will have to be taken from Greek to illustrate the PIE state: Greek *steíchō*, OHG *stīgan* (the Gothic form is *steigan* but the digraph *ei* is always taken to be a long *ī*). All the changes just mentioned are common to all the Germanic languages. Thus far we have been able to deal with the older Germanic languages as a whole, but from now on we must divide them into two groups: East Germanic, comprising Gothic; and all the rest, Old Norse, Old English, Old Low German, Old Frisian, and Old High German, for which some scholars have proposed the name North West Germanic. Our main concern will, of course, be with OHG.

The four vowel system created by the merger of PIE short *a* and *o* was soon to be expanded. The Primitive Germanic short *u* appears to have had two main allophones, each one being determined by the vowel in the following syllable, except before a nasal, when only *u* occurred. When followed by *i, j,* or *u*, Primitive Germanic *u* had the allophone *u*, but when followed by *a, e, o* it was lowered and had the allophone *o*. In the following schema C stands for any consonant except a nasal, and V for any vowel, and *n* stands for a nasal consonant.

phoneme PG/u/

allophones [u]   [o]

CuCu   *CoCa*

CuCi   *CoCo*

CuCj   *CoCe*

CunCV

The allophonic alternation between *u* and *o* was dependent on the nature of the vowel in the following syllable except when a nasal consonant followed. The conditioning factors were the vowels in the following syllables and as long as they remained, *u* and *o* were allophones of one phoneme. This situation changed when, with the fixing of the stress on the root syllable, the now unstressed syllables became weakened to [ə] or else disappeared. The allophonic variation of *u* and *o* could now no longer be maintained by the following vowels and the allophones *u* and *o* were phonemicized, i.e. became phonemes, by a change in the allophonic conditioning factors. The following example will clarify this:

PG *wurdiz* |wurdis| ╱OHG /u/ *wurt*

                      /u/

PG *wordan* |wurdan| ╲OHG /o/ *wort*

Disregarding the final consonants, the difference between the phonemic shape of the two PG words is carried by the vowels *i* and *a*. In OHG the two forms are *wurt* 'fate' and *wort* 'word'. The final syllables have disappeared and the allophones *u* and *o* are now in contrast in identical environments and are therefore phonemes. From our observations it follows that every word with

Primitive Germanic *u* in a stressed syllable followed by *i*, *j*, or *u* or a nasal should have *u* as its reflex in the older Germanic languages, and that when Primitive Germanic *u* was followed by *a*, *e*, *o* it should have *o* as its reflex in the older Germanic languages. This, however, is not always the case. For instance, we find OHG *boc*, *wolf*, and OE *bucc*, *wulf*, and then OHG *fuhs*, *sturm*, and OE *fox*, *storm*. The usual way to explain these discrepancies is that they are the results of analogy, even if in many cases the reason for the analogical levelling of one particular form is unclear.

In the Germanic languages other than Gothic there is a similar phenomenon with regard to PIE *i* and *e*. Here there is no split of a phoneme but a rearrangement of the two phonemes. Some allophones of *i* became *e*, and some allophones of *e* became *i*. After this development *i* and *e* were only in contrast in one position, before *u*, in other positions they were in complementary distribution.

/i/	:	/e/	
i			before a nasal plus a consonant
i			before a following *i* or *j*
		e	before a following *a*, *e*, or *o*
i		*e*	before a following *u*

When the system of unstressed vowels became disturbed, the various allophones of each phoneme became attracted to the phoneme to which they were phonetically most similar. Thus we have Latin *ventus* but OHG *wint*. The unstressed vowels did not disappear in every case, cf. Latin *medius*, Gothic *midjis*. This has been described as PIE *e* being raised to *i* before *i*, *j*, or *n* plus a consonant. Examples of this are more numerous than cases where PIE *i* is lowered to *e* before *a*, *e*, *o*, Latin *vir*, OHG *wer*(*wolf*), PIE **nizdos*, OHG *nest*.

A number of scholars, Twaddell (1945), Beeler (1966), Van Coetsem (1970), and Penzl (1975), assume a PG short vowel system consisting of four phonemes; but Marchand (1957) and Moulton (1961) assume a vowel system containing only three short vowels. According to the latter, /i/ and /e/ did not contrast before *u* but were allophones of one phoneme. Although there is later a raising of *e* to *i* before *u* in OHG (see p. 58), it seems doubtful whether it occurred already in PG. We will follow Penzl and

Van Coetsem and assume a PG short vowel system consisting of four phonemes: /i, e, a, u/.

In the long vowel system which is the basis for the Germanic languages other than Gothic a second long $\bar{e}$ sound is postulated. In Gothic the two words *nēmum* and *hēr* have the same long vowel, but in OHG and the other Germanic languages these two words have different vowel phonemes: OHG *nāmun* (a ninth-century form), *hier*. On this basis scholars have regarded the vowel represented by Gothic *nēmum*, OHG *nāmun*, as Germanic $\bar{e}^1$, and the vowel represented by Gothic *hēr*, OHG *hier*, as Germanic $\bar{e}^2$. The origin of this latter phoneme, Germanic $\bar{e}^2$, is something of a mystery and there is no theory which is accepted by all scholars. The suggestion which held the field for over fifty years was that $\bar{e}^2$ was derived from the PIE long diphthong $\bar{e}i$. The reason that the origin of $\bar{e}^2$ is difficult to find is that the words containing it in the Germanic languages are themselves of diverse origins.

Germanic $\bar{e}^2$ is found as the vowel of the past tense of the reduplicating Germanic verbs which form the seventh class of strong verbs in OHG (see p. 119). In Gothic these verbs are genuine reduplicating verbs, i.e. they formed their past tense by repeating the first consonant of the stem followed by the vowel *ai, haldan, haíhald*, but apart from relic forms like *teta*, the past tense of *tuon*, there is no trace of reduplication in OHG, cf. *haltan, hielt*. In OHG all the verbs of this class agree in having the same vowel in the past tense sg. and pl., whereas the vowel of the infinitive is different: *gān, gieng; stōzan, stiez; lāzan, liez; slāfan, slief*.

Germanic $\bar{e}^2$ also appears in a large number of Latin loan-words: OHG *ziagal, brief*, cf. Latin *tēgula, brevis*. These latter can be discounted as the source of the origin of $\bar{e}^2$ since they are of a later date and their root vowel has merely been assimilated to an already existing phoneme.

The third group is very small and contains the words: OHG *hier, zieri* 'splendid', *skiero* 'swiftly', *wiara* 'fine gold', *stiega* (late Bavarian OHG), and *mieta*, where $\bar{e}^2$ corresponds to *iz* in Gothic, *mizdō*.

One recent theory that has been put forward (see Van Coetsem (1970 and 1972) regards Germanic $\bar{e}^2$ as coming from PIE *ei*. If PIE *ei* was followed by *i, j*, or *u*, except where a nasal intervened, it then merged with PIE long $\bar{i}$, probably through the stage *ii*. When PIE *ei* was followed by *a, e, o* it became $\bar{e}^2$, probably through the stage *ee*. This development is parallel to the development of the short vowels *i* and *e*. However, if this development had taken place then there should be more words with $\bar{e}^2$ when it was followed by *a, e, o*. The reason that there are not is that by analogy the forms with long *i* supplanted the forms with $\bar{e}^2$. According to this explanation the origin of $\bar{e}^2$ is to be found in the last group of words. From this group, though small in number, it spread to the other groups. It has also been suggested that $\bar{e}^2$ arose in the contraction of the past tense forms of the reduplicating verbs: Gothic *haíháit*, contracted form **heet* (the form *heht* appears in OE), and OHG has the form with the reflex of $\bar{e}^2$, *hiez*.

In the development of the vowels, stages of development can be postulated within Primitive Germanic. There was an early Primitive Germanic stage when the merger of PIE short *o* and *a* took place, giving a four term short vowel system: *i, u, e, a*. Possibly the interchange of the reflexes of PIE *i* and *e* took place at this time. The next stage in the development occurs when the Goths migrate to the Black Sea and the other Germanic languages undergo common innovations. The Primitive Germanic short vowel system is increased by the phonemic split of *u* into *u* and *o*, thus creating a five term vowel system. Early Primitive Germanic also had only four long vowels: *ō, ē, ī,* and *ū*. The development of a long *ā* from the sequence [anx] created a five term long vowel system. The PIE diphthongs, *ai, oi, au,* and *ou*, had merged in *ai* and *au*, while probably *eu* and *ei* had not changed. After the migration of the Goths the long vowel systems of the other Germanic languages were changed by the addition of $\bar{e}^2$. This phoneme came into being through the loss of Primitive Germanic *ei*, which merged with long *i* when followed by *i, j,* or *u* but which developed into the new phoneme $\bar{e}^2$ when followed by *a, e, o*. In Gothic this split may also have taken place, but both the resultant sounds merged with already existing phonemes, long *i* and long $\bar{e}^1$.

Further reading

BEELER, M. S., 'Proto-Germanic [i] and [e]: one phoneme or two?', *Language*, 42 (1966), 473–4.

COETSEM, F. VAN, 'Zur Entwicklung der germanischen Grundsprache', in L. E. Schmitt (ed.), *Kurzer Grundriß der germanischen Philologie bis 1500*, vol. i: *Sprachgeschichte* (De Gruyter, Berlin, 1970), 1–74.

—— and H. L. Kufner, *Toward a grammar of proto-Germanic* (Niemeyer Tübingen, 1972).

LUDTKE, H., 'Der Ursprung des germanischen $\bar{e}^2$ und die Reduplikationspräterita', *Phonetica*, 1 (1957), 157–83.

MARCHAND, J. W., 'Germanic short *i and *e: two phonemes or one?,' *Language*, 33 (1957), 346–54.

MOULTON, W. G., 'Zur Geschichte des deutschen Vokalsystems', *Beiträge zur Geschichte der deutschen Sprache und Literatur* (Tübingen) 83 (1961), 1–31.

PENZL, H., *Vom Urgermanischen zum Neuhochdeutschen* (Schmidt, Berlin, 1975).

TWADDELL, W. F., 'The prehistoric Germanic short syllabics', *Language*, 24 (1945), 139–51.

THE DEVELOPMENT OF GERMANIC TO OLD HIGH GERMAN
THE DEVELOPMENT OF THE GERMANIC CONSONANT SYSTEM

The Primitive Germanic consonant system which resulted from the Germanic sound shift (see pp. 31 f.) is the one which underlies all the Germanic languages, but it has undergone changes in the individual Germanic languages themselves. Within the group which comprises all the Germanic languages except Gothic there is a smaller and more controversial group comprising OHG, OE, Old Frisian, and OLG, which is called West Germanic. The main phonological characteristic of this group is the so-called West Germanic consonant gemination. When a stop or a fricative, and in some cases *r*, cf. OHG *nerren*, was followed by an *i* or *j* or a liquid, it became doubled. These geminate or doubled consonants, if they were stops, underwent further development in OHG in the High German sound shift, therefore examples of the consonant gemination can be seen most clearly from OLG.

Gothic	OLG	OHG
ga-skapjan	*skeppian*	*scephen*
satjan	*settian*	*sezzen*
uf-rakjan	*rekkian*	*recchen*
sibja	*sibbia*	*sippa*
bidjan	*biddian*	*bitten*

Gothic	OLG	OHG
hugjan	*huggian*	*huggen*
hafjan	*hebbian*	*heffen*
hlahjan	OE *hliehhan*	**hlahhen*

The Germanic consonant phonemes which had both stop and fricative allophones have become stops in all positions in OHG: OHG *sterban*, OE *steorfan*; OHG *lebēn*, ON *lifa* (the letter *f* is used for a voiced labio-dental fricative); OHG *erda*, OE *erðe*; OHG *taga* (pl.), Dutch *dagen*, with *g* representing a voiced velar fricative, [ɣ].

The second or High German sound shift

All the Germanic languages except OHG retained the series of voiceless stops, *p*, *t*, *k*, which in OHG underwent a radical change and are represented either by affricates, i.e. a stop followed by a fricative at the same, or very similar, point of articulation, or by long voiceless fricatives. Some of the changes have not taken place in every dialect of OHG and so the correspondences have to be specified according to each dialect, or different scribal system, of OHG, and in fact even the dialects of NHG are usually classified according to how Germanic *p*, *t*, *k*, developed. (The map on p. xvi shows the dialects of NHG.)

The situation was probably not very much different in OHG times except of course that there were no German speakers east of the Elbe. These areas were colonized during the Middle Ages. The NHG dialect divisions into Upper, Central, and Low German are, in the main, also valid for OHG.

The following table shows the development in OHG of the Germanic voiceless stops and the long voiceless geminates produced by the West Germanic consonant gemination:

	p	*pp*	*t*	*tt*	*k*	*kk*
Initially	*pf, ph*		*z* [ts]		*k,ch* [k,kx]	
Medially	*f, ff*	*pf*	*z, zz* [s̩]	*z, zz, tz* [ts]	*hh, ch* [xx]	*ck, cch* [kk, kx]
Finally	*f*		*z* [s̩]		*h* [x]	

Germanic *p* is either represented by an affricate [pf], written *ph* or *pf*, or by a voiceless geminate labio-dental fricative, written *f* or *ff*. Geminate *pp* is represented by an affricate *pf*. Examples initially: English *path, plough, penny*, OHG *pfad, pfluog, phenning*; medially, corresponding to a geminate, OLG *skeppian*, OHG *scephen*, OE *æppl*, OHG *aphul*; medially corresponding to a simple stop: OLG *opan*, Gothic *slēpan*, OHG *offan, slāfan*; finally after vowels: OLG *skip*, OHG *skif*; after liquids and nasals: OE *healpan, weorpan*, English *stump*, OHG *helphan, werpfan, stumpf*. After liquids the affricate was replaced by a fricative in the ninth century, e.g. *helfan*. Some affricates remained until MHG, e.g. *scharpf*, but in NHG this has been reduced to a fricative, *scharf*. In NHG the only example of *pf* after a liquid is *Karpfen*.

Germanic *t* is represented by an affricate [ts] written *z, zz*, or *tz*, or else by a voiceless fricative written *z* or *zz*. The exact phonetic nature of the fricative is uncertain, but it was probably voiceless. It was either dental or alveolar, and also probably pre-dorsal, that is the part of the tongue which approached the dental or alveolar region to produce the friction was the front part of the dorsum, or back, of the tongue. The fricative may be symbolized [s̟]. Examples initially: English *tide*, Dutch *twee*, Gothic *tiuhan*, OHG *zît, zwei, ziohan*; medially corresponding to a geminate: OLG *sittian*, English *little*, OHG *sitzen, luzzil*; medially corresponding to a simple stop: English *water*, Gothic *itan, lētan*, OHG *wazzar, ezzan, lāzan*; finally after vowels: English *that, what, foot*, OHG *daz, waz, fuoz*; finally after liquids and nasals: Dutch *zwart*, English *holt, unto*, OHG *swarz, holz, unz*.

Germanic *k* has only been shifted initially and medially when geminate in UG. The expected affricate [kx] only occurs in the southernmost parts of Alemannic and Bavarian, i.e. in the south of Switzerland and Austria. In Alemannic the affricate has been smoothed to a fricative [x] which is current as far north as Freiburg. It is difficult to know how far Germanic *k* was shifted in OHG since the widespread spelling *ch* may represent either a stop, an affricate, or a fricative. However, medially and finally after vowels it has been shifted to a voiceless velar fricative when it corresponded to a simple Germanic *k*. Examples initially: English *corn, kin*, OHG *chorn, kunni*; medially corresponding to a geminate: OLG *wekkian*, OHG *wecken* (the spelling *cch* in some UG sources may reflect an affricate or fricative pronunciation); medially, corresponding to a simple stop: Gothic *brikan, sōkjan, táikns*, OHG *brehhan, suohhen, zeihhan*; finally after vowels: Gothic *sik, mik*, Swedish *tak* 'roof', OHG *sih, mih, dah*. The fricative pronunciation which is to be found for Germanic *k* after nasals and liquids in present Swiss German, *danke, Volk,* is a recent innovation and not part of the original sound shift.

The High German sound shift is an example of a phonemic split. The split of Germanic *p, t* (and *k* in UG) is assumed to have come about by a change in allophones. Germanic voiceless stops developed allophones which at one time were affricates and fricatives. The affricates occurred initially and after consonants, thus the affricate in OHG *aphul* went back to **ppf,* and that in *sitzen* to **ttz,* elsewhere long voiceless fricatives occurred which were later shortened after long vowels and diphthongs. Evidence for **ppf* is provided by spellings in Otfrid such as *uuipphe, giscepphes,* and evidence for **kkx* in Notker's *wecchen;* Notker also distinguishes between the affricate and the fricative by writing the former double after short vowels, e.g. *sizzen,* as against *wazer.* At one time, assumed to be pre-OHG, the affricates and fricatives were in complementary distribution but two changes phonemicized them: firstly, the clusters **ppf* were reduced to *pf,* thus creating an intervocalic phonemic opposition between the two former allophones: *aphul : scaffelōs* 'shapeless'; secondly, the long voiceless fricative merged after short vowels with the long voiceless fricatives which had come into being through the West Germanic consonant gemination: OLG *opan, heffian;* OHG *offan, heffen;* OLG *makon,* OE *hliehhan;* OHG *mahhōn, *hlahhen.* The fricative from Germanic medial *t* did not merge with any existing phoneme in OHG but created a new phoneme. The phonemic pattern can be seen from the following diagram:

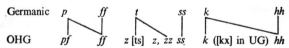

Germanic	*p*	*ff*		*t*	*ss*	*k*		*hh*
OHG	*pf*	*ff*		*z* [ts] *z, zz ss*		*k* ([kx] in UG)		*hh*

The geographical spread of the second or High German sound shift

The extent of the shifting of Germanic *p, t, k* varies from south to north. In the far south, in the High Alemannic and South Bavarian dialects, all the Germanic voiceless stops have been shifted initially, medially, and finally, whereas in Dutch and Low German none of them has been shifted. The material to chart this spread was gathered from the modern dialects in the last century when Georg

Wenker (1852–1911) and Ferdinand Wrede (1863–1934) sent out
a list of forty sentences to be translated into the dialect of each
village. They were sent to every primary school or *Volksschule* of
the German Empire. On the basis of the answers, maps were drawn
showing the extent of the sounds which had undergone the second
sound shift. The geographical distribution of other sounds was also
dealt with. As soon as the material relating to the second sound
shift was available, it was seen that the boundaries which were to
show the extent of the shifted consonants varied according to the
consonant concerned and its position in the word. The lines on the
maps which show the boundary of an area where a certain consonant in a certain position in the word is shifted are called isoglosses (this term can refer to any linguistic feature which is
mapped). The isoglosses of the second sound shift spread out from
south to north in the shape of a fan. The shift of medial Germanic
k and initial and medial Germanic *t* (isogloss 1) defines the whole
of the High German speech area against Dutch and Low German.
The shift of initial *k* (isogloss 5) is much more limited and serves
to mark off High Alemannic from Low Alemannic and Swabian.
The shift of initial and medial geminate *p* (isogloss 4) divides UG
from CG. The latter can be divided into West CG, where initial *p*
remains unshifted, and East CG, where initial *p* is shifted to *pf*
and even to *f* (isogloss 4a). West CG is also divided into two sections: Ripuarian, in which Germanic *p* is unshifted after liquids;
and Moselle Franconian, in which Germanic *p* is shifted in this
position (isogloss 2). Middle Franconian (Ripuarian and Moselle
Franconian taken together) is separated from Rhine Franconian
by an isogloss which shows that the relic words *dat* and *wat* are
shifted in Rhine Franconian but not in Middle Franconian (isogloss 3). It is difficult to be sure how far we can project the spread
of the sound shift in the modern dialects on to OHG. Detailed
work by some scholars has shown how some isoglosses, notably the
dat/das line, originally lay further to the north, as probably did the
Kind/(K)chind line. The other isoglosses can generally be assumed
to be the same as they were in OHG.

It is usually assumed that this geographical distribution of the
sound shift, with more shifted forms in the south than in the north,
reflects its actual spread; it started in the south, in the Alemannic
dialects, and spread northwards. The first shifted forms of which
we have records probably date from the sixth century. Recently it

has been argued that the sound shift is older in the north than was previously assumed, and that perhaps it arose autonomously in the Franconian dialects of CG. Records of very old shifted forms going back to the eighth or ninth century have been discovered, whereas previously most of the shifted forms in these dialects were assumed to date from the twelfth century. These discoveries would give added support to the theory of an autonomous sound shift in the north. The question of the direction of the sound shift has, however, not really been settled and the traditional view of the spread from south to north has many supporters still. This will be the view assumed here.

The shift of Germanic þ to d

Germanic þ was probably a voiceless interdental fricative like the English *th* in *thing*. In the earliest OHG documents it is written *th* and in MHG it is only written *d*: OHG *thū*, MHG *dū* (forms with a short and a long vowel are to be found). It was first written *d* in the eighth century in Bavarian and part of Alemannic. In the ninth century it is written *d* throughout Alemannic and East Franconian. In the tenth century it is written *d* in Rhine Franconian, but in Middle Franconian it is not written *d* until the eleventh century. The orthographic change, which reflects the sound change of voiceless interdental fricative to voiced alveolar stop, spread from the south-east to the north-west.

In Rhine Franconian the shift of Germanic *th* to *d* resulted in a merger with the reflex of Germanic *d* in initial position, e.g. *Otfrid* has *dohter* and *ding*, cf. English *daughter*, *thing*. In East Franconian and UG where Germanic *d* had become *t* (see p. 50) no merger took place. This, of course, is the case in NHG: *Tochter*, *Ding*. These two changes are connected. Chronologically the shift of *th* to *d* occurred after the shift of *d* to *t*. This latter change removed a voiced alveolar *d* from the phonemic system and the shift of *th* to *d* may have come about to fill this 'gap' in the system created by the shift of *d* to *t*. In Germanic there were already two dental or alveolar fricatives, *s* and *þ*; when Germanic *t* became *з* in medial and final position in the second sound shift, there were three. A contributory factor in the shift of *þ* to *d* may also have been the structural pressure to reduce the number of dental or alveolar fricatives in the phonemic system.

The representation of Germanic b/ƀ, d/ð, g/ǥ

In OHG the stop allophones of Germanic b/ƀ, d/ð, g/ǥ were generalized to all positions in the word. The resultant b, d, g also underwent a further development and became written p, t, and k or c respectively. Some scholars regard the change of Germanic d/ð to t as part of the second sound shift. Germanic b/ƀ and g/ǥ are usually written b and g respectively in most OHG documents, except in Bavarian where they are also written p, and k or c, e.g. *Muspilli*: *piutit* (*biutit*), *kotes* (*gotes*). Germanic b/ƀ is written p in all positions in Bavarian: *pein* (NHG *Bein*), *prust, haupit, chalpir, lempir*. During the eleventh century Germanic b/ƀ is spelt b again in medial and final position. OHG Alemannic documents show p for Germanic b/ƀ initially and when doubled, but b intervocalically. In the oldest documents, in the eighth century, Bavarian also shows b medially. Similarly, we find Germanic g/ǥ often written k or c in Alemannic and Bavarian, but not as frequently as p for Germanic b/ƀ. At the beginning of sentences and after voiceless sounds Germanic g/ǥ is written k or c in Bavarian, *calaupa* (NHG *Glaube*), *caplasan* (NHG *geblasen*), but intervocalically it is more often written g, although k and c also occur. In Alemannic we find only k in the St. Gall *Paternoster* and *Credo*, e.g. *kilaubu in kot* in initial and medial position, *take* (NHG *Tage*), while other Alemannic documents only show c finally, *tac*. From the tenth century g is used again and k or c is not used initially and intervocalically. Germanic d/ð is written t in all positions not only in Bavarian and Alemannic, but also in East Franconian (*Tatian*). In other Franconian dialects Germanic d/ð is written d initially, *dages*, but medially also t appears, particularly in South Rhine Franconian, *gotes*. Germanic d/ð when doubled is written tt in UG and East and Rhine Franconian. The change of d to t is one which is reflected in the pronunciation. But is this also the case with the writing of Germanic b/ƀ, g/ǥ as p and k or c? Some scholars are of this opinion and state that p and k or c represent fortis or voiceless sounds which in the tenth century revert to lenis or voiced sounds. This is shown by the use of b and g once again. Since the only evidence for this change is orthographic, it could simply be a change in spelling which did not affect pronunciation. Not all changes in spelling mean that a change in pronunciation has taken place. This orthographic change did not lead to any graphic overlap with the reflexes of the Germanic voiceless stops, since Germanic *p* was written *pf* or *ph* initially; the only initial *p* spellings apart from those of Germanic *b*/*ƀ* were loan-words, e.g. *paradis*, *pīna*. Similarly, there was no overlap with Germanic *k* initially since this was usually written *ch*, e.g. *chalb*, *chind*. Germanic *b*/*ƀ*, *d*/*ð*, *g*/*ǥ* came to be written as *p*, *t*, *c*, representing voiceless sounds in late OHG in final position (see p. 65).

The Germanic fricatives f, s, x

Germanic *f* becomes voiced in all the Germanic languages medially between vowels; this is shown in OHG by writing it *u* or *v*: *reue* 'womb', *neue* 'nephew'. Initially it is spelt *f* which may signify that it was a voiceless sound. It may also be the case that Germanic *s* was voiced medially between vowels. Since the spelling does not change, this cannot be proved with certainty. It is also not clear how far one can say whether OHG *s* initially before vowels stands for a voiced or voiceless sound. In this position the distinction between a voiced and voiceless sound was not phonemic in the case of OHG *s*; probably there was quite a varied phonetic realization of the phoneme in the dialects. The third Germanic fricative *þ*, which has already been dealt with (see p. 49), may have been voiced in an intermediate stage in its development to a voiced stop. This is how some scholars have interpreted the digraph *dh* which is used for it, e.g. *Isidor*: *dhes*, *Weißenburger Katechismus*: *quedhem* ('we talk' cf. English *(be)queath*). Germanic *x* is written *h* initially and finally, *hand*, *ih*. Initially before *l*, *r*, and *w* it is lost during the OHG period, *hring*, *ring*; *hlinēn*, *linēn*; *hwaz*, *waz*. Initially it is assumed to be a mere aspirate as in NHG, but intervocalically it was probably a glottal fricative, possible also voiced, parallel with the intervocalic voicing of Germanic *f* and *s*. Finally after vowels it merged early with the reflexes of Germanic *k*, *sehan*, *sah*; *brehhan*, *brah*. Medially when doubled it also merged with the reflexes of Germanic *k*, *lahhén*, *brehhan*. In the ninth century *hh* was replaced by *ch* intervocalically, *lachén*, *brechan*. Medially the double fricatives *ss* and *ff* occurred in Germanic, OHG *giwissi*, *heffen* (the latter being the sole example of Gmc. *ff* and only occurring in the oldest texts). The occurrence of *ff* was increased by the shift of Germanic medial *p* in the High German sound shift (see p. 45 f.).

THE DEVELOPMENT OF
THE GERMANIC VOWEL SYSTEM

The split of Germanic ai and au

The Germanic diphthongs *ai* and *au* have two reflexes each in OHG: *ai* is represented by *ei* and *ē*, and *au* by *ou* and *ō*. The monophthongs *ē* and *ō* were probably half-open sounds which then became half-close. In OHG the monophthong *ē* occurs only before *r*, Germanic *x*, spelt *h*, and *w*: *ēr*, *ēht* 'possessions', *snēwes*; *ei* appears elsewhere, *stein, heil*. The two reflexes *ei* and *ē* contrast before word-final Germanic *x* and *k*, which had merged in this position: *eih* 'oak': *zēh* past tense of *zīhan* 'to pardon'. The monophthong *ō* appears before Germanic *x*, *hōh*, and alveolars *t, d, s, z, n, r, l*: *rōt, tōd, kōs, gōz, lōn, ōr, kōl* (cf. Latin *caulis*), *ou* appears elsewhere, *loub, loufan, ouga*. The two reflexes contrast before final Germanic *x* and *k*: *hōh* : *ouh* (cf. Gothic *áuk*).

These changes are examples of phonemic splits which came about by allophonic change. Allophones arose under certain conditions, subsequently becoming phonemes by a change in the conditioning factors. At one time Germanic *ai* must have had two main allophones, a half-open monophthong [ɛɪ] before Germanic *x*, *r*, and the semi-vowels *w* and *j*, and a diphthongal allophone, [ei] or [ɛɪ], elsewhere. Similarly, Germanic *au* must have had a half-open monophthongal allophone [ɔɪ] before Germanic *x* and alveolars, and a diphthongal allophone, [ou] or [ɔu], elsewhere. In both cases the allophones were conditioned by the following consonant, or lack of consonant. A change in the quality of the following consonants brought about the change of status of the monophthongal allophones to phonemes. The semi-vowel *j* disappeared in final position and created a phonemic opposition between the monophthongs and diphthongs: OHG *wē* : *ei* represents Gothic *wái* and pre-OHG **aij*. Through the merger of the reflexes of Germanic *x* and *k* in final position the monophthongal and diphthongal allophones also came into contrast: *zēh* : *eih*; *ouh* : *hōh*.

The split of Germanic *ai* received written recognition later than the split of *au* which was first written in the documents of the eighth century. By the end of the eighth century the split of *au* had received orthographic recognition in Alemannic and Franconian. In Bavarian the monophthongal reflex of Germanic *au* was written *ao, frao*, until the beginning of the ninth century. The digraph *au* did not appear until after 825 when it quickly established itself. Again, Bavarian retains longest the spelling *ou* for Germanic *au*, which was the regular reflex of Germanic *au*, except where it became a monophthong.

The oldest OHG texts retain *ai* for the diphthongal reflex of German *ai, ei* did not establish itself until the latter half of the eighth century; in Bavarian not until after 790. The monophthongal reflex of Germanic *ai* was often written *ae* in UG texts and also in *Isidor*. This digraph first appeared in the seventh century, and there are still numerous examples of it in *Isidor* before *r* and *w*, e.g. *aer, aewin* 'eternity'.

From the spread of the changes in the spelling it seems that these changes started in the Franconian dialects, were then quickly taken over by the Alemannic dialects, and only later spread to Bavarian. Although the spread of different spellings for the reflexes of Germanic *ai* and *au* occurs at different times, the phonemic changes they represent seem parallel. Probably both took place at the same time. Generative phonologists have turned their attention to this problem (Vennemann (1972)) and see this change as a lowering of vowels before relatively low consonants.

The spelling of the diphthongal reflex of Germanic *ai* as *ei* has continued into MHG and NHG. What is the phonetic value of *ei*, however, in OHG and MHG? Usually it is taken as representing [ei] or [ɛi], but this is unproven. In the modern CG dialects the reflex of Germanic *ai* is the long vowel [eɪ] which could be derived from MHG [ei]. In UG, however, the reflexes of Germanic *ai* are [oa] in Bavarian and [æi] in Alemannic. Both of these sounds, particularly [oa] in Bavarian, where Germanic *ai* was only written *ei* for a short time, being superseded by *ai* in the twelfth century, are more plausibly derived from an OHG [ai].

The split of Germanic eu

In OHG there are three diphthongs with *i* as the first component, *ie, iu*, and *io*. OHG *ie* is the reflex of Germanic $\bar{e}^2$ (see p. 55), OHG *iu* mostly occurs before *i, j*, or *u* in the following syllable, e.g. *tiuri, (gi-)biutu*, while *io* mostly occurs before an *a, e, o* of the following syllable, *(gi-)biotan, giozo*; elsewhere the latter two diphthongs are in contrast : *liut* : *niot*. Both these diphthongs go back to Germanic *eu*, being the result of a split of allophones into phonemes. Germanic *eu* had two main allophones: *iu* before *i, j*, or *u* and *io*, or *eo*, before *a, e, o*. As in the case of the split of Germanic *u* the loss of unstressed vowels phonemicized the allophones. The reflex of Germanic *eu* before *a, e, o* was first written *eo* but later *io*, which is the main sign used in OHG.

This allophonic structure of *iu* and *io*, determined by the nature of the vowels in the following syllables, is reflected in the development in the CG Franconian dialects. In UG dialects, (including East Franconian), however, the allophonic structure was more complicated since the nature of the following consonant also determined which sound occurred: *io* appeared only before alveolars and Germanic *x* followed by *a, e, o*; in all other cases, that is before labials, velars, and nasals, *iu* occurred: CG Franconian *liogan*, UG *liugan*. *Tatian* has a mixture of forms, *thiuba* but *liogente*. The juxtaposition of the CG Franconian and UG paradigm of the present indicative of the strong verbs shows the difference quite clearly:

CG Franconian	UG	CG Franconian	UG
	Singular		Singular
First pers. *liugu*	*liugu*	(*gi-*)*biutu*	(*gi-*)*biutu*
Second pers. *liugis*	*liugis*	(*gi-*)*biutis*	(*gi-*)*biutis*
Third pers. *liugit*	*liugit*	(*gi-*)*biutit*	(*gi-*)*biutit*
	Plural		Plural
First pers. *liogemēs*	*liugamēs*	(*gi-*)*biotemēs*	(*gi-*)*biotamēs*
Second pers. *lioget*	*liuget*	(*gi-*)*biotet*	(*gi-*)*biotet*
Third pers. *liogant*	*liugant*	(*gi-*)*biotant*	(*gi-*)*biotant*

The verbal endings are dealt with on p. 114 f. This state of affairs existed only in UG in the eighth and ninth centuries. In the tenth century the *iu* before the labials and velars was replaced in writing by *io*. This conditioning may have remained in UG dialects since in NHG there are pairs of words like *die Tiefe* and *die Teufe*, the latter being a word from UG which is used as a mining term for 'depth'. It shows the regular reflex of OHG *iu* in NHG (see p. 69) and not OHG *io*, since the *f* is a labial consonant.

The shift of Germanic ō and ē²

Germanic *ō* and *ē²* are represented in OHG chiefly by the digraphs *uo* and *ie* which are assumed to designate diphthongs. Similar diphthongs are still to be found in modern Bavarian and Alemannic.

In the Franconian dialects of OHG the digraphs for Germanic *ō* appeared after the middle of the eighth century. The main one was *uo*, except in South Rhine Franconian, the dialect of Otfrid, where *ua* was used. At about the same time, or a little later, digraphs appeared in Alemannic sources, *ua* being the main sign used. In Bavarian digraphs did not appear until the ninth century, perhaps not until the first half of the tenth century, but by 950 the main digraph in use was *uo*. In both Alemannic and Bavarian the digraph *oa* was used quite frequently before *uo* and *ua* became the main sign. This digraph may also represent a diphthongal pronunciation. Examples of this shift are: Gothic *bōka*, Otfrid *buah*, OHG *buoh*; Gothic *brōþar*, Otfrid *bruader*, OHG *bruoder*.

Digraphs for Germanic *ē²* start later. In the Franconian dialects they outnumbered the single signs in the ninth century, *ie* being the chief sign. In South Rhine Franconian the digraph *ia* was used. *Isidor* used *ea* which was also typical of Alemannic, where digraphs appeared in the ninth century. In Bavarian the digraph *ie* became the main sign some time in the first half of the ninth century.

There has been much uncertainty as to the phonetic quality of Germanic *ō* and *ē²*. It seems best to regard them both as being open sounds as they are used to render the open *ō* and *ē* of Romance loan-words, but older scholars assumed they were closed sounds. The new open monophthongs from Germanic *ai* and *au* appear to have 'forced' Germanic *ō* and *ē* into becoming diphthongs in order to avoid merging with them. Germanic sounds are in brackets.

Umlaut in OHG

The OHG reflex of Germanic short *a* when followed by *i*, *ī*, or *j*, except before the consonant clusters *ht*, *hs*, was a close *e*. This process whereby a back vowel is fronted before a high front vowel, or semi-vowel, is known as *i*-umlaut, or *i*-mutation. The resultant sound, written *e* in OHG, is considered to be phonetically more close than short Germanic *e*, which is also written *e*. Germanic *a* was not only fronted by *i*-mutation but was also raised. Many present-day dialects keep the two sounds apart phonemically. Most MHG poets were also careful not to rhyme them. However, *i*-mutation did not only affect *a* but all the short and long back vowels and the diphthongs *uo* and *ou*. Even Germanic *e* is assumed to have undergone *i*-mutation. All these vowels developed palatal, or fronted, allophones under the influence of the *i*, *ī*, or *j* which followed, as can be seen from the following diagram (the high front vowels *i* and *ī* as well as *ē* and *ei* were unaffected.)

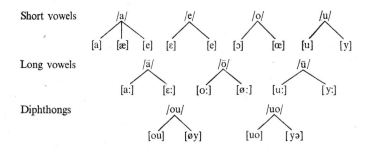

In OHG, however, only the umlaut of short /a/ received orthographic recognition. This is known as primary umlaut (*Primärumlaut*). The other mutated vowel allophones were not written with special signs until MHG, and even then only sporadically. The mutation of the other vowels and diphthongs is known as secondary umlaut (*Sekundärumlaut*). It would be wrong to think that there were two separate umlaut processes. There are rather two stages of one process. Primary and secondary umlaut represent the two different stages of the phonemicization of the umlaut phonemes. Examples of primary umlaut are: OHG *ih faru*, *du feris*, *er ferit*; *gast* (sg.), *gesti* (pl.); *kraft*, *kreftig*. Examples of secondary umlaut are: MHG *wahsen*, *wähset*, OHG *wahsit*; MHG *loh*, *löcher*, OHG *lohhir*; MHG *künne*, OHG *kunni*; MHG *nâmen*, *næme*, OHG *nāmi*; MHG *rôt*, *rœte*, OHG *rōti*; MHG *hûs*, *hiuser*, OHG *hūsir*; MHG *guot*, *güete*, OHG *guoti*; MHG *loufen*, *löufet*, OHG *loufit*. The secondary umlaut of short *a* resulted from the umlaut allophone [æ] not being raised to [e] before the consonant clusters *ht*, *hs*, OHG *mahtig*, *wahsit*. In UG the [æ] allophone of /a/ was also not raised before the clusters *lt* and *rt*, e.g. *haltit*, *arwartit*. In most modern dialects the vowel before these consonant clusters has merged with Germanic short *e*. Only in a few archaic dialects in UG is it a separate phoneme, /æ/.

As in other examples of phonemic split the allophones in complementary distribution become phonemes when the conditioning factors are changed or disappear. In this case the conditioning factors were the *i*, *ī*, or *j* of the following syllable. By MHG all the OHG unstressed vowels, except in some derivational suffixes, e.g. *-lîch*, *-lîn*, where the vowel may have remained long, were reduced to [ə]. Since the semi-vowel *j* had already been lost in the eighth century some scholars assume that all the palatal allophones of back vowels and diphthongs became phonemes at that time. The only clue as to whether this had in fact happened is provided by Notker, who sporadically wrote *iu* for *ū* before OHG *i*, *hūs*, *hiuser* (by Notker's time OHG *iu* had become [yı]), and *oe* for *o* before a following *i*, *froemidiu*. Notker also showed a reduction of unstressed vowels to *e*, *o*, and *a*. Through the loss of unstressed *j* and the merger of *i* and *e* the umlaut allophones could be phonemicized. Generative phonology has turned its attention to this problem (see King (1969), 92–104) and has come to the conclusion that no 'restructuring', i.e. phonemicization of umlaut allophones, took place until MHG. This question has not yet been settled and even generative phonology is revising its original views on this subject (see review of King by Robinson (1973), 331–69).

Another difficult question is: how could the close umlaut vowel, [e], from Germanic short *a* 'pass' the more open Germanic *e* without merging with it? Germanic short *a* appears to have had three allophones in pre-OHG: [æ] before the consonant clusters *hs*, *ht* (and *lt*, *rt* in UG), [ε] which later became [e] before *i*, *ī*, or *j*, and [a] in other positions. Since Germanic short *e* had become *i* before *i*, *j*, or *u* it could only occur in loan-words, e.g. *ketin*, *pelliz*, and in places where it was restored by analogy, pl. *bretir*, gen. dat. sg. *herzin*. In these cases Germanic short *e* seems to have developed a closed [e] allophone and the allophones of Germanic *a* which had become close merged with the allophones of Germanic *e* before *i, ī*, or *j*, since they were phonetically similar, if not the same. Since the allophones of Germanic *a* before *i, ī*, or *j* had merged phonetically with the reflexes of Germanic *e* before *i* or *j* they were regarded as belonging to the latter phoneme and were consequently written *e*. They only merged with Germanic *e* before *i* or *j* and thus seem to bypass the more open [ɛ] allophones which occurred before other unstressed vowels.

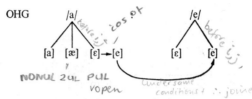

Other vowel changes and the vowels in unstressed syllables

The Germanic long vowel known as *ē*[1], which is represented by long *ē* in Gothic, *nēmum*, is written long *ā* in OHG, *nāmun* (ninth-century form), and shows no variation in the texts.

OHG (and OLG) has *i* as the reflex of Germanic short *e* before the *u* of an unstressed syllable which developed in OHG from a Germanic long *ō*. This chiefly occurs in the first person sg. of strong verbs of Class V, e.g. *geban*, but *ih gibu*. It also occurs in loan-words, OHG *sichur*, from Latin *sēcūrus*. There are some exceptions, *ebur, ernust*, and nouns with the suffix *-unga, werfunga*. Furthermore Germanic short *e* is represented by *i* in OHG before *uu, triuua*, but in the oldest non-Bavarian sources *e* is retained, *treuua*.

In OHG there were five short vowels in word-final position: *gibu guoto, hirta, hirte, suozi*. There is no agreement among scholars as to whether there were also long vowels in this position. Some scholars mark the final vowel long in *taga* nom. pl. but more probably this vowel was short. OHG appears to have had an alternation between a long vowel before a final consonant and a short vowel in absolute word-final position. These can be most clearly seen from the past tense subjunctive of the strong verbs: *ih gābi, du gābīs, er gābi, wir gābīn, ir gābīt, sie gābīn*. Only those vowels which were marked long in OHG manuscripts should be regarded as long. Those few cases where word-final long vowels are marked long, e.g. *hōhī*, are by analogy with other forms, e.g. *hōhīno*, *hōhīn*. Before final consonants, however, long vowels do exist: *zungūn*, *salbōn*, *dannān*, *frāgēn*, *gabīs*. The only sure final long vowel is in the nom. acc. pl. of feminine nouns like *geba* (see p. 107). Notker often writes the pl. form with a circumflex, e.g. *gebâ*. In this case the distinction short vowel : long vowel served to distinguish the sg. from the pl.: *geba* (sg.) : *gebâ* (pl.).

Further reading

BERGMANN, R. and P. PAULY, *Alt- und Mittelhochdeutsch: Arbeitsbuch zum linguistischen Unterricht* (Vandenhoeck & Ruprecht, Göttingen, 1973).

BRAUNE, W., *Althochdeutsche Grammatik*, 13th edn., rev. H. Eggers (Niemeyer, Tübingen, 1975).

EGGERS, H., *Das Althochdeutsche*, *Deutsche Sprachgeschichte*, i (Rowohlt, Reinbek bei Hamburg), 1963.

ELLIS, J., *An elementary OHG grammar* (Clarendon Press, Oxford, 1954).

ESAU, H., 'The medieval German sibilants /s/ and /z/', *Journal of English and Germanic Philology*, 75 (1976), 188–97.

KELLER, R. E., 'The language of the Franks', *Bulletin of the John Rylands Library*, 47 (1964–5), 101–22.

KING, R. D., *Historical Linguists and Generative Grammar* (Prentice-Hall, Englewood Cliffs, N.J., 1969).

MITZKA, W., 'Die ahd Lautverschiebung und der ungleiche fränkische Anteil', *Kleine Schriften* (De Gruyter, Berlin, 1968), 22–9; repr., from *Zeitschrift für deutsches Altertum*, 83 (1951), 107–13.

MOULTON, W. G., *Swiss German Dialect and Romance Patois* (Language Dissertation, 34), suppl. to *Language*, 17 (1941) (Linguistic Society of America, Baltimore).

—— 'The consonant system of Old High German', *Mélanges pour J. Fourquet*, ed. P. Valentin and G. Zink (Klincksieck, Paris, 1969), 247–59.

MUST, G., 'The spelling of Proto-Germanic /f/ in Old High German', *Language*, 43 (1967), 457–61.

PENZL, H., 'The development of Germanic *ai* and *au* in OHG', *Germanic Review*, 30 (1947), 174–81.

—— 'Zur Erklärung von Notkers Anlautsgesetz', *Zeitschrift für deutsches Altertum*, 86 (1955), 196–210.

—— 'Ahd. /f/ und die Methoden der Lautbestimmung', *Zeitschrift für Mundartforschung*, 31 (1964), 289–317.

—— 'The evidence for the change from *th* to *d* in Old High German',

Studies in Languages and Linguistics in Honor of Charles C. Fries
(Ann Arbor, 1964), 169–85.

—— 'Die Phasen der ahd. Lautverschiebung', *Festschrift Taylor Starck*
(Mouton, The Hague, 1964), 27–41.

—— *Lautsystem und Lautwandel in den ahd. Dialekten* (Hueber, Munich,
1971), 115–73.

RAUCH, I., *The OHG diphthongization* (Mouton, The Hague, 1967).

ROBINSON, O. W., 'Review of King, *Hist. Ling. and Gen. Gr.*', *Lingua*,
31 (1973), 331–69.

VENNEMANN, T., 'Sound change and markedness theory: on the history
of the German consonant system', in *Linguistic Change and Generative Theory*, ed. R. P. Stockwell and R. K. S. Macaulay (Indiana
Univ. Press, Bloomington, 1972), 230–74.

—— 'Phonetic detail in assimilation: problems in Germanic phonology',
Language, 48 (1972), 863–93.

VOYLES, J. B., 'The phonetic quality of OHG *z*', *Journal of English and
Germanic Philology*, 71 (1972), 47–55.

THE SCRIBAL SYSTEMS OF OLD HIGH GERMAN

Unlike NHG, OHG is not a uniform standard language, but is
represented by many manuscripts from various different areas
which do not share a uniform orthography. The differences are
not so great that one has to speak of totally different scribal
'languages', but nevertheless they do exist. Usually it is assumed
that the scribal systems from different areas represent different
dialects in OHG. Here we will be concerned mainly with those
points where the OHG scribal systems differ from one another.
Bavarian is only represented by less extensive works and will not
be dealt with.

Differences in the vowel signs

All the OHG written sources generally use the vowel signs
i, e, a, o, u, for both short and long stressed vowels. *Tatian* and
Otfrid make no attempt to distinguish consistently between short
and long vowels. *Isidor*, however, writes long vowels with double
signs, but mostly in closed syllables, e.g. *dhiin* (cf. *dhinan*), *see, iaar,
aloosnin, huus*, and *Notker* uses a circumflex to show that vowels
are long, e.g. *rîche, dû, sâlige, ôra, sêla*. The sign *e*, when it repre-

sents a short vowel, is used to denote two sounds, the half-open Germanic [ɛ], *ezzan*, and the half-close [e] from Germanic *a* by primary umlaut, *gesti* (see pp. 56 f.). The biggest differences are in the representation of the diphthongal reflexes of Germanic *eu*, *ē²*, and *ō*. *Isidor* writes *eo* for Germanic *eu* before *a, e, o, eomanne*, whereas *Tatian* and *Otfrid* have *io* for Germanic *eu*, and *Notker* has *ie* as in MHG; *Isidor, deo, Tatian, Otfrid, dio, Notker, die*. *Notker* and *Tatian* write *ie* for Germanic *ē²*, whereas *Otfrid* writes *ia, hier, hiar* and *Isidor ea, hear*. Germanic *ō* is written *uo* by *Tatian* and *Notker*, whereas *Otfrid* has *ua, guot, guat*. *Isidor* writes *uo* but *oo* in the word *boohhum*. *Isidor* writes *au* for Germanic *au* whereas the other records have *ou*, but only in the environment in which it was not monophthongized (see p. 52). *Isidor, Tatian, Otfrid*, and *Notker* have *ei* for Germanic *ai* (except where it was monophthongized), and *iu* for Germanic *eu* followed by *i, j*, or *u* subject to the UG conditions mentioned on p. 54. They all also have *ā* for Germanic *ē¹*.

Differences in the consonant signs

There are no differences in the monuments in the treatment of Germanic *s* and *f*. Germanic *s* is written *s* in all positions, *sehan, was, disiu*, and Germanic *f* is written *f* initially, *faran*, and finally, *ref* 'womb', but *v* or *u* medially, *reue*.

Most of the differences in spelling are due to different positions in the word. Medial and final Germanic *p* is written *f* or *ff* in all monuments, *slāf, slāfan, skaffen*, but initially it is written *ph* or *pf, phaffo*, but *f* in *Notker, fafo*. *Otfrid* has an unshifted reflex, *pad*. Germanic *t* is always written *z* initially before vowels, *zīt*, but intervocalically there are differences in the reflexes. Both Germanic *p* and *t* occur as geminate consonants between vowels and in this position they developed into affricates, whereas when they were single they became fricatives (see p. 45). In the case of medial Germanic *p* and *pp* a distinction in writing is always made: *slāfan* : *skephen*. The affricate is written *ph* (or *pf*) and the fricative *f*. In the case of Germanic *t* and *tt* this is not always the case. *Tatian* and *Otfrid* make no distinction: *sizzen* (affricate) and *wazzar* (fricative), at least after short vowels. After long vowels and diphthongs the fricative is often written *z, grōze*. The affricate occurred infrequently after long vowels and diphthongs. *Isidor*, however, makes a clear distinction between the affricate and fricative after short vowels, long vowels, and diphthongs: *ezssant, fuozssi* (fricative), and *sitzit* (affricate). *Notker* also makes a distinction between affricate and fricative by writing the latter *z* after short vowels and the former *zz*: *wazer* (fricative), *sizzen* (affricate). This can be seen from the following table:

	Medial Germanic *t* (Gothic *itan*)		Medial Germanic *tt* (OLG *sittian*)	
Tatian, Otfrid	*zz*	*ezzan*	*zz*	*sizzen*
Isidor	*zss*	*ezssant*	*tz*	*sitzenden*
Notker	*z*	*ezen*	*zz*	*sizzen*

These examples are only after short vowels. The medial *zss* of *Isidor* is simplified to *zs* in word final position, *izs*.

Initially before vowels Germanic *k* is always written *k* by *Otfrid*, *kind, kan, kuning, Tatian* only writes *k* before *i* and *e*, *kind, kennen*, elsewhere it is written *c, calb, corn, cuning*. Before liquids and nasals *Otfrid* writes *k*, but *Tatian* has *k* before *n, kneht*, but *c* before *l* and *r, clophōn, crippea*. *Isidor* and *Notker* write initial Germanic *k* as *ch, chomen*. Medially Germanic *k* is written *ch* by *Notker, rîche*, and *Otfrid richi*, and *hh* by *Isidor* and *Tatian, rîhhi*.

Germanic *þ* is written differently in almost every monument. *Tatian* and *Otfrid* write it as *th* initially, *thing*, and *d* medially, *beidiu*; *Isidor* writes it *dh* initially, *dhazs*; medially the signs *d* and *dh* are in free variation, both occurring without any apparent clear indication as to which is the norm. *Notker* writes *d* medially, *nideren*, and *d* initially, *ding*.

Germanic *b/ƀ* and *g/ǥ* are written as *b* and *g* medially in all monuments except in UG where they are sometimes written *p* and *k* (see p. 50). Germanic *d/ð* is written *t* initially and medially by *Tatian* and *Notker, tagun, gotes*. *Isidor* writes it *d* initially, *daghe*, whereas medially *d* and *t* are in free variation. *Otfrid* writes it *d* initially, *dāti*, but *t* medially, *guati*. *Isidor* has the signs *g* and *gh* in complementary distribution, *gh* before or after front vowels, *ghibu, heileghin*, and *g* before or after back vowels, *gote, heilegan*. This is a purely graphic variation and does not reflect any fricative pronunciation. The morpheme OHG *ga-* or *gi-* is always written *chi-* by *Isidor*.

In Notker's works the reflexes of Germanic *b/ƀ, þ* and *g/ǥ* are each written with two signs, *p* and *b*, *d* and *t*, *k* and *g*. These signs are not used in free variation but according to set rules. When the preceding word ends in a vowel or *l*, *m*, *n*, or *r*, they are written *b*, *d*, *g*: *ih antcunde bin dînero listo*; *uber das ander leid, tannân geskah*. In all other cases, including the beginning of sentences, they are written *p*, *t*, *k*: *erwirdîg pist*; *daz ter mano*; *Paulus kehiez*. The reflex of Germanic *d/ð* is always written *t* and is not subject to this alternation, which is known as Notker's Law of Initials or *Anlautgesetz* (Penzl uses *Anlautsgesetz*). The pairs of signs are predictable by rule and various theories have been put forward to account for this phenomenon. It has been regarded as a mere rule of orthography but most scholars nevertheless regard it as having a phonetic basis and call *b*, *d*, *g* lenis sounds and *p*, *t*, *k* fortis sounds. It has been suggested that Notker noticed and wrote these alternations because he was bilingual. Germanic *p* was written *f* and the only other fortis labial stop occurred in loan-words. Germanic *k* was written *ch* by *Notker*. In the case of the reflexes of Germanic *b/ƀ* and *g/ǥ* there is no overlap with other signs if they are written *p* and *k*. This is not the case with the reflex of Germanic *þ* when it is written *t*, since it overlaps with *t* from Germanic *d/ð*.

Further reading

PENZL, H., 'Konsonantenphoneme und Orthographie im ahd. Isidor', *Mélanges de linguistique et de philologie, Ferdinand Mossé in memoriam* (Didier, Paris, 1960), 354–61.
—— 'Die Phoneme in Notkers alemannischem Dialekt', *Germanic Studies in Honor of Edward Henry Sehrt*, Miami Linguistic Series no. 1 (Univ. of Miami Press, Coral Gables, Fla., 1968), 133–50.
—— 'Zur phonemischen Deutung der 'direkten Variation' in ahd. Denkmälern', *Mélanges pour J. Fourquet* (Klincksieck, Paris, 1969), 287–93.
—— *Lautsystem und Lautwandel in den ahd. Dialekten* (Hueber, Munich, 1971), 27–114.
SONDEREGGER, S., 'Das Althochdeutsche der Vorakte der älteren St. Galler Urkunden. Ein Beitrag zum Problem der Urkundensprache in ahd. Zeit', *Zeitschrift für Mundartforschung*, 28 (1961), 251–86.
VALENTIN, P., *Phonologie de l'allemand ancien, les systèmes vocaliques* (Klincksieck, Paris, 1969).

THE DEVELOPMENT OF OLD HIGH GERMAN TO MIDDLE HIGH GERMAN

The merger of OHG io and ie, and of iu with the umlaut of OHG ū

OHG had three diphthongs with *i* as the first component: *io*, *ie*, and *iu*, but in MHG only *ie* occurs. OHG *io* and *ie* have merged in *ie* in MHG: OHG *dionost*, *mieta*, MHG *dienest*, *miete*. OHG *iu* retains the same spelling but has become a long close front rounded monophthong [yː] as in NHG *Bühne*. This new monophthong is also the same sound as the umlaut vowel from OHG long *ū*, OHG *hūsir*, MHG *hiuser*. This merger seems to have taken place by Notker's time since he uses *iu* to designate the umlaut vowel from OHG long *ū*, *hiuser* (OHG *hūsir*) as in MHG. *Notker* also shows the merger of OHG *io* and *ie*, OHG *liod*, *hiez*; *Notker lied*, *hiez*. OHG *io* was not a very frequent phoneme and it was absorbed by the more frequent OHG *ie*. Phonetically the second component of *io* was weakened and became [ə].

Secondary umlaut in MHG

In MHG all the umlaut allophones have become phonemes by the weakening of the vowels in unstressed syllables and the loss of a following *j* (see pp. 56 f.). This change increased the number of vowel phonemes: MHG *über*, *möhte*, *bezzer*, *liute*, *hœren*, *wære*, *güete*, *löufet*, introducing front rounded vowels as phonemes into German. Other Germanic languages have had front rounded vowel phonemes, but in English, for instance, they have been derounded, e.g. NHG *Brücke*, English *bridge*.

Changes in unstressed vowels

In MHG the five short OHG vowels which occurred in word-final position have all merged in *e*, which presumably is phonetically [ə]. Examples are: OHG *taga* (pl.), *ofto*, *gibu*, *hirte*, *turi*; MHG *tage*, *ofte*, *gibe*, *hirte*, *türe*. The OHG long vowels which occurred before final consonants were also reduced to *e*: OHG *zungūn*, *gābin*, *salbōn*, *frāgēn*, *dannān*; MHG *zungen*, *gæben*, *salben*, *vrâgen*, *dannen*. The only diphthong in OHG to occur finally was *iu* which is retained in MHG, but as a long front rounded vowel [yː]. This remains a notable exception to the general weakening of unstressed long and short vowels. The long close vowel *i* was retained in some derivational suffixes in which it probably bore a subsidiary stress, e.g. MHG *-lîche, -lîn, -în*.

The shift of OHG sk to sch

OHG *sk*, sometimes spelt *sc*, is represented by the spelling *sch* in MHG which is widely regarded as being the same sound as in NHG *schon*, a voiceless palato-alveolar fricative. The sound, which is symbolized phonetically as [ʃ], is a new phoneme in MHG. It appears initially, medially, and finally: *schaffen, schrîben, waschen, visch*; OHG *scaffan, scrîban, waskan, fisc*. The shift of OHG *sk* to [ʃ] is difficult to date. The spelling *sch* is found in a few cases in older sources, but it is only in the eleventh century that its frequency increases to any great degree. This change is common to all Germanic languages except Dutch and the Westfalian dialect of German where *sk* has become [sx].

The devoicing of word-final stops

In OHG there were voiced stops in word-final position: *wib, tag, sid*. In MHG the final consonants are written with the same signs as the voiceless stops, *wîp, tac, sît*. The devoicing of OHG *b* and *g* in word-final position does not involve a merger since Germanic *p* has been shifted to *f* in this position, OLG *skip*, OHG *skif*, but the devoicing of final OHG *g* does seem to involve a merger since an OHG final *k* does exist in the words *boc* and *blic*. In these words, however, the voiceless final stop may be a reflex of West Germanic *kk*, since Germanic *k* in this position was shifted to *h*, *brah*. However, the dental stop *d* does merge with OHG *t* when it is devoiced: OHG *sid, zît*; MHG *sît, zît*. This devoicing of final stops in MHG is known as *Auslautverhärtung*. This is the reason why in MHG and NHG there are alternations between medial voiced stops and final voiceless stops, MHG *tac, tage; wîp, wîbe; tôt, tôde*. In NHG this alternation is masked by the spelling since the stem form is always spelt the same: *Tag, Tage; Weib, Weiber; Tod, Tode*.

Further reading

HATTO, A., 'Some OHG vowels in the light of the phoneme theory', *London Medieval Studies*, I (1937), 65–76.

MAYER, A., 'Zum Alter des Übergangs von sk > sch', *Beiträge zur Geschichte der deutschen Sprache und Literatur*, 53 (1929), 288–90.
PENZL, H., 'Umlaut and secondary umlaut in OHG', *Language*, 25 (1949), 223–40.

CLASSICAL MIDDLE HIGH GERMAN

MHG is available to us in many manuscripts from all parts of the German speaking area. Although these manuscripts show variations in spelling, scholars have assumed that the differences, particularly during the twelfth century, were so slight that one may speak of 'classical' MHG. This refers to the language of the poets who wrote about knightly and courtly culture. On the basis of the manuscripts, Karl Lachmann (1793–1851) produced a normalized MHG which is the type of MHG used in most MHG grammars and basic texts.

It is this type of MHG with which we shall concern ourselves here. It must, however, be realized that it is a somewhat artificial reconstruction.

The short vowel system of classical MHG has been reconstructed as follows:

i	*ü*	*u*	*ritter*	*über*	*stube*
e	*ö*	*o*	*bette*	*möhte*	*bote*
ë			*lëse*		
(ä)		*a*	*trähene*		*was*

These nine vowels are phonemes, that is they are all distinctive sounds contrasting with each other. The phoneme /ä/ probably did not exist in CG, and in most dialects it merged early with /ë/. The sign *ë* was introduced by Jakob Grimm in order to distinguish it from the close /e/ which represents the primary umlaut of Germanic short *a*. These two sounds contrasted phonemically in MHG, although the manuscripts do not distinguish between them in writing. In classical MHG it is assumed that that the vowel in *ëzzen* was a half-open [ɛ] and that the vowel in *bezzer* was a half-close vowel [e]. As has been mentioned before, many MHG poets did not rhyme these two *e* sounds and most UG and CG dialects still distinguish these sounds phonemically. In unstressed syllables short *e*, representing [ə], was the most frequent vowel. In some suffixes it was written either *e* or *i*, e.g. *künec, künic*; *irdesch, irdisch.*

The long vowels and diphthongs have been reconstructed as follows:

î	*iu*	*û*	*sîn*	*liute*	*ûf*		*ie*	*liet*	*üe*	*süeze*	*uo*	*buoch*
ê	*œ*	*ô*	*êren*	*hœren*	*ôren*		*ei*	*heil*	*öu*	*löuber*	*ou*	*ouch*
æ		*â*	*wære*		*wâren*							

The spelling of the phonemes *œ, üe, öu* and short *ü* and *ö* in manuscripts was often no different from their unmutated counterparts. The phoneme *öu* was often spelt *eu, vreude.* There may have been some unstressed long vowels in the suffixes -*lîch*, -*lîn*, and -*în* as they often rhymed with MHG stressed long *î*.

The consonant system of MHG has been reconstructed as follows:

	labial	alveolar	palato-aveolar	palatal	palato-velar	glottal
affricates	*pf*	*z* [ts]				
stops { voiceless/fortis	*p*	*t*			*k*	
stops { voiced/lenis	*b*	*d*			*g*	
fricatives { voiceless/fortis	*f*	*s* [s̩] *z* [s̩]	*sch*		*ch* [x]	
fricatives { voiced/lenis	*v*					*h*
nasals	*m*	*n* [n~ŋ]				
liquids		*l r*				
semi-vowels	*w*			*j*		

The affricate *pf* was often written *ph*. The affricate [ts] was written *z* initially, finally, and medially after long vowels and diphthongs: *zît, saz, reizen*, but *tz* medially after short vowels, *sitzen*. It is not clear whether the stop phonemes were distinguished fortis : lenis as in many UG dialects, or voiceless : voiced as in the present standard. The contrast between *f* and *v* only occurred intervocalically, *grâven* : *slâfen*. Initially only *v* appeared which may be voiceless/fortis or voiced/lenis. The voiced : voiceless, or lenis : fortis contrast among the stops and fricatives was neutralized in word-final position where only voiceless/fortis sounds occurred. Intervocalically *s* may have been voiced. Initially before vowels it may have been either voiceless/fortis or voiced/lenis. The contrast between *s* and *z* occurred only in medial and final position: *wîsen* : *wîzen; was* : *waz*. It has been assumed that these two fricatives were both voiceless/fortis and that they were both formed at the same point of articulation. The phonemic feature which distinguished them was that a different part of the tongue was used to narrow the air-stream on its passage through the mouth, thus creating the friction. The *s* was apical, that is articulated with the apex, or tip, of the tongue [ṣ], whereas the *z* was pre-dorsal, articulated with the front part of the back of the tongue, or dorsum [s̱]. The fricative *sch* was probably pronounced in the same way as in NHG. It appeared initially only before vowels, *schône*, and *r*, *schrîben*. Only *s* of the fricatives *s* and *z* appeared initially before vowels and consonants, *sîn, stên, spiln, smerz, snel, swimmen, slâfen*. MHG *ch* was probably a velar fricative in all positions, even after front vowels as in some Swiss German dialects today. MHG *h*, probably a glottal fricative, appeared medially between vowels where it contrasted with the velar fricative *ch*, as well as initially: *sehen* : *brechen* : *hant*. Finally and before *t* and *s* this contrast was neutralized, the resulting sound, probably the velar fricative [x], was written either *h* or *ch*: *sa(c)h, na(c)ht, vu(c)hs*. A velar nasal [ŋ] does indeed exist, but only as an allophone of *n* before *k* and *g*, *sinken, singen*. It is assumed that the cluster *ng* in MHG was pronounced [ŋg]. One of the pieces of evidence for this pronunciation is the fact that medial *ng* becomes *nc* in final position, *sanc* is thus the past tense of both *sinken* and *singen*. The liquids *l* and *r* were alveolar although *r* may have been pronounced as a uvular sound in some dialects. The MHG semi-vowel *w* appeared initially, *wîn*, and medially after vowels and *l* and *r*: *blâwes, houwen; swalwe, varwe*. The palatal semi-vowel *j* appeared initially before vowels, *jâr*, and medially in a few words, e.g. *dræjen*.

Intervocalically long consonants occurred, written *pp, ck, ff, zz: knappe, brücke, schaffen, bizzen*. Since they only occurred after short vowels they were probably allophones. In normalized MHG texts these long consonants appear after short vowels and the corresponding short consonants after long vowels and diphthongs, *schaffen* but *slâfen*. Normally the short counterparts of *pp* and *ck* did not occur intervocalically but only initially, *pîn*, and finally, *wîp*. MHG *ss, tt, mm, nn, ll*, and possibly also *rr*, contrasted with short consonants, i.e. consonant length was phonemically relevant, but only after short vowels: *lesen* : *messe*; *beten* : *betten*; *name* : *amme* 'nurse'; *manec*: *manne*. Examples of contrast in consonant length for the liquids are harder to find.

Unless explicitly stated otherwise, all the MHG sounds mentioned in the text will be regarded as phonemes. In tracing their development to NHG they will be enclosed in the conventional slant lines / / only when their phonemic status is being especially emphasized; they will normally be written MHG *t*, *a*, *s*, etc. The MHG fricatives will often be referred to with two signs, e.g. *ʒ*, *ʒʒ*, *f*, *ff*, and since the two signs are in complementary distribution they will be combined to designate the MHG phonemes /z, zz/, /f, ff/.

Further reading

DE BOOR, H. and R. WISNIEWSKI, *Mittelhochdeutsche Grammatik*, 7th edn. (Sammlung Göschen 41080, De Gruyter, Berlin, 1973).

EGGERS, H., *Das Mittelhochdeutsche, Deutsche Sprachgeschichte*, ii (Rowohlt, Reinbek bei Hamburg, 1965).

OKSAAR, E., *Mittelhochdeutsch* (Almqvist & Wiksell, Stockhom, 1965).

PAUL, H., *Mittelhochdeutsche Grammatik*, 20th edn. ed. H. Moser and I. Schröbler (Niemeyer, Tübingen, 1969).

SACKER, H., *An introductory Middle High German text* (Harrap, London, 1964).

SCHIEB, G., 'Mittelhochdeutsch', in L. E. Schmitt (ed.), *Kurzer Grundriß der germanischen Philologie bis 1500* (Berlin, 1970), 347–69.

WALSHE, M. O'C., *Middle High German Reader* (Clarendon Press, Oxford, 1974).

THE DEVELOPMENT FROM MHG TO NEW HIGH GERMAN

REGULAR SOUND CHANGES

The development of MHG *î, iu, û* and the diphthongs *ei, öu, ou*

The MHG long close vowels *î, iu, û* are represented in NHG by the falling diphthongs [ai], spelt *ei*, [oi], spelt *eu* and *äu*, and [au], spelt *au*. The MHG diphthongs *ei, öu, ou* are also represented in NHG by the same falling diphthongs [ai], [oi], and [au] respectively. Whereas in MHG there was a contrast between *mîn* and *ein*, *vriunt* and *vröude*, *bûch* and *ouch*, there is no contrast in NHG; the vowels in the pairs of words are spelt the same and also pronounced the same: *mein, ein*; *Freund, Freude*; *Bauch, auch*. The MHG phonemic distinctions /î/ : /ei/, /iu/ : /öu/, /û/ : /ou/ no longer exist; the two sets of phonemes have merged in NHG. This can be illustrated as follows.

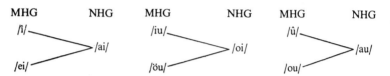

MHG	NHG	MHG	NHG	MHG	NHG
/î/		/iu/		/û/	
	/ai/		/oi/		/au/
/ei/		/öu/		/ou/	

Examples: MHG *mîn, vrî, snîwen, bein, ei*; NHG *mein, frei, schneien, Bein, Ei.*

MHG *iuch, niuwe, diuten, vröude*; NHG *euch, neue, deuten, Freude.*

MHG *bûch, ouch, sû, vrouwe, trûwen, tûbe, toup*; NHG *Bauch, auch, Sau, Frau, trauen, Taube, taub.*

Phonetically MHG *î, iu, û* were diphthongized. They became overlong [ii, yy, uu], then the two parts became differentiated in tongue height, e.g. [ei, øy, ou]. Later [ei] and [ou] were lowered to [ai, au] and [øy] became [oi]. All the CG and UG dialects show diphthongs for MHG *î, iu, û*, except High Alemannic (mostly Swiss German), and the dialect of the west part of Thuringia. The phonetic nature of the diphthongs in the dialects often differs from standard NHG (see maps in Wiesinger (1970)).

The new diphthongs for MHG *î, iu, û* found their first written expression in Carinthian documents of the twelfth century. During the following centuries they spread over the German speech area in a south-east to north-west direction. Diphthongal spellings are found in the whole of Bavaria in the thirteenth century, in East Franconia, Bohemia, and Silesia in the fourteenth century, in Upper Saxony and the eastern part of Thuringia in the fifteenth century, and in Lower Hesse and Middle Franconia in the sixteenth century. The spread of the diphthongal spellings probably does not reflect the actual spread of diphthongal pronunciation which took place earlier and was later reflected in the spelling.

The exact phonetic value of the MHG diphthongs *ei, öu, ou* is uncertain. They may have been pronounced [ei], [øy], [ou], or they may have been pronounced as they are in NHG. The important thing is that in NHG they have merged with the MHG long close vowels *î, iu, û*. This merger is found fully carried through only in the standard language, which is probably due to the fact that when diphthongal spellings were first used in ECG for MHG *î, iu, û* they were the same signs as were used for MHG *ei, öu, ou*. Since both these sets of phonemes were written with the same signs they eventually became pronounced in the same way.

In WCG MHG *iu* merged with MHG *û* in *û* before *w* and was diphthongized to [au]. This development is reflected in NHG *brauen, kauen*, MHG *briuwen, kiuwen*, as against the name *Bräuer* and *wiederkäuen* with the regular development of MHG *iu* to [oi]. These seem to be the only examples reflecting this dialectal development which are to be found in NHG. In *Luke* 'hatch', *Düne* (from Low German), and *Uhr* (from French), the undiphthongized long vowels are retained because these loan-words were borrowed after the diphthongization had taken place. NHG *Friedhof*, MHG *vrîthof*, has not undergone diphthongization because the first part, MHG *vrît-*, was considered to be connected with *Friede*. MHG *dû* and *nû* have also not undergone diphthongization; probably because they had unstressed forms with a short vowel.

There are parallel diphthongizations in English and Dutch but the spelling has not changed from medieval times, English *mine, house* (*ou* is a digraph for OE long *ū* introduced by Anglo-Norman scribes), Dutch *mijn, huis*. Long vowels tend to be unstable and to diphthongize, contrast the 'long' vowels of English *see, do* with the long vowels in German *See, du*, which are 'pure' long vowels.

The monophthongization of the MHG diphthongs *ie, üe, uo*

The MHG diphthongs *ie, üe, uo* are represented in NHG by the long close vowels [iː], [yː], [uː] which are spelt *ie, ü*, and *u* respectively: MHG *lieben, grüene, buoch*; NHG *lieben, grün, Buch*. The spelling has not changed in the case of MHG *ie*. These long monophthongs merged with the MHG short vowels *i, ü, u* when they were lengthened: MHG *siben : lieben*; *über : trüebe*; *stube*:

buobe; NHG *sieben, lieben*; *über, trübe*; *Stube, Bube*. Phonetically this change implies a weakening of the second element of the diphthong, its disappearance, and the consequent lengthening of the first element. This was probably caused by the heavy stress on the root syllable.

Examples:

MHG	NHG
dienest	*Dienst*
süeze	*Süße*
guot	*gut*

The monophthongization appeared first in CG documents in the twelfth century. UG dialects still retain diphthongs of a similar nature to those that are assumed for MHG.

Before certain consonants and consonant clusters the MHG diphthongs *ie, üe, uo* have not only become monophthongs but have also been shortened.

Before nasals:

MHG	NHG
iemer	*immer*
gienc	*ging*
phrüende	*Pfründe* 'benefice, living'

Before MHG *h* plus a consonant:

MHG	NHG
lieht	*Licht*
viehte	*Fichte*
nüehtern	*nüchtern*

Before voiceless consonants:

MHG	NHG
muoter	*Mutter*
vuoter	*Futter*
müezen	*müssen*
muoz	*muß*
krüepel	*Krüppel*

This development represents the situation in many ECG dialects where MHG *ie, üe, uo* are always shortened before voiceless consonants.

The development of the MHG e sounds

In classical MHG there were five *e* sounds, three short and two long. These sounds all contrasted with each other. Examples of words with short *e* sounds are: *bezzer* : *ëzzen* : *mähtic*. The sound written *e* in *bezzer* represents a half-close vowel [e] and the sound written *ë* in *ëzzen* represents a half-open vowel [ɛ]. The sound written *ä* in *mähtic* is more open than the vowel in *ëzzen* but not as open as the *a* in *naht*; it can be symbolized [æ]. The opposition between the half-close /e/ and the half-open /ë/ is not reflected in MHG orthography (see p. 66). The evidence that there was such a contrast in MHG derives from the fact that in many CG and UG dialects such a contrast still exists; also many MHG poets did not rhyme the two sounds. The [æ] sound may have only existed in some UG dialects; in other dialects it merged early with MHG *ë*. Among the long vowels in MHG we have a contrast between the half-close /ê/ [eː], *mêre*, and the half-open /æ/ [ɛː], *lære*.

In NHG the three short MHG vowels have merged in one sound, the half-open [ɛ]. The stressed vowels in NHG *besser, essen, mächtig* are pronounced the same. This is an example of an unconditioned merger. The NHG /e/ phoneme is, however, spelt both *e* and *ä*. Only when the word containing NHG /e/ has a morphologically related word with an *a* as its stem vowel is NHG /e/ written *ä*. This chiefly happens in the case of certain grammatical categories: plural of nouns, *Gast, Gäste*; comparison of adjectives, *lang, länger*; present tense of strong verbs, *wachsen, wächst*; or derivational formations, e.g. *schwach, Schwäche*; *Rache, rächen*.

Historically the sign *ä*, which was sometimes written *å* in Early NHG, comes from UG sources. It apparently did not exist in CG where probably only two short *e* phonemes existed, /e/ and /ë/. When the sign *ä* appeared in CG sources its use became restricted to words which had morphologically related forms with the stem vowel *a* since it did not reflect any difference in pronunciation as it did in UG.

Examples:

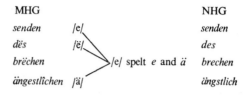

MHG			NHG
senden	/e/		*senden*
dës	/ë/		*des*
brëchen		/e/ spelt *e* and *ä*	*brechen*
ängestlîchen	/ä/		*ängstlich*

The two MHG long vowels /ê/ and /æ/ have also merged in most varieties of NHG in a long half-close /eː/: MHG *êre* : *lære*; NHG *Ehre, Leere*. In some varieties of NHG (including the prescribed standard), particularly in the south and west, there are two long *e* phonemes: *Bären* : *Beeren*, the phoneme spelt *ä* is a half-open /ɛː/, and the other one is a half-close /eː/. This is not, however, a direct continuation of the MHG contrast between /ê/ and /æ/ since the half-open /ɛː/ is found in words from five MHG sources: 1. in *fähig, Käse* it represents MHG /æ/; 2. in *Ähre, Träne* it represents MHG /ä/ when lengthened; 3. in *Bär, Käfig, erwägen* it represents MHG /ë/ when lengthened; 4. in *ähnlich, nähren, zählen* it represents MHG /e/ when lengthened; 5. in *Fäden, Hähne, Läden* it is due to analogical formation. The factor which unites these words is that they are all spelt with *ä*. Where NHG /ɛː/ does exist it is a spelling pronunciation of *ä*, which in some dialects is supported by the fact that a contrast between the reflexes of MHG /ê/ and /æ/ is still maintained.

The lengthening and shortening of vowels

Disyllabic words in MHG had different syllable types from NHG. There were in fact three types (the initial and final consonants will be disregarded): 1. VCCv, e.g. *hazzen, messe, brücke, knappe, ritter, schaffen* (V represents any short vowel, CC a long consonant, and v unstressed *e* as in the final vowel of NHG *bitte*); 2. VCv, e.g. *haben, reden, sagen, lesen, beten*; 3. VVCv, e.g. *âbent, slâfen, brâdem* 'vapour', *vrâgen, râten* (VV represents any long vowel or diphthong). There are two stages in the development from MHG to NHG. The first step was that short vowels before single voiced consonants were lengthened, MHG *siben, stube, eben, haben, oben*; NHG *sieben, Stube, eben, haben, oben*. We will consider the MHG short vowels before MHG *t* later. Syllable type 2 VCv, e.g. *haben*, merged with syllable type 3 VVCv, e.g. *âbent*, giving two syllable types: 1. VCCv *schaffen*, and 2. VVCv *slâfen*, which differed from each other in two ways. Firstly in vowel length; *schaffen* has a short vowel and *slâfen* has a long vowel. Secondly in consonant length; *schaffen* has a long consonant and *slâfen* a short consonant. This change is called the lengthening of short vowels in open syllables, i.e. before single consonants followed by an unstressed vowel (*Tonsilbendehnung*). In NHG there are no long consonants except at the boundaries of words or morphemes, e.g. *nicht tun, Süddeutschland, Schiffahrt*. The second step was that long consonants became redundant and were shortened. In NHG orthography the double consonant, e.g. in *schaffen*, merely signifies that the preceding vowel is short. In NHG length of the vowel alone is sufficient to distinguish between the two types of syllable e.g. [ʃafən], [ʃlaɪfən]; no difference of length of consonants is needed.

The NHG vowels which are the products of the lengthening of MHG short vowels before single voiced consonants have all merged with already existing long vowel phonemes. Phonemically this is an example of a shift with merger. MHG /i, ü, u/ did not merge with MHG /î, iu, û/ since the latter had become diphthongs, but with long close monophthongs which were the result of the monophthongization of MHG /ie, üe, uo/: *siben* : *lieben*; NHG *sieben, lieben*; MHG *übel* : *rüebe*; NHG *Übel, Rübe*; MHG *stube* : *buohe*; NHG *Stube, Bube*. MHG short /a/ merged with MHG long /â/: MHG *sagen* : *vrâgen*; NHG *sagen, fragen*. MHG short /o/ merged with MHG /ô/: MHG *boden* : *tôdes*; NHG *Boden, Todes*. MHG short /ö/ merged with MHG long /œ/: MHG *knödel* : *blœde*; NHG *Knödel, blöde*. MHG short /e/, /ë/ and /ä/, when they were lengthened, merged with MHG /æ/ and /ë/ in a long half-close /eɪ/, or half-open /ɛɪ/, if the resultant phoneme was spelt *ä* (the origin of NHG /ɛɪ/ has been treated on p. 74): MHG *zeln, denen, geben, vrävel(e)*: *lære, sêle*; NHG *zählen, dehnen, Frevel, Leere, Seele*.

Thus far we have avoided dealing with MHG short vowels before single MHG *t*. The reason for this omission is that there are in NHG both short *and* long vowels as the reflexes of MHG short vowels before MHG *t*: MHG *schate, site, beten, bote*; NHG *Schatten, Sitte, beten, Bote*. The regular development is that MHG vowels remain short before MHG *t*, e.g. MHG *site*, NHG *Sitte*. Wherever there is a lengthened vowel it is due either to analogy with other forms, or to the fact that the words became spelt with a single *t*; the vowel before the single *t* followed by unstressed *e* was of course pronounced long in NHG. Only a few words exist which have a long vowel before MHG *t* as the reflex of a MHG short vowel: NHG *Vater, Bote, geboten, beten, kneten, treten, jäten, waten, Spaten, Knoten, Kater*, and *Kröte*. Some of these are verbs and probably have a long vowel by analogy with other verbs in the same class, such as MHG *geben*, whose vowel has been regularly lengthened. This also happens before MHG *m*; NHG *kommen*, MHG *komen*, has not lengthened the vowel, whereas NHG *nehmen*, MHG *nemen*, has a lengthened vowel. The main words which have a lengthened vowel before MHG *m* are: *Schemel* 'stool', *Name, nehmen, schämen, ziemen*. Again a small number compared with those words which have retained a short vowel. To a lesser extent the same situation occurs in the case of short vowels before MHG *l* and *n*. There are long vowels in the case of NHG *spielen, zählen*, but short vowels in NHG *Söller* 'loft', *Füllen*. The MHG forms are *spiln, zeln, sölre* (Latin *sōlārium*), *vülin*. There are long vowels in the case of NHG *dehnen, gewöhnen*, MHG *denen, gewenen*, but short vowels in NHG *Donner, Banner*, MHG *doner, baner*. All these consonants before which there is this mixture of short and long vowels in NHG contrasted phonemically after short vowels with long consonants in MHG: *mite : mitte; nemen : swimmen; manec : manne; spiln : alle*. These short and long consonant phonemes merged after short vowels in long consonants, before which, of course, no lengthening occurred, and were subsequently shortened. Evidence in support of this is provided by some dialects in the south-west of Germany where there are no lengthened vowels before these MHG short consonants. The few cases in NHG in which short vowels were lengthened before MHG *t, m, n, l* are due to other factors such as analogy, or spelling pronunciation (see Russ (1969)).

In monosyllabic words ending in *r* MHG short vowels have been lengthened. This is an example of a conditioned merger: MHG *war* 'observation': *wār* 'true', are pronounced with the same long vowel in NHG, *gewahr, wahr*. The personal pronouns and many words in frequent use were affected by this lengthening of short vowels before final *r*: MHG *er, ir* (NHG *ihr*), *dir, wir, mir, wer, her* (NHG *Heer*), *gar, vor, vür* (NHG *für*). Before *r* plus a dental consonant the vowel was sometimes lengthened and sometimes not: NHG *Erz, Schwert* have a long vowel, but *Herz, fertig* have retained the short vowel. The usual development appears to be that the vowel was lengthened.

By analogy, MHG short vowels which have been lengthened before single voiced consonants have been introduced into forms where this lengthening has not taken place, e.g. in monosyllabic words, or before consonant clusters: the NHG nom./acc. sg. form *Tag* has a long vowel by analogy with oblique forms like *Tage*; NHG past tense sg. *gab* has a long vowel by analogy with the past tense pl.; NHG past tense *legte(n)* and past participle *gelegt* have long vowels by analogy with the infinitive and present forms *lege(n)*. This levelling out of forms with lengthened vowels seems to be confined to certain grammatical categories: case forms in nouns, and tense forms in verbs.

The corollary to this lengthening of short vowels, whether by regular sound-change or by analogy, is the shortening of long vowels before consonant clusters. It occurs most frequently before MHG *ch*, or *h* plus *t*: MHG *brâhte, dâhte, viehte, lieht, schâch, râche*, NHG *brachte, dachte, Fichte, Licht, Schach, Rache*. This shortening also occurred before MHG *z, zz*: MHG *gôz, vlôz, müezen*, NHG *goß, floß, müssen*, and before MHG *ng, vienc, gienc, hienc*, NHG *fing, ging, hing*.

The lengthening of short vowels in open syllables, that is before single voiced consonant, affects all the German dialects except High Alemannic. It is, furthermore, not confined to German but occurs in all the Germanic languages.

The development of MHG w

Thus far the MHG sounds whose development we have followed to NHG have been unaffected by their phonetic environment. MHG *î* is always represented as *ei* in NHG, regardless of either its phonetic environment or its position in the word. In the case of MHG *w*, however, this is not the case. MHG *w* has a different representation in NHG according to its position in words and also according to the sounds it follows.

Initially before vowels MHG *w* was pronounced as a semi-vowel, like English *w*, or else it had already lost the lip-rounding of the semi-vowel and was a bilabial fricative. In this position in NHG it is pronounced as a voiced labio-dental fricative [v], but it is still spelt *w* as in MHG: MHG *wîn, wîp, wâr*; NHG *Wein, Weib, wahr.*

Medially after MHG *l* and *r* it has merged with the MHG MHG voiced bilabial stop *b*, MHG *swalwe, selbe, varwe, gestorben*; NHG *Schwalbe, selbe, Farbe, gestorben.*

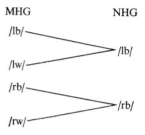

This is an example of a conditioned phonemic merger. The contrast between /b/ and /w/ which existed after *l* and *r* in MHG has been lost in NHG, only /b/ occurs. The spellings *lb* and *rb* found their way into the standard from UG, chiefly Bavarian, sources. Although the CG dialects also have this merger, the resultant sound is a fricative, and not a stop as in the UG dialects.

In MHG in medial position *w* also appeared after certain long vowels and diphthongs: *blâwes, bûwen, niuwe, vröuwen, vrouwe.* In this position it has either been lost, as in *bauen, neue, freuen, Frau*, or it has combined with MHG long *â* to form a diphthong and merged with NHG /au/ from MHG *û* and *ou*: MHG *blâwes*, NHG *blaues.*

In the case of nouns like MHG *sê* with gen. *sêwes*, the *w* has been lost by analogy: NHG *Sees.* In the case of MHG *êwic*, the *w* was probably regarded as being in syllable initial position (MHG *ê* was a word in its own right meaning 'eternity, law') and the *w* was shifted to the voiced labio-dental fricative [v]. The only clue we have as to when MHG *âw* became a diphthong is when the use of the digraph *aw* is extended in Early NHG to cover MHG *ou* or the diphthong from MHG *û*, e.g. *haws*, for *Haus.* Because of the loss of MHG *w* or the merger of MHG *âw* with NHG /au/ there are no words which have medial [v] for MHG *w* (the only exception being *ewig*). Where medial [v] does occur in NHG the words come either from Low German, e.g. *Möwe, stowen* 'to stew', or in the case of NHG *Löwe* it is a spelling pronunciation from a variant Early NHG form *löwe* which existed side by side with *leu, lau.* In initial position in MHG *w* could form consonant clusters with *t, twingen, z* [ts], *zwível,* [k], written *qu, quelle,* and *s, swimmen.* In NHG the words with initial *tw* in MHG have either merged with words beginning with *qu:* MHG *twalm, twer, twarc, twirl, twarz;* NHG *Qualm, quer, Quark, Quirl* 'whisk', *Quarz,* or with those beginning with *zw-:* MHG *ge-twerc, twerh, twingen;* NHG *Zwerg, Zwerch-(fell)* 'diaphragm', *zwingen.* There were not many words with initial *tw-* in MHG. They were either assimilated to the larger groups with initial *zw-* or *qu-* or else they died out; for example, MHG *tweln* 'to live, dwell', and MHG *twahen* 'to wash'. In the modern dialects ECG shows almost exclusively a merger of MHG /tw/ with /kw/ *qu,* while UG dialects show a merger with /zw/.

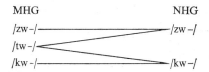

MHG	NHG
/zw–/	/zw–/
/tw–/	
/kw–/	/kw–/

Recently words with initial *tw-* have re-entered NHG: the English loan-words *Tweed, Twill, Twinset, twisten,* and the new formation *Twen* 'someone in his or her twenties'.

The MHG sibilants and their development in NHG

The sounds generally known as sibilants, because of the acoustic effect of hissing they produce, are the alveolar fricatives *s* and *z* and the palato-alveolar fricative *sch.* In MHG four sibilants occurred medially between vowels: *lesen : messe : wazzer, grôze : vische.* It is not certain what phonetic value they had. MHG *sch* was probably pronounced as in NHG and MHG *s* in *lesen* was probably voiced. In NHG it has certainly become voiced intervocalically. Since the spelling has not changed since OHG we cannot say with certainty when *s* became voiced. MHG short vowels before voiced consonants were lengthened (see pp. 74 f.), and the fact that short vowels were lengthened before MHG *s* seems to point to the fact that *s* was already voiced by that time. The fricatives written *ss, zz, z* (the latter only appearing after long vowels and diphthongs) were all voiceless and were doubtless pronounced at the same point of articulation. They differed in that in the articulation of medial *ss* and final *s* the apex (tip) of the tongue made the friction against the alveolar ridge. In the articulation of MHG *z*, *zz* the front part of the dorsum, the back of the tongue, made the friction against the alveolar ridge. Medial MHG *ss* and final *s* may be described as voiceless apico-alveolar fricatives, and MHG *z*, *zz* as voiceless dorso-alveolar fricatives. Which part of the tongue makes the friction is no longer of phonemic importance in NHG where we distinguish only three sibilant phonemes medially between vowels: a voiced /z/; voiceless /s/ and /ʃ/. MHG initial pre-vocalic and medial *s* has shifted to [z], and MHG medial *ss* and final *s* have merged with MHG *z*, *zz*. Phonemically this is an example of a shift with merger.

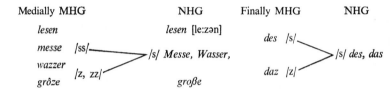

The NHG voiceless alveolar fricative [s] which resulted from the merger of MHG /ss/ and /z, zz/ medially and /s/ and /z/ finally is written *ss*, *ß*, or *s*. Finally it is written *ß* (this sign comes from *s*, in its older form of ſ, plus *z*) if it alternates with a voiceless medial [s], e.g. *groß*, *große*, *gewiß*, *gewisse*, but *s* if it alternates with a voiced medial [z], e.g. *las*, *lasen*. Medially both *ss* and *ß* represent the voiceless [s]. Their present distribution, *ss* after a short vowel, *wissen*, and *ß* after a long vowel or diphthong, *fließen*, *reißen*, was not established until the eighteenth century.

This merger appears to have taken place first in the Alemannic dialects at about the end of the twelfth century, for in German documents of the period none of them shows a clear distinction in writing between *ss* and *z*, *zz*. In the northern and central part of Bavarian and East Franconian the merger of MHG *ss* and *z*, *zz* seems to have occurred by the middle of the thirteenth century. In the ECG area documents in German do not appear until later, thus we cannot date the merger with any real certainty. It probably began in the second half of the thirteenth century.

A few words have found their way into standard NHG which show a voiced [z] for medial MHG *z*, *zz* instead of the regular voiceless [s]. These words fall into two groups: one in which

MHG *z* occurs after nasals: *Binse, Gemse, Gesimse* 'cornices', and a second group in which it occurs after vowels: *losen* (cf. *Los*), *kreisen* (cf. *Kreis*), *Ameise, mausern* 'to moult'. The vowel between MHG *z, zz* and the nasal was lost and MHG *z, zz* became voiced and merged with MHG *s*: MHG *bineze, gense*, NHG *Binse, Gänse* (pl.). The remaining words were often spelt with *ss*, or even *ß*, into the eighteenth century. Their subsequent spelling with a single medial *s*, *kreisen*, led to the pronunciation with a voiced fricative [z].

In initial position in MHG only two sibilants occurred, *s* and *sch*: *sündet* : *schündet* ; *stên, spiln, smerz, snel, swimmen, slâfen*. The fricative phoneme MHG *z, zz* did not occur in this position. Pre-vocalically in MHG voice or strength of articulation was not a phonemic feature in fricatives; the two contrasting sibilants in this position were distinguished by point of articulation, *s* being alveolar and *sch* palato-alveolar. In some parts of Germany initial pre-vocalic *s* was probably voiced, whereas in other areas it was voiceless as is the case today. In standard NHG MHG pre-vocalic initial *s* is represented by a voiced [z], but in the southern dialects of German it is voiceless. Before initial consonants MHG *s* has merged with MHG *sch*: NHG *schnell, Schmerz, schwimmen, schlafen*. This has also happened before *t* and *p* but the spelling has not changed, NHG *stehen, spielen*. Initially before vowels MHG *s* has been shifted to a voiced alveolar fricative but before initial consonants it has merged with MHG *sch*. The whole pattern is an example of a split with merger.

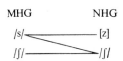

Finally after *r* MHG *s* has also merged with *sch*: MHG *mürsen, bars*; NHG *morsch, Barsch*. There are, however, some exceptions, MHG *vers, verse, hirse*; NHG *Vers, Färse*, 'heifer', *Hirse* 'millet'. This change also happens to MHG *z, zz* when it comes to stand after *r*, but the only example is NHG *Hirsch*, MHG *hirez*.

NHG has one sibilant phoneme which has come into the language since MHG times through French loan-words, the voiced palato-alveolar [ʒ]. It occurs initially, written *g* before *e, i*, e.g. *Genie, genieren, Giro* (Italian), and *j* before *a* e.g. *Jalousie, Journal*.

In NHG it also occurs medially after long vowels, e.g. *Etage, Loge, Garage, Page. Jalousie, Jargon, Loge* and *Page* are the oldest examples, dating from the seventeenth century.

The development of MHG v

MHG *v* contrasted with MHG *f, ff* in medial position: *grâven* : *slâfen*. In NHG the two sounds have merged in the voiceless labio-dental [f]: *Grafen, schlafen*. The number of words in MHG which had *v* in medial position was not very great. The following NHG words had medial *v* in MHG: *Eifer, elf, Geifer* 'spittle', *Höfe* (pl.), *Käfer, Neffe, Ofen, Schaufel, Schiefer* 'slate', *schnaufen, Tafel, Teufel, Ufer, Ungeziefer* 'vermin', *Waffel, Wolf, Zweifel*. It is not easy to tell when this merger took place, as the phonemes are still kept apart in Early NHG; MHG *v* is written *f* and MHG *f, ff* is written *ff*.

In initial position MHG *v* contrasted with the semi-vowel *w* : *vîn* : *wîn*. It is not certain whether initial MHG *v* was voiced or voiceless. Either alternative is equally possible. It probably contrasted with MHG *w* by point of articulation, *v* being labio-dental and *w* a bilabial semi-vowel or fricative, as it is in many UG dialects. In NHG, however, the reflex of MHG *v* is voiceless being spelt *v* or *f* before vowels, *Vater, Vogel, fahren, fein*, but always *f* before consonants, *frisch, fließen*, the only exception being *Vlies*. There is one word in NHG spelt with a medial *v*, *Frevel*, which is pronounced as a voiceless [f].

<pre>
MHG   NHG
grâven /v/ ──────┐
                 ├──> /f/ Grafen, schlafen
slâfen /f, ff/ ──┘
</pre>

The development of MHG h

MHG *h* was pronounced both medially and initially: *sehen* [sɛhən], *hant*. Medially it was pronounced as an aspirate or a glottal fricative. The letter *h* also occurred before *s*, *wuohs*, but here it was pronounced as a voiceless velar fricative as in NHG *Nacht*. In NHG the *h* in intervocalic position is no longer pronounced; *sehen* is pronounced [zeɪən] or [zeɪn]. Only in very careful pronunciation, in church or on the stage, is *h* pronounced in this position, e.g. *siehe* as [ziːhə]. In MHG *h* contrasted medially with the velar fricative *ch* : *sehen* : *brechen*; *sâhen* : *brâchen*. In NHG this contrast is maintained in orthography but *h* has been lost in pronunciation whereas *ch* is pronounced as a voiceless palatal or velar fricative, depending on the preceding vowel. In final position in MHG only the velar *ch* appeared. Words which had a medial *h* had other forms with a final *ch*, e.g. *sehen, sach*; *schuohes, schuoch*. In NHG the forms with *h* have been levelled out in the whole paradigm except in *hoch*, comparative *höher, schmähen* (verb), *Schmach* (noun) and *nach* beside *nahe*. Thus we have in NHG *sehen* [zeɪən], *sah* [zaɪ]; *Schuhes, Schuh* [ʃuɪ]. The final sounds in MHG *doch* and *noch* have the same origin as MHG *sach* (Gmc. *h*), but the fricative pronunciation has been retained because there were no inflected forms with a medial *h*. Gmc. *h* seems to have been articulated very weakly. In the modern Germanic languages it has been retained only in initial position before vowels as an aspirate.

After MHG medial *h* had been lost in pronunciation it was still retained in writing as it showed that the preceding vowel was long, *sehen, Stahl*. The sign *h* consequently came to be used where it was not historically justified, for example NHG *gehen* goes back to MHG *gên*. It was first used as a length sign in CG in the first part of the sixteenth century after MHG *ê*, or *e* when lengthened, Early NHG *ehre, nehmen*. In the eighteenth century the grammarians prescribed its use finally, *Stroh* (MHG *strô*), and before *l, m, n*, and *r*: *Stahl, lahm, Hahn, wahr*. All vowels except [iɪ], which was written *ie* (but in some cases *ieh, sieht*), could be followed by *h*. There were also other means of indicating vowel length, e.g. doubling the vowel, *Meer*. A long vowel need not be specially marked in NHG if it is followed by a single consonant in an open syllable, *geben*.

NHG *blühen, drehen, krähen, mühen, Ruhe* correspond to MHG *blüejen, dræjen, kræjen, müejen, ruowe*. This is not a shift of intervocalic MHG *j* or *w* to *h*, but merely another orthographic use of *h* to represent the hiatus between the long stressed vowel and the unstressed vowel coming immediately after it. In MHG all these verbs had alternative forms without medial *j*.

When MHG *h* occurred before *s* or *t* it was sometimes written *h* and sometimes *ch*. In NHG it is always written *ch*: MHG *naht, lieht, vuhs, sehs*; NHG *Nacht, Licht, Fuchs, sechs*. The pronunciation, however, is different in NHG; before *t* the reflex of MHG *ch* is pronounced [x], but before *s* it is pronounced [k]; the voice-

less velar fricative has become a voiceless stop. This is an example
of a phonemic shift. As there was no medial or final cluster [ks]
in MHG there was no merger and hence no need for the spelling
to be changed. Verbs with medial [ks] in NHG e.g. *drucksen* 'to
hesitate', *knicksen, mixen* are of more recent origin. In the northern
part of Germany MHG *hs* has been assimilated to *ss*. This is also
the case in Dutch, NHG *Ochsen*, Dutch *ossen*.

MHG	NHG
/ch/ [x]: /h/ ⟶	*ch* [x]: *h*
hs ⟶	*chs* [ks]

The development of the MHG nasals in NHG

MHG had only two nasal phonemes, a bilabial /m/ and an alveolar
/n/ : *mîn* : *nein*. The velar nasal [ŋ] also occurred, but only as an
allophone of /n/ before the velar stops *k* and *g*, *sinken, singen*
[siŋgən]. In NHG the velar nasal is a separate phoneme: *schwimmen* : *sinnen* : *singen* [ziŋən]; *schwamm* : *sann* : *sang* [zaŋ]. From
being an allophone, or variant, in MHG, the velar nasal has become a phoneme in NHG. This is an example of a phonemic split.
This change came about when the MHG voiced velar stop [g] was
assimilated to the preceding velar nasal, resulting in a new long
phoneme /ŋŋ/ which contrasted with MHG /nn/. When long
consonants were shortened, MHG /nn/ and /n/ merged, and MHG
/ŋŋ/ became /ŋ/.

A similar change affected the MHG cluster *mb*, comprising a
bilabial nasal plus a voiced bilabial stop. MHG *kumber* has come
Kummer in NHG. The stop in the cluster *mb* was assimilated to
the nasal, [mm] and the long nasal was subsequently shortened.
Phonemically, however, this change is a merger, not a split. The
[mm] which resulted from the assimilation of the *b* in *mb* merged
with an already existing long [mm]: MHG *kumber* : *swimmen*;
NHG *Kummer, schwimmen*. At first these assimilations took place
in medial position. By analogy the assimilated forms were then
levelled out to final position; MHG has *singen, sanc*; *tumbes, tump*,
but NHG has *singen, sang*; *dummes, dumm*.

A corresponding merger of MHG *nd, nt,* and *nn* does not take
place in standard NHG. Perhaps this is because of the weak verbs
whose stems ended in a nasal. An assimilation in the past tense

of *nt* to *nn* where *t* was part of the tense ending would have severely disrupted the system of tenses. In Low German dialects such an assimilation has taken place, NHG *Kinder*, LG *kinner*.

MHG	NHG

sinnen, singen /n~ŋ/ —————— /n/ *sinnen*

swimmen /mm/ ————— /ŋ/ *singen*

lember /mb/ —————————→ /m/ *schwimmen, Lämmer*

The development of MHG [x], spelt (c)h

Since some UG dialects, notably Swiss German, do not have any allophonic variation of [x] after back vowels and [ç] after front vowels—only the voiceless velar fricative occurs regardless of the quality of the preceding vowel—it is assumed that this variation did not exist in MHG. It is not clear when it arose, as the spelling has remained the same in NHG, e.g. MHG *buoch, sprechen*; NHG *Buch, sprechen*. This change is an assimilation of a velar fricative to the front articulation of the preceding vowel. There are no exceptions to this, but there are two points to note: the palatal [ç] appears after uvular [ʀ], e.g. *durch*, and always in the diminutive suffix *-chen*, even after back vowels, e.g. *Frauchen, Kuhchen*. In the first case it is to be assumed that when the velar [x] became fronted the *r* was still dental, i.e. a front consonant, which would not have hindered the fronting of [x]. The case of the diminutives is more difficult, but in most cases the stems before the diminutive suffix ended in *-e*, MHG *brievechen*. One can say that MHG [x] was probably palatalized after unstressed [ə], which was later lost.

The development of MHG r

It is a common assumption that OHG and MHG *r* was a dental trill or fricative. In NHG, however, this pronunciation has largely been superseded by a uvular trill or fricative [ʀ], which is gaining ground in the standard. Many speakers fluctuate in their use of a dental or uvular pronunciation of the initial consonant in a word such as *richtig*. Sometimes there is no real trill articulation but only dental or uvular friction of varying degrees (see p. 19). The development of MHG *r* depends on its position in the word. We will consider three positions: initially, *richtig, breiten*; postvocalically, either before a consonant, *Karte*, or finally, *der*; and in the final sequence *-er*, *Vater*.

Initially the dental trill has been replaced by a uvular trill or similar sound. In its latest edition (1969) *Deutsche Aussprache* prescribed pronunciation allows this pronunciation the same status as that of the dental trill, but for the first time! There is no increase or decrease in the number of phonemes, but simply a change in the phonetic realization of MHG *r*. After vowels MHG *r* is usually a uvular frictionless continuant, but in colloquial speech this tends to be vocalized to a half-open central vowel, symbolized as [ɐ], which is lower than [ə]. This vowel either forms a diphthong [deɐ] with the preceding vowel, or else it disappears after lengthening a preceding *a*, thus for some speakers NHG *Karte* and *Kate* 'cottage', are pronounced the same, [kaːtə]. In *-er* the vocalization of the *r* leads to the creation of new vowel, thus *bitter*, ending in [ɐ], contrasts with *bitte*, ending in [ə]. This development, though common in everyday speech, has not yet affected the written language. A strict phonemic analysis of colloquial German would possibly want to set up /ɐ/ as a separate phoneme, but it could also be said to be an allophone of /r/.

It has traditionally been thought that the uvular [ʀ] was a borrowing from French, which occurred during the eighteenth century when most of the German nobility used French among themselves. It has been shown, however, that there is evidence for a uvular [ʀ] pronunciation in parts of Germany before French influence can be made responsible. There is even some evidence that a uvular [ʀ] might have been in use in OHG; *r* has the effect of monophthongizing Germanic *ai* like the high back consonants *x* and *w* (see Penzl (1961)). The development of uvular [ʀ] is probably an independent change in Germany, as it is in parts of Northumberland in the North of England, and it found support in the presence of a French [ʀ] among the nobility.

The loss of unstressed e before -st and -t

Unstressed *e* in MHG regularly appeared in the inflectional endings of both weak and strong verbs: *hilfes(t)*, *hilfet*; *vrâges(t) vrâget*, *vrâgete*; and also in adjectives, *nacket*, and nouns, *dienest*. In NHG this unstressed *e* has been lost: *hilfst*, *hilft*; *fragst*, *fragt*, *fragte*; *nackt*; *Dienst*. This process is called syncope. It has been retained, however, in those cases where the stem of the word ended in an alveolar stop, e.g. NHG *redest, redet, redete*; *rettest, rettet, rettete*. (The loss of final unstressed -*e*, which is irregular, is dealt with on pp. 92 f.) Among the strong verbs, not only was the *e* lost after stems ending in dentals, but also the *t* of the third person sg., e.g. *raten, rät*. If the stem ended in *d* the *t* was retained in spelling, *lädt*. This only happens with strong verbs whose stem ends in an alveolar stop which change their stem vowel in the second and third person sg., e.g. *halten, hält*, but cf. *binden, bindet*. Originally the syncope of unstressed *e* was more general and occurred even after *t* or *d*, Early NHG *redt*, but the *e* has been restored in NHG except in cases like *rätst, rät*; *lädst, lädt*.

IRREGULAR SOUND CORRESPONDENCES

MHG long â corresponding to NHG long [oː]

In the previous sections we have been able to make generalizations about the correspondence between MHG and NHG sounds; thus MHG *î* corresponds to NHG *ei*. Sometimes there may be more than one reflex of a MHG sound as in the case of MHG *w*, which is represented by [v] initially, by *b* after *l* and *r*; medially it has been lost after long vowels or diphthongs. Nevertheless the correspondences are still regular, that is we can deal with them in general statements. There are cases, however, where we can merely enumerate the examples of a sound correspondence, for instance the vowels in NHG *Lohn* and *ohne* are the same synchronically, but historically they are different; *Lohn* comes from MHG *lôn* whereas *ohne* comes from MHG *âne*. In the case of the latter word we have MHG *â* corresponding to long [oː] in NHG. However, this does not happen to every MHG *â*; most of them remain, e.g. MHG *jâr*, NHG *Jahr*. We cannot say that MHG *â* corresponds to NHG long [oː], or even that it does so in certain positions; the only way of dealing with the correspondence MHG *â* : NHG [oː] is by listing the words in which it occurs. The existence of irregular sound correspondences is due to the fact that NHG is a standard language which has drawn its vocabulary from many sources. Thus words from dialects where a regular correspondence of MHG *â* to [oː] exists may have been borrowed by the standard which does not have this regular correspondence. Thus in many dialects, MHG *â* has become an open or a closed long *o*, or even a diphthong. Words have found their way into the standard from these dialects, although it is impossible to say exactly which dialects are involved. The following are a list of the main words which have NHG [oɪ] for MHG *â*:

MHG	NHG	MHG	NHG
âne	*ohne*	*brâdem*	*Brodem* 'vapour'
mâne	*Mond*	*tâhele*	*Dohle* 'jackdaw'
mânôt	*Monat*	*quât*	*Kot*
mâhe	*Mohn*	*wâc*	*Woge*
âme	*Ohm*	*slât*	*Schlot*

In NHG *Brombeere, Docht* the vowel has also been shortened, cf. MHG *brâmber, tâht*.

Rounding and derounding

In a certain number of words in NHG there is a front rounded vowel, either *ü* or *ö*, where in MHG there was an unrounded vowel, *i* or *e*. The number of examples where NHG *ö* corresponds to MHG *e* is greater than the number of examples of NHG *ü* corresponding to MHG *i*:

MHG	NHG	MHG	NHG
swern	*schwören*	*welben*	*wölben*
zwelf	*zwölf*	*leffel*	*Löffel*
schepfen	*schöpfen*	*lewe*	*Löwe*
leschen	*löschen*	*pekeln*	*pökeln*
stenen	*stöhnen*	*derren*	*dörren*
ergetzen	*ergötzen*	*helle*	*Hölle*
flistern	*flüstern*	*wirz*	*Gewürz*
wirde	*Würde*		

These words reflect the situation in the Alemannic dialects and East Franconian where this rounding has regularly taken place before certain consonants. In CG dialects and Bavarian derounding has taken place (Bavarian does also have rounding in certain circumstances). Some MHG words with *ü* or *ö* correspond to NHG words with *i* or *e*. All that can be done is to give a list of the words which have undergone this change. Derounding has mostly affected MHG *ü*.

MHG	NHG	MHG	NHG
fündling	*Findling*	*gümpel*	*Gimpel* 'bullfinch'
sprütze	*Spritze*	*küssen*	*Kissen*
bümez	*Bimsstein*	*bülez*	*Pilz*
nörz	*Nerz* 'mink'		

In Early NHG rhyme technique it was quite permissible, as indeed it is in NHG, to rhyme front rounded with front unrounded vowels, e.g. *Flügel* : *Siegel*; *säumt* : *keimt*. This became acceptable because Thuringian, Upper Saxon, and Silesian poets made no distinction between front rounded and front unrounded vowels in their speech. They transferred this lack of distinction to their rhymes. The Silesians did not rhyme the reflexes of MHG *iu, öu,* and *ei* since they distinguished between them in speech. The North German poets adopted this tradition in their rhymes although it did not reflect their speech habits. A few examples from seventeenth-century poetry show this tradition quite clearly:

> *Germanie ist tot, die Herrliche, die Freie;*
> *Ein Grab verdecket sie und ihre ganze Treue.*
> > (Paul Fleming 1609–40)

> *Wenn das Glück uns blüht und grünet,*
> *Sind wir schön und hübsch bedienet:*
> > (Paul Gerhardt 1607–76)

> *Herr, vor dem unser Jahr als ein Geschwätz und Scherzen,*
> *Fällt meine Zeit nicht hin wie ein verschmeltzer Schnee?*
> *Laß doch, weil mir die Sonn' gleich in der Mittagshöh',*
> *Mich noch nicht untergehn gleich ausgebrennten Kerzen!*
> > (Andreas Gryphius 1616–64)

MHG *ü* and *u* corresponding to NHG *ö* and *o*

Phonetically MHG *ü* and *u* have been lowered to NHG *ö* and *o*. In some words, e.g. NHG *König, Sohn*, MHG *künec, sun*, they have also been lengthened. The following are the main examples of this change:

MHG	NHG	MHG	NHG
nunne	*Nonne*	*sunne*	*Sonne*
günnen	*gönnen*	*künnen*	*können*
sunder	*sondern*	*münech*	*Mönch*
sumer	*Sommer*	*vrum*	*fromm*
rôrtumel	*Rohrdommel* 'bittern'	*mügen*	*mögen*

These forms mostly have a nasal after the vowel which is lowered and they probably come from the CG dialects.

Interchange between voiced and voiceless stops

There are a large number of words in NHG which have *d* corresponding to MHG *t*. The following examples show this correspondence initially.

MHG	NHG	MHG	NHG
tam	*Damm*	*tampf*	*Dampf*
teich	*Deich*	*tengeln*	*dengeln* 'to whet'
tihten	*dichten*	*tiutsch*	*deutsch*
till	*Dill*	*tump*	*dumm*
tunkel	*dunkel*	*tâhele*	*Dohle*
toter	*Dotter*	*trache*	*Drache(n)*

The correspondence MHG *t* : NHG *d* also occurs medially.

MHG	NHG	MHG	NHG
dulten	*dulden*	*geltes*	*Geldes*
milte	*Milde*	*schiltes*	*Schildes*
bortes	*Bordes*	*herte*	*Herde*
kleinôtes	*Kleinodes*	*rietes*	*Riedes*

There is also a smaller number of words which in NHG have *t* but which in MHG had *d*:

MHG	NHG	MHG	NHG
dôsen	*tosen*	*dôn*	*Ton* 'sound'
dorpære	*Tölpel*	*Düringen*	*Thüringen*
under	*unter*	*hinder*	*hinter*

This interchange is not regular and occurs only in a set number of words. In most of the CG and UG dialects the MHG voiced and voiceless stops, except *g* and *k*, have merged in unaspirated voiceless stops. This is known as consonant weakening or lenition (*Konsonantenschwächung*) since it also affects fricatives. Among the CG dialects only Silesian, the northern part of Thuringian, Ripuarian, the northern part of Thuringian, and the western part of Moselle Franconian do not show this merger. Among the UG dialects Upper Bavarian and High Alemannic still distinguish between the two sets of consonants. Because of this merger of the reflexes of MHG *d* and *t*, words beginning with MHG *d* and *t* came to be written with the historically wrong letter in some cases. In the written Chancery languages of all dialect areas the distinction between *t* and *d* was always maintained, but there was uncertainty in many cases as to whether a word should be written with *t* or *d*. The decisions by the scribes which run counter to the regular development are represented by these lists of words with NHG *t* for MHG *d* and NHG *d* for MHG *t*. There is also a similar interchange between the reflexes of MHG *b* and *p*. Some MHG words, mostly Romance loan-words, which were written with *b*, are written with *p* in NHG:

MHG	NHG	MHG	NHG
bülez	*Pilz*	*bâbest*	*Papst*
bech	*Pech*	*belliz*	*Pelz*
		bredigen	*predigen*

There are no examples of MHG *p* being represented by NHG *b*. This change may be due to the fact that MHG *p* and *b* merged in many CG and UG dialects, but it is more likely due to the influence of the Latin spelling of the loan-words, e.g. Latin *picem* (*pix*), Med. Latin *pāpa*, *pellīcia*, *predicāre*, but *bōlētus* for *Pilz*.

There is no interchange between the reflexes of MHG *g* and *k* since they are always kept apart, even in those dialects which have consonant weakening. The NHG word *gucken* owes its initial voiceless [k] in pronunciation to its similarity to the Low German word *kieken* 'to look'.

The addition of a [t] in NHG after certain consonants

In some words in NHG there is a final [t] which has no counterpart in MHG. This is called an epenthetic or excrescent [t].
Normally it is found after final *n* and *s* which is preceded by an
unstressed vowel. It does not occur if the *n* or *s* is part of a grammatical ending, e.g. MHG *tagen* dat. pl., *wir gaben* past tense pl.,
tages gen. sg. It also occurs sporadically after *ch*.
   Examples after *n*:

MHG	NHG	MHG	NHG
mâne	*Mond*	*ieman*	*jemand*
nieman	*niemand*	*irgen*	*irgend*
allenhalben	*allenthalben*	*eigenlich*	*eigentlich*

Examples after *s*:

MHG	NHG	MHG	NHG
ackes	*Axt*	*obez*	*Obst*
sus	*sonst*	*moras*	*Morast*
palas	*Palast*	*ieze*	*ietzt*

Examples occurring after *ch* are: MHG *dornach, habich, predich*;
NHG *Dornicht, Habicht, Predigt*. An epenthetic [t] has also developed in NHG *Saft*, MHG *saf*; but this is an isolated example.

The loss of unstressed final vowels

In UG and Low German dialects all unstressed final vowels not
followed by a consonant have been lost, whereas in CG they have
been retained. This change, which is called apocope, affected a
large number of grammatical categories: plural in nouns, adjective
inflection, adverbs, and the past tense of weak verbs. Owing to the
loss of the final unstressed vowels the third person sg. of the
present and past tense of weak verbs became the same in UG
dialects: *er sagt, er sagt'*; the past tense fell into disuse, the perfect
taking its place. The standard language, based on ECG usage,
has resisted this radical reduction of final unstressed vowels.
The only cases where it shows radical apocope are: among the
MHG adverbs, MHG *lîhte*, NHG *leicht*, in the nom. sg. of many
nouns, MHG *hane*, NHG *Hahn*, MHG *herze*, NHG *Herz*, MHG
vrouwe, NHG *Frau*, and in most particles, MHG *abe, mite*, NHG

ab, mit. Even in these cases there are exceptions, e.g. *der Käse, das Erbe,* many masc. weak nouns, *der Junge, der Bote,* and the preposition *ohne.*

Further reading

BROOKE, K., *An introduction to Early New High German* (Blackwell, Oxford, 1955).

EGGERS, H., *Das Frühneuhochdeutsche, Deutsche Sprachgeschichte,* iii (Rowohlt, Reinbek bei Hamburg, 1969).

FLEISCHER, W., *Strukturelle Untersuchungen zur Geschichte des Nhd.* (Akademie, Berlin, 1966).

FOURQUET, J., 'The two e's of MHG, a diachronic phonemic approach', *Word,* 8 (1952), 122–35.

—— 'Perspective sur l'histoire du vocalisme allemand', *Travaux de l'Institut de linguistique* (Paris), 1 (1956), 109–24.

HOTZENKÖCHERLE, R., 'Entwicklungsgeschichtliche Grundzüge des Nhd.', *Wirkendes Wort,* 11 (1962), 321–31.

JOOS, M., 'The medieval sibilants', *Language,* 28 (1952), 222–31; repr. in M. Joos (ed.), *Readings in Linguistics,* i (Univ. of Chicago Press, 1957), 372–8.

LINDGREN, K. B., *Die Apocope des mhd. -e in seinen verschiedenen Funktionen, Annales Acad. Scient. Fennicae,* ser. B. Tom. 78, 2 (Helsinki, 1953).

—— *Die Ausbreitung der nhd. Diphthongierung bis 1500, Annales Acad. Scient. Fennicae,* ser. B. Tom. 123, 2 (Helsinki, 1961).

MICHEL, W.-D., 'Die graphische Entwicklung der s-Laute im Deutschen', *Beiträge zur Geschichte der deutschen Sprache und Literatur* (Halle), 81 (1959), 456–80.

MOSER, H. and H. STOPP (eds.), *Grammatik des Frühneuhochdeutschen,* vol. i, 1 ed. K. O. Sauerbeck (1969); vol. i, 2 ed. H. Stopp (1973) (Winter, Heidelberg).

MOSER, V., *Frühneuhochdeutsche Grammatik,* 2 vols. (Winter, Heidelberg, 1929).

PENZL, H., 'Old High German ⟨r⟩ and its phonetic identification', *Language,* 37 (1961), 480–6.

—— 'The history of the third nasal phoneme of Modern German', *Publications of the Modern Language Association of America,* 83 (1968), 340–7.

—— 'Die mhd. Sibilanten und ihre Weiterentwicklung', *Linguistic Studies offered to A. Martinet,* vol. 2 (*Word,* 24 (1968), 204–13).

—— 'Die Entstehung der frühnhd. Diphthongierung', in *Studien zur deutsch–Sprache und Literatur des Mittelalters, Festschrift für H.*

Moser zum 65. Geburtstag, ed. W. Besch *et al.* (Schmidt, Berlin, 1974), 345–57.

Russ, C. V. J., 'Die Ausnahmen zur Dehnung der mhd. Kurzvokale in offener Silbe', *Zeitschrift für Dialektologie und Linguistik*, 36 (1969), 82–8.

Sanders, W., "Hochdeutsch /ā/—"Ghostphonem" oder Sprachphänomen', *Zeitschrift für Dialektologie und Linguistik*, 39 (1972), 37–58.

Von Bahder, K., *Die Grundlagen des nhd. Lautsystems* (Strasburg, 1890).

Wagner, K., 'Die Geschichte eines Lautwandels ks ⟨chs⟩ s', *Teuthonsista*, 2 (1925–6), 30–46.

Wiesinger, P., *Phonetisch-phonologische Untersuchungen zur Vokalentwicklung in den deutschen Dialekten, Studia Linguistica Germanica*, 2, 2 vols. and vol. of maps (De Gruyter, Berlin, 1970).

Zwierzina, K., 'Mhd. Studien 8. Die e-Laute in den Reimen der mhd. Dichter', *Zeitschrift für deutsches Altertum*, 44 (1900), 249–316.

II · MORPHOLOGY

GENERAL INTRODUCTION

MORPHOLOGY comprises the study of both the inflection and derivation of words, and as a grammatical term became widely used only in the historical grammars of the nineteenth century. The classical division of grammar dating back to the Greeks and Romans was a division into accidence, which dealt with the different inflected forms of words, and syntax, which dealt with the order and function of words in sentences. Word formation, or derivational morphology (also called lexical morphology), which today is regarded as part of morphology, had no real status in classical grammar.

The usual distinction made between inflection and derivation is that inflection deals with the different forms of a word according to its syntactic uses: e.g. *mensa*, nominative, subject case, *mensam*, accusative, direct object case, *mensae*, dative, indirect object case. Word formation, or derivation, on the other hand, deals with new words which usually belong to different parts of speech from the words from which they were formed: e.g. *sings*, *singing* are both inflected forms from the lexical unit 'sing', whereas *singer*, *song* are different words, and not merely inflected forms of 'sing'. Word formation deals with suffixes and prefixes which have a lexical meaning, e.g. addition of the suffix *-er*, accompanied in most cases by mutation of the stem vowel, designates the person who performs a task: thus the noun *der Bäcker* is derived from the verb *backen*. Alternatively the suffix may signal the fact that the word concerned belongs to a different part of speech: *falsch*, adjective, *Falschheit*, noun, and *fälschen*, verb. Certain exceptions to this principle are presented by the feminine suffix *-in*, the collective prefix *Ge-*, as well as numerous verbal prefixes which do not create words belonging to different parts of speech, although they are words with a clearly different meaning: *König, Königin*; *Berg, Gebirge*; *sehen, besehen, versehen, aussehen*. In the history of German such derivational formations are regarded as belonging to the history of the vocabulary, whereas inflection, which is what will be understood by morphology in this work, deals with the different forms of the same lexical units and their development for each part of speech. The syntactic use of the words and forms is dealt with in W. B. Lockwood, *Historical German Syntax*. Although many linguists have criticized the traditional parts of speech, this has chiefly been due to the fact that the latter have often been defined on semantic grounds and not according to the form of the words themselves. In this book labels such as 'noun', 'verb', and so on will be retained as convenient terms of reference.

Traditionally the basic unit of morphology has been the word, but modern structuralist linguists have suggested that the basic unit should rather be the morpheme. In the word *un/accept/able*, or *un/trag/bar*, the portions between the slant lines would be said to represent morphemes: the smallest meaningful units into which an utterance can be divided. However, problems in defining the morpheme have been legion. It has been shown that morphemes very often have little or no meaning. The German prefix *ver-* often has a pejorative meaning, *verschlafen* 'to oversleep', *vergucken* 'to see wrongly', but what meaning does it have in *verheiraten, verloben*? What 'meaning' do the morphemes *-er* and *-e* have in the strong and weak adjective declension: *ein guter Mann, der gute Mann*? They are automatically determined by the type of article or other word used in front of them. In the word *Schönheit* the morpheme *-heit* merely signals the fact that the word concerned belongs to the noun class. In view of these problems many linguists simply define the morpheme as the minimum grammatical unit, without any specific reference to meaning. Other problems arise with regard to the division of words into morphemes. Words like *boys* or *Tage* can easily be divided into the morphemes *boy* and *-s, Tag* and *-e*, but what about *sang*? Various possibilities of dividing this and similar forms, e.g. *took, men*, were suggested: *s . . . ng* and *a*; *sing* and a replacive morpheme, '*i* is replaced by *a*'; and *sang* plus a zero variant of the past tense morpheme. All this was motivated by the desire to maintain the parallelism between *sang* and *sagte*; the latter being clearly divisible into *sag-* and *-te*. Linguists now would regard *sang* as being an indivisible unit which is the result of a rule changing the form *sing-* into *sang*, replacing *i* by *a*, as in *trinken, trank*. It must be clearly recognized that although in many cases words can be easily divided into morphemes this is not always the case in languages like English and German. Processes such as *i* becoming *a* present no problem if the word is taken as the basic unit of morphology for they can be portrayed in the old-fashioned list of word forms called the paradigm: *sagen, sagte, gesagt*; *singen, sang, gesungen*, which illustrates clearly the similarities and differences between the two types of verb.

Although the concept of the morpheme is the child of modern structuralist linguisitics it should not be assumed that traditional grammar was unaware of the fact that the word consisted of smaller elements. Prefixes and suffixes were recognized and the setting up of a paradigm such as *mensa, mensam, mensae, mensae, mensā* implies that there are inflectional endings although it does not specify exactly where they are to be separated from the other part of the word. In our account of morphology we will describe German words as consisting of a stem and an ending, e.g. in *Tages, Tag-* would be the stem and *-es* the ending. In older stages of the Indo-European languages the stem consisted of a root followed by a stem-forming element (see p. 99). Most stems in German are bound, that is they do not appear on their own, the stem [taɪg-] ending in a voiced consonant (since we are concerned with the pronunciation of the morpheme we have enclosed it in phonetic brackets) does not occur on its own but only together with an ending. Some stems have different forms, but unlike word forms which express different syntactic functions, these are determined by the adjacent sounds: the stem [taɪg-], with a voiced [g] appears before vowels, [taɪgəs, taɪgə], whereas the form [taɪk], with a voiceless final consonant, appears at the end of words before a pause (the spelling *Tag* disguises this difference in pronunciation). Endings can also have varying forms. In NHG the endings *-et* and *-t* for the third person sg. and second person pl. of weak verbs are determined by the final consonant of the stem. If the stem ends in any consonant other than *d* or *t*, then the ending is *-t*: *sagt, packt, bebt, kippt, hofft, reist, mischt, lacht*, but if the final consonant of the stem is *d* or *t* then the ending *-et* is used: *redet, rettet*. The linguists who used the morpheme as a basic morphological unit gave the name allomorph to these different shapes of morphemes. It was also said that the alternation, for example between [g] and

[k] in *Tages*, *Tag*, was a morphophonemic, or morphophonological, alternation. Some linguists do not use the term allomorph but take a basic form for each morpheme, called its underlying form, and derive its variant forms from it by rules, e.g. [taɪk] is produced from underlying [taɪg-] by a rule that devoices a voiced stop in word-final position.

So far we have only mentioned ways of describing the word structure of a language at a given time but we must also consider the historical aspect which will be our main concern. The chief mechanism in morphological change has always been regarded as 'analogy', that is one word is remodelled on the pattern of another word. In MHG, strong verbs of Class II, such as *biegen*, have the stem vowel *iu* in the present indicative sg. and *ie* in the present indicative pl., but in NHG the only stem vowel in both sg. and pl. is *ie* [iː]. The sg. has been remodelled on the pattern of, or by analogy with, the plural. Another way of expressing this is to say that the vowel of the pl. has been extended, or levelled out, in the sg. The usual result of analogy is to make a morphological paradigm regular, or expressed another way, to eliminate allomorphs or morphophonemic alternations. Another mechanism akin to analogy is the extension of the use of an inflectional ending to other words where it was not originally used. A prime example of this is the spread of the ending -*er*, originally part of the stem, accompanied by stem vowel mutation where possible, as a plural ending from a small number of neuter nouns to nearly all neuter nouns. In MHG only a small number of neuter nouns had -*er* as a pl. ending: *blat, ei, huon, kalp, lamp, rint, ris, rat, tal*, but in NHG this ending has spread to most neuter nouns and even to some masc. ones, e.g. *Geist, Mann, Wald*. This type of change often results in another ending being lost or becoming less frequent. In the history of English the pl. ending -*en* was originally used with many more nouns than is the case today but it has mostly been replaced by -*s*. The examples mentioned so far have dealt with endings or parts of words but there are also cases where a whole word is extended in its use and thus replaces another word, e.g. the NHG reflexive pronoun *sich* was originally only used in the sg. as the acc. form, the dat. being MHG *im(e)*, but in NHG *sich* is now also used as the dat. form and has thus replaced MHG *im(e)* in this function. As well as being extended or restricted, inflectional endings may be completely lost, e.g. the MHG strong adjective ending -*iu* no longer occurs in NHG but has been replaced by *-e*. It does not seem very common that new inflectional endings arise in the history of a language, and if indeed they do they are often borrowings, such as the pl. in NHG, which was originally borrowed from French and possibly Low German, but it is now used with some native German words (see p. 146). Another possible way for new endings to arise is through a false division of the ending from the stem. The NHG pl. ending *-er* was originally part of the stem but is now a pl. ending. Through these mechanisms of morphological change grammatical categories may be lost, restricted, or strengthened. Sometimes it is not easy to draw the line between morphological change and purely mechanical sound change: in MHG most distinctions in case have become no longer recognizable since the vowels which showed these distinctions have merged in *-e*. But is this a morphological change, the elimination of case distinctions, or a phonological change, reduction of unstressed vowels to *-e*? Most of the changes in the following section will be dealt with in terms of the mechanisms described here.

Further reading

MATTHEWS, P. H., 'Recent developments in morphology', in J. Lyons (ed.), *New Horizons in Linguistics* (Penguin, London, 1970), 96–114.
—— *Morphology: An Introduction to the Theory of Word Structure* (Cambridge Univ. Press, 1974).
PALMER, F., *Grammar* (Penguin, London, 1971).
SAMUELS, M. L., *Linguistic Evolution* (Cambridge Univ. Press, 1972), Chs. 4 and 5.

OLD HIGH GERMAN AND THE DEVELOPMENT FROM INDO-EUROPEAN

NOUNS IN INDO-EUROPEAN

From a study of the forms in the various Indo-European languages it has been assumed that Primitive Indo-European nouns consisted of three parts: a root, which usually bore the meaning of the whole word, a stem-forming element, which served to indicate which class the noun belonged to, and an inflectional ending, which showed the number and case of the noun. For example, in the Latin noun *hostis*, *host-* is the root, *-i-* the stem-forming element, and *-s* the inflectional ending.

According to whether the stem-forming element of a noun ended in a vowel or a consonant, nouns can be divided into vocalic or consonantal stems: thus *host-i-s* and *fruct-u-s* with vowels as stem-forming elements, called thematic vowels, are called vocalic stems, whereas *nom-in-is* with a stem-forming element ending in a consonant, is called a consonantal stem. The root plus the stem-forming element make up the stem of the IE noun to which the inflectional ending is added. In Old and Middle High German the descendants of the vocalic stems are usually called strong declension nouns and the descendants of the consonantal stems are usually called weak declension nouns. Depending on the vowel of the stem-forming element IE nouns can be arranged in various classes: long *ā* stems, Latin *mens-a-m* (the vowel has been shortened before *m*), Greek *chŏr-ā-n*; *o* stems, Greek *log-o-s* (in Latin *hort-u-s* the original *o* has become *u*); *i* stems, Latin *host-i-s*, Greek *pól-i-s*; *u* stems, Latin *man-u-s*, Greek *pêch-u-s*. The long *ā* and the *o* stems had the sub-classes *jā*, *wā* and *jo*, *wo* stem when an IE *j* or *w* appeared in front of the vowel stem-forming element. The stems of the consonantal nouns most frequently end in *-in*, *nom-in-is*, but some also ended in stops, or *-s*, or *-r*, cf. Latin *ped-is*, *gener-is* (this intervocalic *r* comes from IE *s*, Sanskrit *janas-as*), *matr-is*.

Nouns in IE belonged to one of three genders: masculine, feminine, and neuter. They were characterized by three numbers: singular, dual, and plural, and by eight cases: nominative, vocative, accusative, genitive, dative, ablative, locative, and instrumental.

In the Germanic languages the IE declension of nouns has been considerably modified. Through the loss and the weakening of unstressed vowels, case endings and class indicators (the stem-forming elements) have been obliterated to a large extent, and the eight cases of IE have been reduced to four: nominative, accusative, genitive, and dative, with relics of a fifth case, the instrumental. The dual number has been lost.

The IE *ā*, *o*, *u*, and *i* classes have left clearer traces of their thematic vowels in Gothic: Gothic *gib-ō-s*, Germanic *ō* stem (IE long *ā* has become long *ō* in Germanic), as well as the sub-classes with *j* and *w*, *har-ji-s*, *sái-wi-s*, but there are also traces of these in OHG, for example, *sē-we-s*. It is convenient, however, for historical reasons, to retain the classification into IE *ā*, *o*, *u*, and *i* stems to show their origins. (Some books use the classification into

Gmc. *ō* and *a* stems, since Gmc. *ō* and *a* are the reflexes of IE *ā* and *o*, but this will not be used here.)

Further reading

BUCK, C. D., *Comparative Grammar of Latin and Greek* (Univ. of Chicago Press, 1933; 9th impression 1963), 168–208.

HUDSON-WILLIAMS, T., *A short introduction to the study of comparative grammar (Indo-European)* (1935; repr. Univ. of Wales Press, Cardiff, 1961), 46–61.

KRAHE, H., *Indogermanische Sprachwissenschaft*, 5th edn. (Sammlung Göschen 64, De Gruyter, Berlin 1969), ii: *Formenlehre*, 6–32.

LOCKWOOD, W. B., *Indo-European Philology* (Hutchinson, London, 1969), 85–116.

PALMER, L. R., *The Latin Language* (Faber, London, 1954), 232–52.

SZEMERÉNYI, O., *Einführung in die vergleichende Sprachwissenschaft* (Wissenschaftliche Buchgesellschaft, Darmstadt, 1970), 143–76.

THE DEVELOPMENT FROM INDO-EUROPEAN TO GERMANIC

Wherever possible Latin and Greek examples will be used to show the IE forms and only the development of those case forms which survived into Germanic will be treated.

In the nom. sg. *hostis*, both the thematic vowel and inflectional ending have been lost in OHG, *gast*. In Gothic only the inflectional ending has been retained, *gasts*, and this has become *r* in Old Norse, *gestr*. The same thing happens with the IE *o* and *u* classes, Latin *lupus*, OHG *wolf*, but the descendants of the *u* class have retained their *u* in most cases, late Latin *pecus*, Gothic *faíhu*, OHG *fihu*. The OHG representatives of the IE *ā* class retain the ending *-a* with the vowel shortened in final position, Gothic *giba*, OHG *geba*, cf. Latin *terra*. In the *n* stems, the most frequent example of the consonant stems, the final *-n* is lost in the nom. sg. OHG *gumo*, cf. Latin *homō* (*n* is retained in Latin following an *e*, cf. *nōmen*).

The acc. sg. in Latin, *lupum, hostem, manum, hominem*, has lost both its thematic vowel and its inflectional ending, e.g. OHG *wolf, gast*. Only in Primitive Scandinavian records in Runic inscriptions are there relics of it as *-a, steina*. In OHG the nom. and acc.

sg. of all vocalic declensions have the same form: *gast, sunu, hirti, tag*. The IE *ā* declension, Latin *mensam*, has lost its ending but retained the thematic vowel, reduced to a short *a*, OHG *geba*, which has also become the nom. form. The OHG acc. form in the *n* declension masc. is *gumin*, with the loss of the inflectional ending, cf. Latin *hominem*, which differs from the nom. sg. form OHG *gumo*.

The IE gen. sg. ending *-es*, Latin *hostis*, OHG *gastes*, is closest in form to the original IE ending. In the *n* declension, Latin *hominis*, the vowel of the ending has been lost giving OHG *gumins*. In the *ā* declension, older Latin *familiās*, the *s* has been retained in Gothic, *gibōs*, and it has become *r* in Old Norse, *skarar*; in OHG it has disappeared, giving *geba*, the same form as the nom. and acc. sg.

The IE dat. sg. ending *-ai*, Latin *mensae*, becomes *ē* in PG but is shortened to *e* in OHG *gaste*. In the *n* declension it was lost, Latin *hominī*, OHG *gumin*. The ending *-u* in OHG *gebu*, a noun of the IE *ā* declension, represents an IE instrumental case.

The IE nom. pl. ending, thematic vowel plus the ending *-s*, Latin *hostes*, has lost the final *-s* in OHG, *gesti*, but it has been retained in Gothic, *gasteis*, and in Old Norse where it has become *r, gestir*. This is also true of the IE *ā, o*, and *u* stems, which in OHG may be represented by the forms *gebā* (probably with a long final vowel), *taga*, and *suni*, (with *-i* from *i* stems). The *n* declension in OHG has the nom. pl. form *gumun*, which represents the IE ending *-ōnes* with the loss of *-es*.

In the IE acc. pl. form, thematic vowel plus the ending *-ns*, the ending has been lost in all the Germanic languages except Gothic, *dagans, gastins*. OHG nouns of all classes have the same ending for the nom. and acc. pl., retaining merely reflexes of the thematic element, vowel or consonant: *taga, gesti, gebā, gumun*.

The IE gen. pl. ending, thematic vowel plus *-m*, Latin *hostium*, is represented in OHG by *-o, worto, gestio*, later *gesto*. The OHG *ā* stem form, *gebōno*, owes its *-no* to the feminine *n* stems where it was the regular form. From there it was transferred to the masc. and neuter *n* stems.

In the IE dat. pl. ending, thematic vowel plus *-mis*, Old Church Slavonic *rabomu* 'servant', Lithuanian *vyrams* 'man' the *-is* has been lost, OHG *tagum, gestim, sunum, gumōm*. There is a relic of the ending *-is* in the Runic form *gestumʀ* where *s* has become ʀ. Latin has another dat. pl. ending *-bus* which is also found in

Sanskrit as *-bhas*. In the ninth century OHG *-m* becomes *-n*, giving the dat. pl. forms *tagun, gestin, sunun, gumōn*.

Further reading

KRAHE, H., *Indogermanische Sprachwissenschaft*, ii: *Formenlehre* (Sammlung Göschen 780, De Gruyter, Berlin, 1959), 6–49.
PROKOSCH, E., *A comparative Germanic grammar* (Philadelphia, 1939), 225–58.

NOUN INFLECTION IN OLD HIGH GERMAN

Most treatments of OHG noun inflection deal with it exclusively from the historical point of view, i.e. they review each stem class after the other, IE *ā* stems, *o* stems, and so on, and deal with the etymological descendants of the members of these classes in OHG, even though the stem-forming elements have for the most part disappeared. An attempt will be made here to divide OHG nouns into classes purely from their forms in OHG, but for reference we will state from which IE classes each OHG class has descended. The OHG forms quoted will be those of the ninth century, from *Tatian* or *Otfrid*.

Considering OHG purely descriptively the nouns can be divided into three classes on the basis of their gen. sg. endings. Class I, with the gen. sg. ending *-es, tages, gastes, sunes, hirtes, sēwes*, comprises historically the descendants of the IE *o, i, u, jo*, and *wo* stems respectively; Class II, with the gen. sg. ending in a vowel, contains only fem. nouns, *geba, ensti, hōhī, sunta* which are historically the descendants of the IE *ā, i*, long *ī*, and *jā* stems. These two classes traditionally comprise the strong declension; Class III, with the gen. sg. ending in *-n, hanin, zungūn, ougin*, comprises the descendants of the IE *n* stems and is traditionally called the weak declension. The classes do show some differences in their endings for other cases but these are less significant. Owing to the fact that the definite article, the main designator of gender, has a much more restricted use in OHG and that not all classes have nouns of all three genders, a classification according to gender is only of secondary importance.

The forms of the singular

Nouns of Class I have a gen. in -es and a dat. in -e: (masc.) *tages,*
tage; *hirtes, hirte*; *sunes, sune*; *sēwes, sēwe*; (neuter) *wortes, worte*;
nezzes, nezze. There is only one form for the nom. and acc. but it is
not possible to predict its form from the other cases, except in the
case of nouns like *sēwes*, where the nom. and acc. form has no ending but the *w* of the stem changes to *o* in final position, *sēo*.

With the other nouns there are three possibilities: either the
nom. and acc. will end in a consonant, *tag*, or -*i*, *hirti* (the latter
being historically a *jo* stem), or -*u*, *sigu* 'victory' (an old *u* stem of
which in OHG there are only seven masc.: *witu, hugu, situ, fridu,
metu, sigu,* and *sunu,* which only retains its final -*u* in the oldest
sources, and one neuter, *fihu*). To this class also belong the nouns
in -*er* signifying relationships, *fater, bruoder,* and short monosyllabic consonantal stems such as *man,* all of which occur in
OHG with and without -*es* in the gen. and -*e* in the dat.; their
other cases being formed like those of *tag.* The minor group of
consonantal stems in -*nt*, of which there are only two, *friunt* and
fiant, have dat. forms without -*e* but they always have -*es* in the
gen. Class. I only contains masc. and neuter nouns. The full paradigms of nouns in this class are:

	Masculine				Neuter	
N/A	*tag*	*hirti*	*sēo*	*sigu*	*wort*	*nezzi*
G	*tages*	*hirtes*	*sēwes*	*siges*	*wortes*	*nezzes*
D	*tage*	*hirte*	*sēwe*	*sige*	*worte*	*nezze*

Class II nouns, such as OHG *geba*, which form the large majority
in this class have their gen. ending in a vowel, *geba*, which is also
the same form as the nom. and acc. The dat. form of *geba* is *gebu*,
which in UG sometimes occurs in the gen. There are some examples of nom. forms occurring with and without -*a*: *hwîl, hwîla*;
buoz, buozza. The forms with -*a* are acc. forms which have ousted
the original nom. forms without endings; the latter being mostly
found in set phrases, cf. *Ludwigslied*, l. 3: *thes warth imo sâr buoz*
('He was immediately recompensed for this'). The other nouns
which belong to this class have their gen. in -*i* or -*î*, *ensti, hôhî*.
Nouns like *hôhî* have the same form in all other cases and are historically a sub-class of the *n* declension. Nouns like *ensti*, historically *i*

stems, have the same form for the dat. case. In the nom. and acc.
they all lose the -*i* except for the case of a few short syllable *i* stems;
kuri 'choice', *turi* (fem) and *risi*, *wini* 'friend', *quiti* 'speech'
(masc.). Since they have retained the final -*i* they undergo umlaut
or *i*-mutation in all forms of the sg. and pl. in MHG, *türe*, NHG
Tür, whereas the nouns which have no -*i* in the nom. and acc. do
not undergo mutation in these cases. If the nom. and acc. has *a* as a
stem vowel, this becomes *e* before the final -*i* of the gen. and dat.
by *i*-mutation, e.g. N/A *anst*, G/D *ensti*. There are also a few
consonantal stems (cf. Latin *noct-is*, with no thematic vowel) of
which only *naht* is left by the ninth century. The full paradigms
are:

N/A	*geba*	*anst*	*hōhī*
G	*geba*	*ensti*	*hōhī*
D	*gebu*	*ensti*	*hōhī*

Original *jo* stems such as masc. *hirti*, neuter *nezzi* also had *i* in the
dat. sg. in early OHG, *hirtie*, *nezzie*, while fem. *jā* stems had *e* or *i*
throughout the sg. in early OHG, *suntea*, *suntia* (nom. acc. and
gen.), *suntiu* (dat.)

Class III, unlike the other classes, has a sub-grouping according
to gender. The masc. and neuter nouns have a gen. and dat. ending
in -*in*, *hanin*, *ougin*, -*en* in Franconian, while the fem. nouns have
the ending -*ūn* for the gen. and dat., *zungūn*. The acc. case shows
three different forms, one for each gender: -*un*, *hanun*, for the
masc. nouns, -*on* in Franconian; -*ūn*, *zungūn*, for the fem. nouns;
and -*a*, *ouga*, for the neuter nouns, which is also their nom. ending.
The fem. nouns also have the ending -*a* in the nom. *zunga*, while
the masc. nouns have the ending -*o*, *hano*. The full paradigms are:

	Masculine	Feminine	Neuter
N	*hano*	*zunga*	*ouga*
A	*hanun*	*zungūn*	*ouga*
G	*hanin*	*zungūn*	*ougin*
D	*hanin*	*zungūn*	*ougin*

The forms of the plural

In Class I, the gender distinction, masc. versus neuter, determines
the plural endings. Even within the masc. group, however, there
are two sub-classes according to whether the stem vowel *a* of the

sg. is modified to an *e*, i.e. whether it undergoes *i*-mutation: *gast—gesti*, as against *tag—taga*, which does not. The ending of the gen. is the same for both sub-classes, *-o*, *gesto*, *tago* (in earlier OHG the ending *io* was also found in those nouns descended from the *i* and *jo* stems, *gestio*, *hirtio*). The nouns which modify their stem vowel, the descendants of the *i* stems, have the ending *-i* in the nom. and acc. and the ending *-in*, earlier *-im*, in the dat. Those nouns which do not modify their sg. stem vowel, the descendants of the *o*, *jo*, and *wo* stems, have the ending *-a* in the nom. and acc. and the ending *-un*, earlier *-um*, in the dat.: *taga*, *hirta* (earlier *hirte*), *sēwa*; *tagun*, *hirtun*, *sēwun*. There are other nouns, those with a stem vowel other than short *a*, which take the pl. endings *-i*, *-o*, *-in*, but which do not show any mutation of the stem vowel until MHG, *fuoz*, sg., *fuozi* pl., or whose stem vowel is not susceptible to *i*-mutation, *scrit* sg., *scriti* pl.

The neuter nouns are also subdivided according to whether the stem vowel of the sg. is modified if it is an *a*, e.g. *lamb—lembir*, before the *-ir* which is historically not a plural ending but an IE stem forming element *-is-*. Ony a few nouns have this plural ending in OHG: *kalb*, *huon*, *rind*, *farh* 'piglet', *ei*, *luog* 'lair'. Some neuter nouns have both a pl. form which is the same as the sg. and the pl. in *-ir*: *rad*, *grab*, *loub*, *krūt*, *bret*, *holz*, *abgot*, *loh*, *bant*, *feld*, *hūs*. Most neuter nouns have no ending in the nom. and acc.; only the definite article shows whether they are plural: *daz wort— diu wort*; *das nezzi—diu nezzi*, or if they are the subject of the verb, the verbal ending. The gen. and dat. are formed by adding the endings *-o* and *-un*, earlier *-um*, respectively to the nom. and acc.: *lembiro*, *lembirun*; *worto*, *wortun*; or *-o* and *-in*, earlier *-io* and *-im*, *nezzi*, gen. *nezzo*, dat. *nezzin*. The short *i* stems have gen. in *-io*, later *-o*, *quitio*, *quito* and dat. in *-im*, later *-in*, *quitim*, *quitin*.

	Masculine				Neuter		
N/A	*gesti*	*taga*	*hirta*	*sēwa*	*wort*	*lembir*	*nezzi*
G	*gesto*	*tago*	*hirto*	*sēwo*	*worto*	*lembiro*	*nezzo*
D	*gestin*	*tagun*	*hirtun*	*sēwun*	*wortun*	*lembirun*	*nezzin*

The Class II nouns like *geba* have a long *ā* in the nom. and acc. pl., *gebā*, and the ending *-ōn* in the dat., earlier *-ōm*. The gen. ending is *-ōno*, *gebōno*, which is similar to the ending of nouns such as *hōhī* which merely add *-no* to the sg. form, *hōhīno*, and have the same form as the sg. for the nom. and acc. The dat. ending of *hōhī* is *-n, hōhin*. Nouns like *anst—ensti* have the same form in the nom. and acc. pl. as the gen. and dat. sg., *ensti*. The gen. is *ensto*, earlier *enstio*, and the dat. *enstin*, earlier *enstim*. The noun *naht* has the same form as the sg. for the nom. and acc. *naht*. The gen. is formed in the same way as the other nouns, i.e. *nahto*, but the dat. has the ending *-un, nahtun*, like the *o* stems of Class I. The gen. and dat. of *kuri* and *turi* are the same as those of the masc. short *i* stems. The full paradigms are:

N/A	*gebā*	*hōhī*	*ensti*
G	*gebōno*	*hōhīno*	*ensto*
D	*gebōn*	*hōhin*	*enstin*

Class III nouns also differ in the pl. according to gender. The masc. and neuter nouns have the ending *-un, -on* in Franconian, in the nom. and acc., *hanun, ougun*; the fem. nouns have *-ūn, zungūn*. The endings for the gen. and dat. are the same for all three genders: *-ōno* for the gen., *hanōno, ougōno, zungōno*; and *-ōn*, earlier *-ōm*, for the dat., *hanōn, ougōn, zungōn*. The full paradigms are:

	Masculine	Feminine	Neuter
N/A	*hanun*	*zungūn*	*ougun*
G	*hanōno*	*zungōno*	*ougōno*
D	*hanōn*	*zungōn*	*ougōn*

Further reading

BRAUNE, W., *Althochdeutsche Grammatik*, 13th edn., ed. H. Eggers (Niemeyer, Tübingen, 1975), §§ 192–243.

SCHATZ, J., *Althochdeutsche Grammatik* (Vandenhoeck & Ruprecht, Göttingen, 1927), §§ 301–75.

SONDEREGGER, S., *Althochdeutsche Sprache und Literatur* (Sammlung Göschen 8005, De Gruyter, Berlin, 1974), 174–89 (a short but well set out display of paradigms clearly showing dialect differences).

ADJECTIVES AND ADVERBS IN OLD HIGH GERMAN

In German, adjectives in attributive position inflect in two ways according to the determiner, i.e. the article or pronoun which

also mixed paradigm declension

precedes them: NHG *der gute Mann* (weak declension), as against *ein guter Mann* (strong declension).

Originally in IE this was not the case. The noun and its attributive adjective had the same endings; the adjective took its gender, case, and number from the noun it modified. Masc. and neuter adjectives were usually inflected like *o* stem nouns, Latin *dominus bonus, prātum bonum*, while the fem. adjectives were inflected like *ā* stem nouns, *puella bona*. There were also *i* stem adjectives, Latin *brevis*, and in Greek, *u* stems, *hēdús*. This close association of form with nouns led to adjectives for a long time being regarded merely as a subdivision of the noun.

In OHG, as in the other older Gmc. languages, there developed a twofold distinction in adjective declension between strong and weak adjectives, the latter having the same endings as those of Class III nouns, the *n* or weak declension. The strong declension in OHG has endings which come from both the strong nouns and the declension of pronouns. The masc. and neuter gen. sg., *blintes*, and the fem. acc. sg., *blinta*, have the ending of the strong declension nouns, cf. *tages, wortes, geba*, as do the uninflected nom. forms of all genders and the neuter acc. sg., *blint*, cf. *tag, anst, wort*. The other forms of the sg. and all the pl. endings are from the personal or demonstrative pronouns. The weak adjective inflection had its beginnings in IE when attributive nouns were formed from adjectives by an *n* suffix, e.g. Latin *rūfus* 'red-haired', *Rufō* (gen. *Rufōnis*) 'the red-haired man'. Nouns with this form came to be used as adjectives in Germanic. The full sg. and pl. paradigms of strong adjectives are:

c.f. gothic og ios
? paradigms

			Masculine	Feminine	Neuter
sg.	N		blint, blintēr	blint, blintiu	blint, blintaz
	A		blintan	blinta	blint, blintaz
	G		blintes	blintera	blintes
	D		blintemo	blintero	blintemo
pl.	N		blinte	blinto	blintiu
	A		blinte	blinto	blintiu
	G		blintero	blintero	blintero
	D		blintēn	blintēn	blintēn

In early OHG the dat. sg. forms ended in *-u*, *blintemu, blinteru*, and the dat. pl. in *-ēm*, *blintēm*. Both the inflected and uninflected nom. sg. forms occur in attributive position. An inflected neuter nom.

acc. sg. from occurred in Gothic, *blindata*, but the inflected masc. and fem. nom. forms are OHG innovations. In Notker's writings the masc. and fem. nom. acc. pl. is *-e*, *blinde*. The paradigms of the weak adjective declension are exactly the same as those of the weak, or Class III, nouns (see pp. 105 ff.).

		Masculine	Feminine	Neuter
sg.	N	*blinto*	*blinta*	*blinta*
	A	*blintun*	*blintūn*	*blinta*
	G	*blintin*	*blintūn*	*blintin*
	D	*blintin*	*blintūn*	*blintin*
pl.	N	*blintun*	*blintūn*	*blintun*
	A	*blintun*	*blintūn*	*blintun*
	G	*blintōno*	*blintōno*	*blintōno*
	D	*blintōn*	*blintōn*	*blintōn*

The dat. pl. form for all genders was earlier *blintōm*.

Adjectives were usually uninflected in predicative position and could always be distinguished from adverbs in that the latter ended in *-o*, *starko*. The suffix *-līhho* was also used to form adverbs from adjectives, *wār—wārlīhho*. This was originally a deri- vational suffix used for forming compound adjectives, e.g. *eban*, adjective, *ebanlīh*, compound adjective, and adverb *ebanlīhho*, with the regular adverbial ending *-o*. In OHG instead of merely the ending *-o* in *ebanlīhho* being regarded as the adverbial ending, the longer suffix *-līhho* came to be regarded as having this function.

One of the main formal characteristics of adjectives is that they inflect in the comparative and superlative. In OHG many adverbs had a comparative form different from that of adjectives. There were two comparative endings for adjectives, *-iro* accompanied by mutation, and *-ōro* without mutation. In the comparison of adverbs *-ōro* was always used. The ending *-iro* with modification of the stem vowel *a* to *e* was usually added to simple *jo* stem adjectives: *suozi—suoziro*; *engi—engiro*, cf. adverb *ango*. In the case of those adjectives which were *o* stems, both endings were found: *hōh—hōhiro*, *hōhōro*; *reht—rehtiro*, *rehtōro*. The ending *-ōro* was added to adjectives formed with derivative suffixes and those adjectives having more than one syllable: *sālīg—sālīgōro*; *tiurlīh— tiurlīhhōro*. The form of the superlative was determined by the form of the comparative; if the comparative ending was *-ōro* then the superlative was -*ōsto*: *saligōsto, tiurlīhhōsto*, and if the ending was -*iro* then the superlative ending was -*isto*: *engisto, suozisto*. In the case of *o* stem adjectives, the fluctuation between -*iro* and -*ōro* in the comparative gave rise to a fluctuation in the superlative between the endings -*isto* and -*ōsto*.

As in all the Gmc. languages some adjectives and adverbs in OHG formed their comparative and superlative by suppletion, i.e. the comparative and superlative endings are added to a different stem from the positive. The following examples show this quite clearly.

Positive	Comparative	Superlative
guot	*bezziro*	*bezzisto*
wola 'well' (adv.)	*baz*	*bezzist*
ubil	*wirsiro*	*wirsisto*
mihhil	*mēro*	*meisto*
luzzil	*minniro*	*minnisto*

Both the comparative and superlative forms, whatever their ending, were inflected as weak adjectives.

The numerals in OHG will be described together with the MHG numerals on pp. 131 f. in the section ADJECTIVE INFLECTION IN MIDDLE HIGH GERMAN.

Further reading

BRAUNE, W., *Althochdeutsche Grammatik*, 13th edn. (Niemeyer, Tübingen, 1975), §§ 244–69.

CURME, G. O., 'The origin and growth of the weak adjective declension in Germanic', *Journal of English and Germanic Philology*, 9 (1909–10), 439–82.

SCHATZ, J., *Althochdeutsche Grammatik* (Vandenhoeck & Ruprecht, Göttingen, 1927), §§ 376–407.

SONDEREGGER, S., *Althochdeutsche Sprache und Literatur* (Sammlung Göschen 8005, De Gruyter, Berlin, 1974), 189–95.

PRONOUNS IN OLD HIGH GERMAN

The pronouns in the IE languages vary a great deal in form from language to language and use a great many different roots, the origins of which will not be dealt with here. The personal pronouns function as the subject or object of verbs and comprise first, second, and third person pronouns, the latter having separate masc., fem., and neuter forms. They inflect for number and case.

| | First Person | | Second Person | | | | Third Person | | | |
| | sg. | pl. | sg. | pl. | | | sg. | | | pl. | | |
					Masc.	Fem.	Neut.	Masc.	Fem.	Neut.
N	*ih*	*wir*	*dū*	*ir*	*er*	*siu*	*iz*	*sie*	*sio*	*siu*
A	*mih*	*unsih*	*dih*	*iuwih*	*inan*	*sia*	*iz*	*sie*	*sio*	*siu*
G	*mīn*	*unsēr*	*dīn*	*iuwēr*	*sīn*	*ira*	*es*	*iro*	*iro*	*iro*
D	*mir*	*uns*	*dir*	*iu*	*imo*	*iru*	*imo*	*in*	*in*	*in*

The form *du* also occurs with a short vowel. The early OHG forms for the dat. pl. third person was *im*, and for the third person sg. masc. and neuter, *imu*. The gen. forms of the personal pronouns represent the stems of the possessive adjectives, of which *mīn*, *unsēr*, *dīn*, *iuwēr*, and *sīn*, the latter from the reflexive pronoun *sih*, are declined like strong adjectives, while *ira* and *iro* remain uninflected. For the neuter *es*, *sīn* is used as the possessive adjective. The following paradigm shows the declension of *mīn*:

			Masculine	Feminine	Neuter
sg.	N		*mīn, mīner*	*mīn, mīniu*	*mīn, mīnaz*
	A		*mīnan*	*mīna*	*mīn, mīnaz*
	G		*mīnes*	*mīnera*	*mīnes*
	D		*mīnemo*	*mīnero*	*mīnemo*
pl.	N		*mīne*	*mīno*	*mīniu*
	A		*mīne*	*mīno*	*mīniu*
	G		*mīnero*	*mīnero*	*mīnero*
	D		*mīnēn*	*mīnēn*	*mīnēn*

The early OHG forms of dat. sg. *mīnemo* and *mīnero* were *mīnemu* and *mīneru* and of *mīnēn*, *mīnēm*. Franconian has shortened forms for the first and second person pl. of the possessive adjectives: masc. sg. N *unsēr*, A *unsan*, G *unses*, D *unsemo*, and so on.

The demonstrative pronoun *desēr* and the definite article *der*
were mostly used as modifiers of nouns, but *der*, sometimes accompanied by the particles *dar*, *dā*, also functioned as a relative
pronoun. The OHG demonstrative *jener* is declined like a strong
adjective. The paradigms of *desēr* and *der* are as follows:

		Masc.	Fem.	Neuter		Masc.	Fem.	Neuter
sg.	N	*desēr*	*disiu*	*diz* (*z* = [ts])	pl.	*dese*	*deso*	*disiu*
	A	*desan*	*desa*	*diz*		*dese*	*deso*	*disiu*
	G	*desses*	*desera*	*desses*		*desero*	*desero*	*desero*
	D	*desemo*	*deseru*	*desemo*		*desēn*	*desēn*	*desēn*

		Masc.	Fem.	Neuter		Masc.	Fem.	Neuter
sg.	N	*der*	*diu*	*daz*	pl.	*die, dia*	*dio*	*diu*
	A	*den*	*dia*	*daz*		*die, dia*	*dio*	*diu*
	G	*des*	*dera*	*des*		*dero*	*dero*	*dero*
	D	*demo*	*dero*	*demo*		*dēn*	*dēn*	*dēn*

The early OHG nom. sg. masc. was *dese*. In the nom. fem. sg.
and nom. acc. pl. neuter the original *e* of the stem, *desiu*, was raised
to *i* before the ending *-iu*. A rare masc. gen. sg. form *desse* is found
in *Muspilli*. The early OHG forms for *desemo* and *desēn* were
desemu and *desēm* respectively. The early OHG form for *demo*
was *demu*. The early OHG form for dat. sg. fem. *dero* was *deru*.
Later the dat. fem. sg. form *dero* is also used for the gen. Of the
two forms in the masc. nom. acc. pl. *die* is the main form in
Tatian and *Otfrid* but *dia* occurs in other texts. The dat. pl. form
dēn, early OHG *dēm*, was shortened to *den* in OHG. The indefinite article *ein* is declined like a strong adjective in OHG with the
uninflected forms in the nom. sg. in all genders and the acc. sg.
fem. and neuter, e.g. *ein man*, *ein geba*, *ein wīb*.

The interrogative pronoun *wer* inflects only in the sg.:

	Masculine, Feminine	Neuter
N	*wer*	*waz*
A	*wenan*	*waz*
G	*wes*	*wes*
D	*wemo*	*wemo*
		(early OHG *wemu*)

Before the ninth century these forms occur with initial *h*, *hwer*,
hwaz. The indefinite interrogative pronoun is *sō wer* 'who(so)ever',

sō waz 'what(so)ever'. Other interrogative pronouns are *wedar* 'which of two' and *welīh* 'which', both being declined like strong adjectives. OHG *solīh* 'such' was originally the indefinite form of *welīh*, cf. *sō wer* from *wer*.

There were also a number of indefinite pronouns: *sum, sumelīh* 'some one', *einig* 'anyone', *etilīh* 'many a one', *iogelīh, jeder* 'each'; *nihein, dihein* 'any', which were declined like strong adjectives; *man* 'one', *ioman* 'anyone', *wiht* 'anything' (the latter occurring in *Otfrid* and *Tatian* but only with a negative particle in the sentence, a more usual form is *iowiht*), and their negative counterparts *nioman, niowiht*, which function as subjects or objects.

In OHG there was a special form for the reflexive pronoun only for the third person sg. and pl. acc. case: *sih*, and for the gen. sg.: *sīn*. The other forms were provided by the third person personal pronouns. Reflexive pronouns for the first and second person sg. and pl. were provided solely by the acc. and dat. forms of the personal pronouns, e.g. *mih, mir, unsih, uns*.

Further reading

BRAUNE, W., *Althochdeutsche Grammatik*, 13th edn. (Niemeyer, Tübingen, 1975), §§ 282–300.

SCHATZ, J., *Althochdeutsche Grammatik* (Vandenhoeck & Ruprecht, Göttingen, 1927), §§ 416–28.

SONDEREGGER, S., *Althochdeutsche Sprache und Literatur* (Sammlung Göschen 8005, De Gruyter, Berlin, 1974), 201–7.

THE VERB IN OLD HIGH GERMAN

In IE the verb was a very highly inflected part of speech. It had three numbers: singular, dual, and plural; three moods: indicative, subjunctive, and optative; and three voices: active, middle, and passive. There were six tenses for each of the moods and voices: present, imperfect, future, aorist, perfect, and pluperfect. All the possibilities of combination are not present in all the IE languages but the Latin and Greek verbal systems give a good idea of the complexity of the verbal forms.

In the older Gmc. languages this complex system has been considerably simplified. There are only two tenses: present and past (later a perfect and a future were developed using auxiliary verbs); two moods: indicative and subjunctive; and two voices: active and passive. Usually in the Germanic languages the passive is formed by an auxiliary verb plus the past participle, e.g. *Tatian*, Ch. I, v. 2: *Alliu thuruh thaz vvurdun gitán* ('All things were made by Him'). Only in Gothic are there remains of a passive formed by inflecting the verb stem, e.g. *nimada* 'I am taken', cf. *niman* 'to take'. Verbs in the Gmc. languages fall into two main categories, strong and weak. The strong verbs are those which form their past tense by changing their stem vowel, e.g. NHG *singen—sang—gesungen*, whereas weak verbs form their past tense by adding a dental suffix, e.g. NHG *sagen—sagte—gesagt*. (The tenses and moods formed with the help of auxiliaries are dealt with in Lockwood, *Historical German Syntax*, pp. 114 ff.).

Strong verbs in Old High German

The endings of the present tense of the verb in IE were as follows:

	Singular		Plural	
First person	*-o	Latin *legō*	*-omes	Latin *legimus*
Second person	*-es(i)	Latin *legis*	*-ete	Latin *legitis*,
				Greek *férete*
Third person	*-et(i)	Latin *legit*	*-ont(i)	Latin *legunt*

The initial vowels of the IE endings are called thematic or stem vowels. Most verbs in IE had a thematic conjugation. The Latin form *legitis* owes its final -*s* to the corresponding sg. form. The regular development of the IE forms can be seen in the early OHG forms: *gibu, gibis, gibit, gebemēs, gebet, gebant* (the ending -*ēs* is not PIE and has never been satisfactorily explained). The vowel before -*mēs* was either *e* or *a*; the latter being more frequent in UG. In later OHG the ending -*st* appears for the second person sg.; this is probably the result of a wrong division of the inverted verb plus personal pronoun in the interrogative construction, e.g. *gibistu? = gibis du?* From this form -*st* instead of -*s* was incorrectly separated off and used in non-interrogative sentences, e.g. *du gibist*. In the ninth century the long form *gebemēs* was replaced by the short forms *gebēm, gebēn*, which are possibly from the subjunctive.

The endings for the past tense are as follows: *ih, er gab, du gābi, wir gābun*, earlier *gābum*, *ir gābut*, *sie gābun*. Except for the second person sg., which has not been fully explained (it may be an old IE aorist form), all the endings are regular developments from the IE perfect tense forms. ON and Gothic have the regular development from IE for the second person sg., *-t*, *gaft*, cf. Latin perfect tense *vidis-tī*.

The subjunctive is used in OHG for 'will', 'wish', and 'potentiality', combining the functions of the IE optative and subjunctive which are only formally distinct in Greek and Sanskrit. Historically, however, the OHG subjunctive forms are, rather misleadingly, the reflexes of IE optative forms. No clear cases of reflexes of IE subjunctive forms exist in OHG. We will retain the traditional designation of subjunctive. The IE sign for the optative, the mood of 'wishing' and 'potentiality', was **ie* or **i*, Latin *sīmus*, or **oi* as in the Greek paradigm of *lúō* 'I loose': *lúo-oi-mi*, *lú-oi-s*, *lú-oi*, *lú-oi-men*, *lú-oi-te*, *lú-oi-en*. In OHG the IE **oi*, which had become *ai* in Gmc., was monophthongized to a long *ē* and shortened in word final position: *ih*, *er bere*, *du berēs*, *wir berēn*, earlier *-ēm*, *ir berēt*, *sie berēn*. In the first person pl. the indicative ending *-emēs* and the subjunctive endings *-ēm*, *-ēn* are confused in many texts. The fluctuation was finally resolved in the ninth century when the ending *-ēn* is used in both the indicative and the subjunctive and the ending *-emēs* dies out. The past tense of the subjunctive in OHG was formed by adding *-ī* to the pl. stem of the past tense of the indicative, e.g. *gāb-*, *gābī-*, and then adding the personal endings: *ih*, *er gābi*, *du gābīs*, *wir gābīmes*, *ir gābīt*, *sie gābīn*. The oldest ending for the first person pl. was *-īm*, then *-īmes* was used; *Otfrid* and *Tatian* use *-īn*. The long *ī* represents IE **ie*. In the first and third person sg. the *ī* was usually shortened in word-final position.

The method of forming the past tense by changing the vowel of the present tense, e.g. NHG *singen*, *sang*, *gesungen*, is known as vowel gradation, or *Ablaut*. In Gothic there are relics of another method, reduplication, the repetition of the initial consonant of the stem followed by a vowel, e.g. *háitan*, past tense *haíháit*. In OHG this process is no longer productive, but the past tense form *teta*, from *tuon*, seems to be a relic of it.

Vowel gradation takes the form of a systematic use of differences in certain vowels in order to show grammatical function. In the Gmc. languages it was largely restricted to verbs and the formation

[handwritten marginal note: ie .ai in main particle formation. not a vowel in stress syllable doesn't conform to sound-change we've been dealing with]

of nouns from verbs, cf. NHG *schreiten—Schritt*. In IE there were two types of vowel gradation: qualitative, where the vowels concerned differed in quality, Latin *tegō—toga* (*e* and *o* were the only vowels concerned); and quantitative vowel gradation, where vowel length was significant, Latin *sedeō—sēdī*. In these two types of vowel gradation three grades were distinguished: full, or normal, grade, *e, o*; lengthened grade *ē, ō*; and vanishing grade, represented by the absence of the vowel. In IE the vowels that could be modified by vowel gradation were either followed by stops, *s* (the only fricative in IE), or the semi-vowels *i, u* [j, w], the nasals *m, n*, and the liquids *l, r*. These last three groups of sounds are known as resonants. When the vowels were followed by *i, u* [j, w], the resulting combination is best regarded not as a diphthong but as a cluster of vowel plus resonant. The vanishing grade is most easily seen from the vowel gradation before a resonant, in this case before *i*: Greek *leipō* 'I leave' present tense, *léloipa* perfect tense, and *élipon* (vanishing grade) aorist tense.

Descriptively OHG has seven classes of verbs which form their past tense by changing the stem vowel, but only six of these classes represent vowel gradation in IE, and, of these, five represent a vowel gradation of *e* with *o* in IE. In OHG the IE vowel alternations have been obscured by sound changes but with the pattern for each vowel gradation class (*Ablautreihe*) its development from IE will be given. (Details of the sound changes in the vowels from IE to OHG will be found on pp. 38 ff. and 52 ff.)

infinitive		first sg. pres.	sg. past	pl. past	past participle
Class Ia	*rītan*	*rītu*	*reit*	*ritun*	*giritan*
Ib	*zīhan* 'to accuse'	*zīhu*	*zēh*	*zigun*	*gizigan*

Historically this class represents the vowel gradation of IE *e* with *o* before the resonant *i* [j]. IE *ei*, which in Gmc. and OHG became *ī*, alternates in the infinitive and present tense with IE *oi*, which became *ei* in OHG (*ái* in Gothic), in the past tense sg. with *i*, the vanishing grade in the past pl. and past participle. The sub-class Ib contains those verbs whose stems end in *h* or *w*, before which the diphthong *ei* has become *ē* in OHG in the past sg. (see p. 52). The verb *spīwan* has the past tense sg. form *spēo*; medial OHG *w* becomes vocalized to *o* in word final position (see also p. 103).

Examples of Class Ia: *snidan, strītan, stīgan, slīchan, bīzan, risan, grīfan*, and of Class Ib: *dīhan* 'to thrive', *līhan*.

[handwritten: I.E   eu   zu   ou   u]

Class IIa:	biogan	biugu	boug	bugun	gibogan
IIb:	ziohan	ziuhu	zōh	zugun	gizogan

This class represents IE *e/o* vowel gradation before the resonant *u*[w]. IE *eu* before an *a* of the following syllable became *io* in OHG, and before *u* it became *iu*. The *ou* of the past sg. represents Gothic *áu, báug*. If the stem ended in an alveolar, *d, t, z, s,* or *h*, then the past sg. was monophthongized to *ō: biotan—bōt; giozan—gōz; kiosan—kōs* 'to choose', as in Class IIb (see p. 52). Those verbs whose stems ended in *w* had *iu* in the infinitive and present tense and *ū* in the past pl. and past participle: *kiuwan, kiuwu, kūwun, gikūwan*; in the sg. past the final *w* is deleted, *kou*. The past tense pl. forms *bugun, zugun* represent the vanishing grade of resonant which in the case of the past participle forms *gibogan, gizogan* has undergone a lowering from *u* to *o* before the *a* of the following syllable.

Examples of Class IIa: *liogan, klioban* 'to cleave', *triofan, kriochan*, and of Class IIb, *siodan* 'to boil', *riozan* 'to weep', *friosan, firliosan*.

[handwritten: Indo European]

Class IIIa:	bintan	bintu	bant	buntun	gibuntan
IIIb:	helfan	hilfu	half	hulfun	giholfan

This class also represents the IE *e/o* vowel gradation, in this case before a nasal or a liquid followed by a consonant, or before a double nasal, e.g. *rinnan*. The different vowels of the infinitive, *bintan, helfan*, are due to the fact that IE *e* was raised to *i* either before a nasal plus consonant, (see p. 41), or before a double nasal. The vowel in the past sg. represents IE *o* which became *a* in Gmc. and the vowel in past pl. and past participle shows the vanishing grade as in Classes I and II. The *u* before the nasal or liquid in the past participle is a Gmc. development of IE *n* and *l* which functioned as vowels when they occurred between obstruents, e.g. [CṇC, CḷC]. IE vocalic [ṇ] and [ḷ] developed to *un* and *ul* in Gmc. The *u* was lowered to *o* before the *a* of the following syllable except when a nasal intervened, *giholfan* but *gibuntan*. The verb *werdan* 'to become', which was used as an auxiliary verb to a limited extent in OHG (see Lockwood, *Historical German Syntax*, pp. 11 f. and 143 ff.), belongs to Class IIIb. The verbs *brestan* 'to

[right margin handwritten table, Class IIIa:]

	Infinitive	Pret.sg.	Pret pl.	Past part.
I.E	bhendhonom	bhondhe	bhṇdhṃe	bhṇdhonos
Gmc	bendanam	banda	bundum	bundanaz
OHG	bintan	bant	buntum	gibuntan

[bottom handwritten table:]

ss IIIb

	Infinitive	Pret.sg.	Pret plural	past participle
I.E	*Kelbonom	Kolba	Klbme	klbonos
Gmc	helpanam	halpa	hulpum	hulpanaz
OHG	helfan	half	hulfun	giholfan

burst' and *dreskan* also belong to Class IIIb, probably because historically the *r* came before the consonant cluster, cf. OE *berstan, þerscan.*

Examples of Class IIIa: *singan, rinnan, findan, sinkan, dinsan* 'pull', and of Class IIIb: *sterban, werdan, smelzan, bergan.*

Class IV: *neman* | *nimu* | *nam nāmun* | *ginoman*

This class represents the IE *e/o* vowel gradation before a single nasal or liquid. The development of the forms from IE is regular. The long *ā* of the past pl. *nāmun*, represents IE *ē*, Gmc. *ē¹*, cf. Gothic *nēmum*; it represents the lengthened grade of IE *e*. The past participle shows a lowering of *u*, from an IE syllabic nasal or liquid, to *o* before an *a* of the following syllable. The verbs *brechan, stechan,* and *treffan* are usually regarded as belonging to this class since they share the same vowel patterning as the other verbs, although their stem ends in a fricative.

Examples of Class IV: *beran, helan* 'to hide', *queman, stelan, klenan* 'to smear'.

Class V: *geban* | *gibu* | *gab gābun* | *gigeban*

The forms of this class have exactly the same origin as those of Class IV, except for the past participle. In Class V, however, the stem final consonant is always an obstruent, i.e. a stop or a fricative. In the past participle the vowel is that of the normal grade, *e*, inserted by analogy with the infinitive and the pl. present, to avoid two obstruents occurring together. The verbs *liggen, bitten,* and *sitzen,* cf. OLG *sittian,* are also included in this class. They differ from other verbs in their infinitive (see p. 122) and present tense forms which have stem final double consonants caused by an original *j* which has been lost in OHG.

Examples of Class V: *sehan, ezzan, tretan, lesan, quedan* 'to talk', *weban.*

Class VI: *faran*   *faru*   *fuor fuorun*   *gifaran*

This class shows only two stem vowels, *a* and *uo*, which historically represent a quantitative vowel gradation between IE short *o* and long *ō*. IE short *o* became *a* in Gmc.; IE long *ō* remained in Gothic, *fōr, fōrum,* but was diphthongized to *uo* in OHG (see p. 55). The verbs *heffen, skepfen,* and *swerien* also belong to this class and only differ from the other verbs in that they have *e* for *a* (see p. 122) in the infinitive and present owing to an original *j* in the endings.

Examples of Class VI: *tragan, wahsan, stantan, graban, watan, malan.*

Class VIIa	*heizan*	*heizu*	*hiez hiezun*	*giheizan*
VIIb	*loufan*	*loufu*	*liof liofun*	*giloufan*

This class contains those verbs which historically formed their past tense by reduplication. The stem vowel of Class VIIa is *ei, a,* or *ā,* and that of Class VIIb is *ou, ō* before dentals, *stōzan, scrōtan* 'to cut', or *uo.* The *ie* of the past tense comes from Gmc. *ē²* and the *io* from Gmc. *eu.*

Examples of Class VIIa: *gangan, skeidan* 'to sever', *rātan, lāzan, blāsan,* and of Class VIIb: *houwan, blōzan* 'to sacrifice', *ruofan.*

The second person sg. imperative form is the stem of the verb. In the cases where the verb changes its stem vowel from *e* to *i* in the present tense, the same change also takes place in the imperative: *nim,* cf. infinitive *neman, ih nimu,* but *far,* cf. *faran, ih faru.*

Grammatical change

Cutting across the classification into vowel gradation classes is the phenomenon called grammatical change (*Grammatischer Wechsel*), the alternation of certain pairs of medial and final consonants, one being found in the infinitive, present, and past tense sg., and the other in the past tense pl. and past participle. (The historical origin of this is explained on pp. 33 f.)

(1) *d* alternates with *t*: *snīdan, sneid, snitun, gisnitan; siodan, sōd, sutun, gisotan; līdan, leid, litun, gilitan; werdan, ward, wurtun, giwortan; findan, fand, funtun, gifuntan; quedan, quad, quātun, giquetan.*

(2) *s* alternates with *r*: *rīsan, reis, rirun, giriran; firliosan, firlōs, firlurun, firloran; friosan, frōs, frurun, gifroran; lesan, las, lārun, gileran.*

(3) *h* alternates with *g*: *dīhan, dēh, digun, gidigan; slahan, sluoh, sluogun, gislagan; dwahan, dwuoh, dwuogun, gidwagan.* In the

late eighth and early ninth centuries the forms *sluoh, dwuoh,* were replaced by *sluog* and *dwuog.*

There are other alternations but there are only a few clear examples of each: *f* alternating with *b*: *heffen, huob* (this is the only past tense sg. form of this verb recorded), *huobun, (ir)haban; h* alternating with *w*: *lihan, lēh, liwun, giliwan*; and *h* alternating with *ng*, which also occurs in the past tense sg.: *hāhan, hiang, hiangun, gihangun; fāhan, fiang, fiangun, gifangan.*

Weak verbs in Old High German

The weak verbs in OHG may be divided into classes on the basis of their infinitive endings: Class I verbs end in -*en, zellen*; Class II verbs end in -*ōn, salbōn*; and Class III verbs in -*ēn, sagēn*. The personal endings of the verbs in the present tense differ slightly in each class.

		Class I	Class II	Class III
sg.	1	*ih zellu*	*ih salbōn*	*ih sagēn*
	2	*du zelis(t)*	*du salbōs(t)*	*du sagēs(t)*
	3	*er zelit*	*er salbōt*	*er sagēt*
pl.	1	*wir zellēn*	*wir salbōn*	*wir sagēn*
	2	*ir zellet*	*ir salbōt*	*ir sagēt*
	3	*sie zellent*	*sie salbōnt*	*sie sagēnt*

The stem vowel remains the same throughout the present; there is no vowel alternation as there is with strong verbs. The first person sg. of verbs of Classes II and III ended in -*m* in early OHG, *ih salbōm, sagēm.* The double *ll* in the present tense of *zellen* is due to an original *j* which caused the gemination of the preceding consonant (see p. 44). The second and third person sg. did not originally have a *j* and thus show no gemination. The present subjunctive shows gemination throughout.

As with strong verbs, the short endings of the first person pl., -*ēm, -ēn,* replaced the earlier longer endings, e.g. *wir zellemēs, wir salbōmēs, wir sagēmēs,* in the ninth century. The personal endings for the present subjunctive are the same for all three classes: -*e,* -*ēs(t), -e, -ēn, -ēt, -ēn,* which are attached to the stems *zell-, salbō-, sagē-,* e.g. *zelle, zellēs(t), zelle, zellēn, zellēt, zellēn.* However, the forms *salbōe, sagēe*, etc. are only found in UG; usually the *e* of the ending is dropped, thus giving forms which are the same as the present indicative except in the first and third person sg., *ih, er salbo, sage* (with the vowel shortened in word-final position), and the third person pl., *sie salbōn, sagēn*.

The past tense of all three classes is formed by adding the endings: *-ta, -tōs(t), -ta, -tun, -tut, -tun* to the present stem. Many Class I verbs have either an *-i-* between the stem and the ending, e.g. *nerita*, in which case the past tense has the same stem vowel as the present, *nerren* 'to save', or there is no *-i-*, *zalta*, in which case the stem vowel of the infinitive, if it is *e*, corresponds to *a*: *zellen— zalta*. This correspondence of *e* to *a* is the exact opposite of um-umlaut, cf. *gast—gesti*, and is known as *Rückumlaut*. Historically this process is the result of the early loss of *-i-* after originally long syllables, e.g. those containing a diphthong, a long or short vowel followed by a consonant cluster: *ougen, ougta; hōren, hōrta; sterken, starcta*. The *-i-* which was lost at an early date did not cause mutation in the past tense, whereas if it remained, i.e. after short syllables and in the infinitive and present tense, it did cause mutation: *nerita, nerren*. In OHG only the *Rückumlaut* of *e* to *a* is expressed orthographically, in MHG more vowels are involved (see pp. 56 f.). The paradigms of the past tense indicative are as follows:

		Class I		Class II	Class III
sg.	1	*ih zalta*	*ih nerita*	*ih salbōta*	*ih sagēta*
	2	*du zaltōs(t)*	*du neritōs(t)*	*du salbōtōs(t)*	*du sagētōs(t)*
	3	*er zalta*	*er nerita*	*er salbōta*	*er sagēta*
pl.	1	*wir zaltun*	*wir neritun*	*wir salbōtun*	*wir sagētun*
	2	*ir zaltut*	*ir neritut*	*ir salbōtut*	*ir sagētut*
	3	*sie zaltun*	*sie neritun*	*sie salbōtun*	*sie sagētun*

The past subjunctive is formed by taking the past stem: *zalt-, nerit-, salbōt-, sagēt-*, and adding the endings: *-i, -īs, -i, -īn, -īt, -īn*, which are the same as those for the past subjunctive of strong verbs. The origin of the past tense dental ending of weak verbs is obscure; it may well be a weakened form of the verb 'to do' which has lost its full meaning and become a tense suffix.

Examples of Class I: *retten, teilen, brennen, gilouben*; of Class II: *dionōn, machōn, dankōn, offanōn*; and of Class III: *folgēn, frāgēn, lernēn, sorgēn*.

The nominal forms of strong and weak verbs

The present participle of strong verbs is formed by adding -enti to the stem: nem-, nementi (in the earliest OHG the form was ne-manti, the final i mutated the a to e). In earlier Alemannic -inti is also found. The present participle of weak verbs is formed by adding -ti to the infinitive: zellenti, salbōnti, sagēnti. The present participle can be declined like a weak or strong adjective. The past participle is in most cases formed by adding the prefix gi- to the past stem of weak verbs, gizalt, gisalbōt, gisagēt, or to the past pl. stem of strong verbs and adding the suffix -an, rit-, giritan. Many verbs with inseparable prefixes have no gi-, binoman. The prefix gi-, Gothic ga-, was originally used as a perfective verbal prefix throughout the verbal paradigm, and not merely with the past participle, to signify a completed action, cf. Gothic ga-baíran (inf.), gabar ina . . . jah galagida ina in uzētin, '[she] bore him and laid him in a manger', Luke 2:7 (past tense). Some strong verbs in OHG which already have a perfective meaning do not take gi- in the past participle, e.g. queman, findan, treffan, and the originally strong verb bringan which developed weak past tense forms. The past participle of both strong and weak verbs is declined like a strong adjective. The infinitive of strong verbs ends in -an: rītan, biotan, and it could also be inflected like a Class I declension, jo stem, noun, e.g. gen. werfennes, dat. zi traganne. The j, which has been lost in OHG, caused the gemination of the n to nn (see p. 44). Sometimes the inflected forms also show umlaut, because of the j, -ennes, -enne, but usually the forms were -annes, -anne by analogy with the -an of the uninflected form, werfan, tragan. The infinitive of the weak verbs ended in -en, -ōn, and -ēn; these could also inflect in the gen. and dat. Strong verbs from Classes V and VI with an infinitive in -en have alternative forms with -an, e.g. bittan, skepfan.

Irregular verbs

(a) Preterite-present verbs

This group comprises nine verbs whose forms are historically those of the past tense but which are used in OHG (and other Gmc. dialects) to designate the present. Consequently, they have formed new past tense forms on the model of weak verbs. The fact that they were originally strong verbs can be seen from the forms of the present tense. They show the vowel alternation between sg. and pl. (the only exception is *muozan*), e.g. *er weiz, wir wizzun*, cf. *er beiz, wir bizzun*, and the same form for the first and second person sg., *ih, er kan*, cf. *ih, er nam*, both of which are characteristic of the past tense of strong verbs. Historically preterite-present verbs come from the strong verb vowel gradation Classes I to VI.

From Class I: *wizzan*, present: *ih weiz, du weist, er weiz, wir wizzun, ir wizzut, sie wizzun*, cf. *ih beiz, wir bizzun*. The subjunctive is *wizzi*, conjugated like *gābi* (see pp. 114 f.). In OHG there were several forms for the past tense: *wissa*, which is UG, and *wessa, westa*, which are Franconian and used by *Tatian* and *Otfrid*. The past tense endings are the same as those of the weak verbs, e.g. *ih westa, du westōs(t), er westa, wir westun, ir westut, sie westun*. This is the only preterite-present verb with a past participle in OHG, *giwizzan*.

From Class II: the only present forms of the MHG verb *tougen* 'to avail' in OHG are *toug* and *tugen*, cf. *ih boug, wir bugun*, the sole past tense form is *tohta*, third person sg.

From Class III: *kunnan*, present: *ih kan, du kanst, er kan, wir kunnun, ir kunnut, sie kunnun*, cf. *ih ran, wir runnun*. The subjunctive is *kunni*. The past tense is *ih konda, du kondōs(t), er konda, wir kondun, ir kondut, sie kondun*. The only sg. present form of the verb *unnan* 'to grant' occurs in the form with the prefix *ir-*, (*ih*) *irban* 'I do not allow'; the pl. is complete, *wir unnun, ir unnut, sie unnun*. The subjunctive is *unni*. The past tense is *onda*. The verb 'to dare', which has no infinitive in OHG, has the present forms: *ih gitar, du gitarst, er gitar, wir giturrun, ir giturrut, sie giturrun*. The subjunctive is *giturri* and the past tense *ih gitorsta, du gitortōs(t), er gitorsta, wir gitorstun, ir gitorstut, sie gitorstun*. The verb *durfan* has the present forms: *ih darf, du darft, er darf, wir durfun, ir durfut, sie durfun*. The subjunctive is *durfi* and the past tense forms are: *ih dorfta, du dorftōs(t), er dorfta, wir dorftun, ir dorftut, sie dorftun*.

From Class IV: *scolan*, present: *ih scal, du scalt, er scal, wir sculun, ir sculut, sie sculun*. The subjunctive is *sculi*. In late OHG *Notker* uses the forms without a *c*: *sol, solt, sol, suln, sult, suln*. The forms of the past tense are: *ih scolta, du scoltōs(t), er scolta, wir scoltun, ir scoltut, sie scoltun.* Notker uses forms without *c.* This verb is regarded as belonging to Class IV but the *u* of the present pl. is not to be found in strong verbs of that class, cf. *ih stal, wir stālun.* The *u* may have come from the past participle (see pp. 117 f.) before it was lowered to *o* before *a*, or it may be the result of re-modelling *scolan* on the analogy of verbs like *kunnan*, which had *a* in the present sg. and *u* in the pl.

From Class V: *mugan*, present: *ih mag, du maht, er mag, wir mugun, ir mugut, sie mugun.* The subjunctive is *mugi.* The oldest forms of this verb in OHG have the stem vowel *a* in the infinitive and pl. present: *magan, wir magun, ir magut, sie magun.* The subjunctive *megi* shows mutation of *a.* The past tense is: *ih mohta, du mohtōs(t), er mohta, wir mohtun, ir mohtut, sie mohtun.* The stem vowel *a* also existed in early OHG in all the past tense forms, *mahta*, etc. It is usually assumed that *mugan* was from Class V, cf. *ih gab, wir gābun*, and that the *u* came from *sculun* (Class IV). Its historical class is, however, considered uncertain by some scholars.

From Class VI: *muozan* has the present forms: *ih muoz, du muost, er muoz, wir muozun, ir muozut, sie muozun.* The subjunctive is *muozi.* The past tense forms are *ih muosa, du muosōst, er muosa, wir muosun, ir muosut, sie muosun.*

(b) The verb 'to be'

This verb shows three different stems in the form of its conjugation. A stem with *s-*, representing IE **es-* (cf. Latin *esse*), is used in the present subjunctive for all persons in the sg. and pl., e.g. *ih sī, wir sīn*, the infinitive, *sīn*, and for the third person sg. and pl. in the present indicative, *er ist, sie sint.* Another stem, beginning with *b-*, representing an IE stem **bhō* (cf. Latin *fuī*, where IE **bh* becomes *f* initially), is used to form all the other persons in the present indicative except for the third person sg. and pl. The present tense of the verb 'to be' is as follows:

Indicative		Subjunctive	
sg.	pl.	sg.	pl.
ih bin	*wir birun*	*ih sī*	*wir sīn*
du bis(t)	*ir birut*	*du sīs(t)*	*ir sīt*
er ist	*sie sint*	*er sī*	*sie sīn*

The first person sg. indicative ended in -*m* in early OHG as did the first person pl. indicative and subjunctive. The third stem, represented by *wesan*, a strong verb of Class V, is used for the imperative second person sg., *wis*, and second person pl., *weset*, the present participle, *wesanti* (a past participle is not recorded in OHG), the infinitive form *wesan*, which had to compete with *sīn* (*Otfrid* uses *wesan* and *sīn* equally but *Notker* mostly uses *sīn*). The past tense is supplied wholly by the forms of *wesan* with an alternation of final -*s* and medial -*r*-, *ih was*, *wir wārun* (see p. 119 for other examples). The endings are the same as those of the past tense of any strong verb, both in the indicative and the subjunctive:

Indicative		Subjunctive	
sg.	pl.	sg.	pl.
ih was	*wir wārun*	*ih wāri*	*wir wārīn*
du wāri	*ir wārut*	*du wāris(t)*	*ir wārīt*
er was	*sie wārun*	*er wāri*	*sie wārīn*

(c) Other irregular verbs

The verbs *tuon*, *gēn*, and *stēn*, together with *wellen* and *habēn* (*hān*), will be treated in this section. The first three verbs, together with *sīn*, which has been dealt with in section (b), are called athematic verbs. The ending of their first person sg. present is -*m*, which has become -*n* in the ninth century, representing IE *-*mi*, cf. Greek *dídōmi* 'I give', which has been added to the root without any intervening thematic vowel (for 'thematic vowel', see p. 99). In early OHG all these verbs had the ending -*mēs* for the first person pl. present indicative. The verb *tuon* conjugates as follows in the present:

Indicative		Subjunctive	
sg.	pl.	sg.	pl.
ih tuon	*wir tuon*	*ih tuo*	*wir duen* (*Otfrid*)
du tuos(t)	*ir tuot*	*du tues*	*ir tuot*
er tuot	*sie tuont*	*er tuo*	*sie tuon*

This verb shows a variety of forms in texts; the paradigm presented here is from *Tatian*. The first person pl. subjunctive only occurs in *Otfrid*, who also has the form *duest* for the second person sg. subjunctive.

The past indicative shows clear relics of reduplication in the form for the first and third person sg., *teta* (see p. 115). The other forms, as well as those of the past subjunctive, are the same as those of a regular strong verb of vowel gradation Class V. The paradigms are as follows:

	Indicative		Subjunctive	
	sg.	pl.	sg.	pl.
	ih teta	*wir tātun*	*ih tāti*	*wir tātīn*
	du tāti	*ir tātut*	*du tātīs(t)*	*ir tātīt*
	er teta	*sie tātun*	*er tāti*	*sie tātīn*

The present participle is *tuonti* and the past participle *gitān*. The imperative second person sg. is *tuo*, and the second person pl. is *tuot*.

The verbs *gēn* and *stēn* are shortened forms of the strong verbs *gangan* and *stantan* which have the regular past tense of Class VIIa, *gieng*, and VI, *stuont*. They are both conjugated exactly alike. The present paradigms are:

	Indicative		Subjunctive	
	sg.	pl.	sg.	pl.
	ih gēn	*wir gēn*	*ih gē*	*wir gēn*
	du gēs(t)	*ir gēt*	*du gēs(t)*	*ir gēt*
	er gēt	*sie gēnt*	*er gē*	*sie gēn*

These verbs also occur with the stem vowel *ā* throughout their present indicative *gān, stān*, but only in Alemannic; the forms with *ē* are found in Franconian, including East Franconian (*Tatian*), Bavarian, and always in the present subjunctive. Apart from these present tense endings they are exactly like verbs of vowel gradation Class VII. In early OHG the form *stuot* is used in the past tense as well as *stuont*, and in late OHG the form *gie* is used in the past tense as well as *gieng*.

The verb *wellen* has the present tense sg. forms: *ih willu, du wili, er wili*, which are historically optative forms. The present pl. forms are the same as those of the weak verbs of Class I: *wir wellēn, ir wellet, sie wellent* (see p. 120). A new subjunctive was formed from the infinitive with the same endings as those of the weak verbs of Class I: *ih welle, du wellēs(t), er welle, wir wellēn, ir wellēt, sie wellēn*. Like the preterite-present verbs, it has formed a new weak past tense, *ih wolta*, which is conjugated like *zalta*. In Franconian the *o* from the past tense was also transferred to the forms with the stem vowel *e* in the present, and the infinitive, *wollen*.

The auxiliary *habēn* was conjugated like a regular weak verb of Class III. In OHG, however, it also had a contracted infinitive, *hān*, and other contracted forms in the present which did not occur frequently until the eleventh century: *ih hān, du hās(t), er hāt, wir hān, ir hāt, sie hānt*. The past tense is *habēta*, conjugated like *zalta*, although *hapta* also occurs, and the past participle is *gihabēt*. The present and past subjunctive are the same as those of Class III weak verbs (see pp. 120 f.).

Further reading

BALL, C. J. E., 'The Germanic dental preterite', *Transactions of the Philological Society* (1968), 162–88.

BARNES, M. and H. ESAU, 'Germanic strong verbs: a case of morphological rule extension?', *Lingua*, 31 (1973), 1–34.

BRAUNE, W., *Althochdeutsche Grammatik*, 13th edn. (Niemeyer, Tübingen, 1975), 301–85.

SCHATZ, J., *Althochdeutsche Grammatik* (Vandenhoeck & Ruprecht, Göttingen, 1927), §§ 429–550.

MIDDLE HIGH GERMAN AND THE DEVELOPMENT FROM OLD HIGH GERMAN

NOUN INFLECTION IN MIDDLE HIGH GERMAN

In general the MHG system of noun inflection is the same as that for OHG, although several sub-classes have been eliminated, chiefly through sound change. Through the merger of OHG unstressed *-u, -o, -a*, and *-i* with *-e* (phonetically [ə]), many forms which in OHG represented different cases came to have the same form in MHG; for instance, OHG nom. and acc. sg. *hirti*, dat. sg.

hirte, nom. and acc. pl. *hirta*, gen. pl. *hirto*, are all represented by *hirte* in MHG.

In Class I the merger of OHG *-u* and *-i* meant that in MHG the nom. and acc. sg. of nouns in this class either ended in a consonant, *tac*, *gast* (*o* and *i* stems), or in *-e*, *hirte*, *sige*, OHG *hirti* (*jo* stem), *sigu* (*u* stem). This resulted in the disappearance of the relics of the *jo* and *u* stems. The OHG minor consonantal stems, *friunt*, *fiant*; *fater*, *bruoder*; *man* have become assimilated into Class I. Relics of gen. forms without *-(e)s* and dat. forms without *-e* do still occur in MHG but not frequently. Another change in this class was the loss of the final *-o* after long vowels and diphthongs in the nom. and acc. sg. of the IE *wo* stems: OHG *sēo*, MHG *sê*, although in the gen. and dat. sg. and throughout the pl. the intervocalic *w* was retained: MHG *sêwes*, *sêwe*, dat. pl. *sêwen*. The sg. paradigms of nouns of OHG Class I have been reduced to two sub-classes, one whose members end in a consonant, the other whose members end in *-e*. Disyllabic and monosyllabic nouns of both sub-classes ending in a liquid and having a short stem vowel, have no *-e* endings in their declension, e.g. *nagels*, *zils*, dat. *nagel*, *zil*.

			Class Ia			Class Ib		
		Masculine			Neuter	Masculine	Neuter	
N/A	*tac*	*gast*	*nagel*	*sê*	*wort*	*hirte*	*netze*	*zil*
G	*tages*	*gastes*	*nagels*	*sêwes*	*wortes*	*hirtes*	*netzes*	*zils*
D	*tage*	*gaste*	*nagel*	*sêwe*	*worte*	*hirte*	*netze*	*zil*

In Class II the OHG distinction between the nom. acc. and gen. sg. form *geba* and the dat. sg. form *gebu* was eliminated. In MHG the form *gebe* is the only form of the sg. in all cases. The gen. and dat. sg. of nouns like *anst*, e.g. OHG *ensti*, ended in *-e* in MHG, *enste*. The sg. paradigms of Class II nouns in MHG still contain the same two sub-classes as in OHG:

	Class IIa	Class IIb
N	*gebe*	*anst*
A	*gebe*	*anst*
G	*gebe*	*enste*
D	*gebe*	*enste*

MHG nouns of this class which ended in *l*, *zal*, *nâdel*, or *r*, *tür*, had no final -e throughout their sg. declension. The original short fem. *i* stems, OHG *turi, kuri*, have a mutated vowel throughout the sg. and pl.

Nouns of Class III in MHG, the weak nouns, were divided into sub-classes on the basis of grammatical gender. In MHG, through the reduction of the five OHG case endings -*o*, -*a*, -*un*, -*in*, and -*ūn* to two, -*e* and -*en*, the only difference in gender shown by endings was in the acc. sg. where the neuter nouns ended in -*e*, *herze*, and the masc. and fem. nouns ended in -*en*, *boten, zungen*. Nouns of this class had only two forms in the sg., one ending in -*e* for the nom. (also for the acc. in the case of neuter nouns), and the ending -*en* for all the other cases.

	Masculine	Feminine	Neuter
N	*bote*	*zunge*	*herze*
A	*boten*	*zungen*	*herze*
G	*boten*	*zungen*	*herzen*
D	*boten*	*zungen*	*herzen*

The merger of unstressed vowels in MHG also affected the pl. forms of nouns. The mutated vowels which in OHG had been variants, or allophones, conditioned by an -*i*, -*ī*, or *j* in the following syllable became phonemes in MHG by the merger of unstressed -*i* and the other vowels in [ə] (*j* in unstressed position had been lost already in OHG). There was thus in the pl. in MHG not merely an alternation between *a* and *e*, *gast—geste* (this had been present in OHG), but also between other vowels: *u—ü, sune* sg.— *süne* pl., OHG *sunu, suni*; *â—æ, tât—tæte*, OHG *tāt, tāti*; *o—ö, loch* sg.—*löcher*, OHG *loh, lohhir*; *ô—œ, nôt—nœte*, OHG *nōt, nōti*; *û—iu* [yı], *hûs—hiuser*, OHG *hūs, hūsir*. (For the origin of *i*-mutation see pp. 56 f.) Nouns of Class Ia can be further sub-divided into those that mutate their stem vowel in the pl. and those that do not. This reflects the original distinction among the masc. nouns between *o* and *i* stems, and among the neuter nouns between *o* and -*is* stems (see p. 105). The noun *sun*, CG *sune*, OHG *sunu* (a *u* stem), was declined like an *i* stem in the pl. The masc. nouns which undergo *i*-mutation in the pl. take the ending -*e*, **geste**, and the neuter nouns take the ending -*er*, **lember**. Masc. nouns which do not undergo *i*- mutation simply take the ending -*e*, **tage**, while neuter nouns which do not undergo *i*-mutation do not change, the difference in number between sg. and pl. being shown by the article: *daʒ wort—diu wort*, or by the sg. or pl. form of the verb.

The nouns of Class Ib are not subject to *i*-mutation since they contain front vowels as their stem vowels. In MHG, the question of whether a noun is subject to *i*-mutation in the pl. is not predictable from its phonetic shape but must be shown in the dictionary. The OHG gen. pl. ending *-o* was reduced to *-e* and the OHG dat. pl. endings *-un* and *-in* were reduced to *-en*. Nouns like *nagel, nâdel, ʒal*, and *ʒil* had no *e* endings in the pl.; their dat. pl. ended in *-n*. The nom. and acc. OHG form of the *wo* stems, *sēwa*, merged in MHG with the gen., OHG *sēwo*, in *sēwe*. The dat. pl., OHG *sēwun*, became *sêwen* in MHG.

	Class Ia						Class Ib		
	Masculine				Neuter		Masc.	Neuter	
N/A	tage	geste	negel	sêwe	worte	lember	hirte	netze	ʒil
G	tage	geste	negel	sêwe	worte	lember	hirte	netze	ʒil
D	tagen	gesten	negeln	sêwen	worten	lembern	hirten	netzen	ʒiln

In Class II the nom. and acc. pl. endings *-ā, -i*, OHG *gebā, ensti*, were reduced to *-e* in MHG, *gebe, enste*. The nouns of this class, like those of Ia, are also divided into two groups according to whether they undergo *i*-mutation in the pl. or not, e.g. *sorge* sg. and pl., *kraft* sg., *krefte* pl. This difference coincides exactly with the division of this class in the sg. into IIa and IIb, the latter division reflecting the original distinction between *a* stems and *i* stems. Original *i* stems with front stem vowels, e.g. *list, pfliht*, do not undergo *i*-mutation. Nouns like OHG *hōhī*, belonging to a sub-class of the *n* stems, and OHG *sunta*, old *ja* stem, have a mutated stem vowel throughout the sg. and pl., e.g. *hœhe, hœhen*; *sünde, sünden* as do MHG *tür(e), kür(e)*, original short *i* stems. If they remained in this class they were members of sub-class IIa. Some of them became members of Class III. The gen. pl. ending *-ōno*, was reduced to *-en*, OHG *gebōno*, MHG *geben* (to *-n* for nouns like *ʒal*), and the other gen. ending *-o* was reduced to *-e*, OHG *ensto*, MHG *enste*. The two OHG dat. pl. forms *-ōn* and *-in*, *gebōn, enstin*, were reduced to *-en*, MHG *geben, ensten*. Apart from the *i*-mutation of the stem vowel the only differences in the pl. between Classes IIa and IIb was that the gen. ending was *-en* for nouns of Class IIa and -*e* for nouns of Class IIb. This class contains only feminine nouns.

	Class IIa		Class IIb
N	*gebe*	*zal*	*enste*
A	*gebe*	*zal*	*enste*
G	*geben*	*zaln*	*enste*
D	*geben*	*zaln*	*ensten*

As with the sg. forms the most radical changes took place in Class III where the four separate OHG case endings -*un*, -*ōn*, -*ūn*, -*ōno* were reduced to a single ending, -*en*. In OHG there was no gender distinction in the gen. and dat. pl. and the levelling of the other endings to -*en* eliminated any gender distinction in endings throughout the pl. In the nom. and acc. pl. the definite articles could show the gender of a noun, *die* for masc. and fem., and *diu* for neuter (see p. 136).

All these changes had the effect of eliminating many of the sub-classes of OHG, retaining the three main classes particularly in the sg. Only Class III has nouns of all three genders but with the falling-together of case endings the task of distinguishing gender as well as case in nouns became increasingly the function of the definite and indefinite articles.

Further reading

PAUL, H., *Mittelhochdeutsche Grammatik*, 20th edn., ed. H. Moser and I. Schröbler (Niemeyer, Tübingen, 1969), 135–57.

STOPP, H. and H. MOSER, 'Flexionsklassen der mhd. Substantive in synchronischer Sicht', *Zeitschrift für deutsche Philologie*, 86 (1967), 70–101 (this article presents a different synchronic description from the one suggested in this section).

ADJECTIVE INFLECTION IN MIDDLE HIGH GERMAN

Owing to the merger of all the OHG unstressed vowels except -*iu* in -*e*, and the merger of final -*m* and -*n*, many changes occurred in the endings of the strong declension of adjectives in MHG.

The acc. sg. masc. and the dat. pl. of all genders merged in -*en*,

OHG *blintan, blintēn,* MHG *blinden.* (The change of *t* to *d* after nasals is limited to a few words, cf. OHG *fintan,* MHG *finden.*) The gen. and dat. sg. fem. and the gen. pl. of all genders merged in *-er,* which was also the ending of the nom. sg. masc.: OHG *blintera, blinteru, blintēr,* MHG *blinder;* the nom. and acc. pl. masc. and fem. and acc. sg. fem. all merged in *-e:* OHG *blinte, blinto, blinta,* MHG *blinde.* The neuter nom. and acc. sg. endings were reduced to *-ez:* OHG *blintaz,* MHG *blindez;* and the dat. sg. masc. and neuter became *-em,* OHG *blintemo,* MHG *blindem.* All OHG unstressed final vowels after *-er* and *-em* are lost in MHG, thus making the inflectional endings of adjectives monosyllabic in the whole paradigm. The strong declension is as follows:

		Masculine	Feminine	Neuter
sg.	N	*blint, blinder*	*blint, blindiu*	*blint, blindez*
	A	*blinden*	*blinde*	*blint, blindez*
	G	*blindes*	*blinder*	*blindes*
	D	*blindem*	*blinder*	*blindem*
pl.	N	*blinde*	*blinde*	*blindiu*
	A	*blinde*	*blinde*	*blindiu*
	G	*blinder*	*blinder*	*blinder*
	D	*blinden*	*blinden*	*blinden*

The thirteen different OHG endings have been reduced to seven. Only the masc. and neuter gen. sg. ending *-es* has remained unchanged. The OHG ending *-iu* for the nom. fem. sg. and nom. acc. neuter pl. became [yı] in MHG. The OHG weak adjective endings, as in the weak noun inflection, have been drastically reduced from five to two: *-e* and *-en,* as can be seen from the following sg. paradigm. The pl. has *-en* throughout.

	Masculine	Feminine	Neuter
N	*blinde*	*blinde*	*blinde*
A	*blinden*	*blinden*	*blinde*
G	*blinden*	*blinden*	*blinden*
D	*blinden*	*blinden*	*blinden*

The OHG comparative and superlative endings: *-iro, -ōro* and *-isto, -ōsto* have merged in *-er* and *-est(e)* in MHG. The only clue as to which was used in OHG is whether the stem vowel of the adjective has been mutated in MHG or not. As in OHG most monosyllabic adjectives have a mutated vowel in the comparative and superlative, while polysyllabic, or compound, adjectives have no mutated vowel in these forms. Some adjectives, however, have forms with and without a mutated vowel: *alter, elter, junger, jünger, hôher, hœher*. Adverbs, however, never have a mutated vowel in the comparative, but there are some forms with a mutated vowel in the superlative. Some adjectives form their comparative and superlative by suppletion (see p. 110 for the OHG forms). The most common are:

Positive	Comparative	Superlative
guot	*bezzer*	*bezzest(e)*
wol (adv.)	*baz*	*best(e)*
übel	*wirser*	*wirsest(e)*
michel	*mêre*	*meiste*
lützel	*minre*	*minste*

Since numerals are inflected according to both the weak and strong adjective declension they are being dealt with in this section. In OHG they were only inflected according to the weak adjective declension. Of the cardinal numerals only *ein, zwei*, and *drî* were inflected in attributive position in MHG. In OHG the cardinal numerals from four to twelve could be inflected, but only in predicative position. In the meaning 'one', *ein* was declined like the strong adjective declension of *blint* but the uninflected form *ein* was generally used in the nom. and acc. sg.: *ein man, ein vrouwe, ein wîp*. The numerals 'two' and 'three' were declined as follows. Where the OHG forms differ from the MHG ones the former are given in brackets.

	Masc.	Feminine	Neuter	Masc.	Feminine	Neuter
N/A	*zwêne*	*zwâ, zwô*	*zwei*	*drî*	*drî (drîo)*	*driu*
G		*zweier (zweio)*			*drîer (drîo)*	
D		*zwei(e)n (zweim)*			*drî(e)n (drîm)*	

For the nom. and acc. fem. in OHG *Tatian* and *Otfrid* have *zwâ*, whereas *Notker* has *zwô*. In MHG both forms occur but *zwô* is the more frequent. The form *drîe*, with an adjectival ending -*e*, also occurs in the nom. and acc. masc. and fem. in MHG. The forms *zweier, drîer* have the ending of the strong adjective declension. The form *zweien* seems only to occur in later MHG, but the parallel form *drîen* is found as early as the twelfth century. The numerals in MHG are very similar to those in OHG as will appear from the following list:

Cardinal numbers		Ordinal numbers	
OHG	MHG	OHG	MHG
ein	*ein*	*ēristo*	*érste*
zwei (neuter)	*zwei*	*ander*	*ander*
drî (masc)	*drî*	*dritto*	*dritte*
fior	*vier*	*fiordo*	*vierde*
finf	*finf*	*finfto*	*finfte*
sehs	*sehs*	*sehsto*	*sehste*
sibun	*siben*	*sibunto*	*sibende*
ahto	*ahte*	*ahtodo*	*ahtede, ahte*
niun	*niun*	*niunto*	*niunde*
zehan	*zehen*	*zehanto*	*zehende*
einlif	*eilf*	*einlifto*	*eilfte*
zwelif	*zwelf*	*zwelifto*	*zwelfte*
drîzehan	*drîzehen*	*drittozehanto*	*drîzehende*
zweinzug	*zweinzic*	*zweinzugōsto*	*zweinzigeste*

The MHG form of the ordinals from *drîzehende* onwards with the cardinal number as the first part begins in Notker's writings. In OHG the word for 'one hundred' was *zehanzug* which has become *zehenzic* in MHG. Notker also uses the form *hunt* but in the twelfth century the word *hundert*, a borrowing from OLG *hunderod*, comes to be the only form. In OHG both the suffixes -*zug* and -*zig* occurred but in MHG -*zic* is the only suffix used. In the numeral for 'thirty' the suffix -*zic* begins with a fricative and not an affricate [ts], *drîzic*, cf. NHG *dreißig*.

Further reading

PAUL, H., *Mittelhochdeutsche Grammatik*, 20th edn., ed. H. Moser and I. Schröbler (Niemeyer, Tübingen, 1969), 157–66 and 182–3.

PRONOUNS IN MIDDLE HIGH GERMAN

The personal pronouns have undergone the following changes in MHG: the OHG acc. pl. first person, *unsih*, is superseded by the dat. pl. form, *uns*. The vowel in the third person sg. neuter nom.

and acc. neuter, OHG *iz*, was replaced by *e* to give MHG *ez*, which originally was probably an unstressed form. The acc. sg. fem. third person, OHG *sia*, and the nom. and acc. pl. fem., OHG *sio*, became *sie* in MHG, merging with the nom. and acc. pl. masc., OHG *sie*. The gen. and dat. sg. fem. and the gen. pl., OHG *ira*, *iru*, *iro*, became *ir(e)* in MHG, eliminating any distinction between the fem. gen. forms of the sg. and pl. and between the gen. and dat. cases in the fem. sg. The acc. sg. masc., OHG *inan*, was replaced by the shorter form *in* in MHG. The dat. sg. masc. and neuter occur both as *ime* and *im*, but the latter is the more frequent form. The following paradigms illustrate the inflection of the personal pronouns:

	First Person		Second Person		Third Person					
	sg.	pl.	sg.	pl.	sg.			pl.		
N	*ich*	*wir*	*du*	*ir*	*er*	*siu*	*ez*	*sie*	*sie*	*siu*
A	*mich*	*uns*	*dich*	*iuch*	*in*	*sie*	*ez*	*sie*	*sie*	*siu*
G	*mîn*	*unser*	*dîn*	*iuwer*	*sîn*	*ir(e)*	*es (sîn)*	*ir(e)*	*ir(e)*	*ir(e)*
D	*mir*	*uns*	*dir*	*iu*	*im(e)*	*ir(e)*	*im(e)*	*in*	*in*	*in*

The gen. forms are mostly used as the base forms for the possessive adjectives but are also used on their own to express the possessive. The neuter gen. sg. *es* is mostly used with indefinite antecedents. The possessive pronouns are still declined like the strong adjectives (for changes in inflectional endings, see p. 132), but they are frequently uninflected in the nom. sg. of all genders and the acc. sg. neuter. The *ir(e)* is normally uninflected in all cases. The paradigm of *mîn* may be given as an example:

	Singular			Plural		
	Masculine	Feminine	Neuter	Masc.	Fem.	Neuter
N	*mîn, mîner*	*mîn, mîniu*	*mîn, mînez*	*mîne*	*mîne*	*mîniu*
A	*mînen*	*mîne*	*mînez*	*mîne*	*mîne*	*mîniu*
G	*mînes*	*mîner*	*mînes*	*mîner*	*mîner*	*mîner*
D	*mînem*	*mîner*	*mînem*	*mînen*	*mînen*	*mînen*

In the demonstrative pronoun OHG *deser*, the stem vowel *e* has been replaced throughout by *i*. The MHG form *dirre* for the nom. sg. masc., gen. and dat. sg. fem., and the gen. pl. all genders arose through the assimilation of the *s* of the OHG stem to the *r* of the

ending, cf. OHG *desera, deseru, desero,* and the loss of the intervening vowel. For these cases the form *diser* also occurs in MHG.
The forms *diser, dise* also occur for the masc. nom. sg. The regular
masc. neuter gen. sg. form *disses,* OHG *desses,* occurs in CG, but
usually the medial *-ss-* has been shortened to *-s-, dises.* The masc.
and fem. nom. acc. pl., OHG *dese, deso,* have the same form in
MHG, *dise,* and the dat. pl. of all genders, OHG *desēn,* earlier
desēm, has merged with the acc. sg. masc., OHG *desan,* in MHG
disen. In the declension of the definite article the nom. and acc. pl.
masc. and fem. and the acc. sg. fem., OHG *die, dio, dia,* have
merged in the one form *die* in MHG, pronounced with a diphthong
[iə]. The gen. and dat. sg. fem., OHG *dera, deru,* and the gen. pl.
of all genders, OHG *dero,* have become *der(e)* in MHG. For the
dat. sg. masc. and neuter both the forms *deme* and *dem* exist, but the
latter is the more usual. The paradigms of both these pronouns are
as follows:

| | Singular | | | Plural | | |
	Masculine	Feminine	Neuter	Masculine	Feminine	Neuter
N	*dirre*	*disiu*	*ditz(e)*	*dise*	*dise*	*disiu*
A	*disen*	*dise*	*ditz(e)*	*dise*	*dise*	*disiu*
G	*dises*	*dirre*	*dises*	*dirre*	*dirre*	*dirre*
D	*disem*	*dirre*	*disem*	*disen*	*disen*	*disen*

| | Singular | | | Plural | | |
	Masculine	Feminine	Neuter	Masculine	Feminine	Neuter
N	*der*	*diu*	*daz*	*die*	*die*	*diu*
A	*den*	*die*	*daz*	*die*	*die*	*diu*
G	*des*	*der(e)*	*des*	*der(e)*	*der(e)*	*der(e)*
D	*dem(e)*	*der(e)*	*dem(e)*	*den*	*den*	*den*

The MHG interrogative pronouns were *wer,* acc. *wen, weder*
'which of two', *welch,* and its correlative *solch.* The indefinite
interrogatives, OHG *sō wer, sō waz,* have been contracted to *swer,
swaz* in MHG. With the exception of *sum,* which died out during
MHG, the same indefinite pronouns are used in MHG as in
OHG: MHG *einec, etelich, jeder, nechein, dechein* (declined like
strong adjectives); *man, ieman, nieman, niht (niewiht).* The form
iht 'something' may either be a MHG formation from *niht,* or else
come from OHG *iewiht* with monophthongization and subsequent
shortening of the vowel. It has the variant forms *ieht, iet.* The

forms for the reflexive pronoun third person are the same as in OHG, except for regular sound changes: sg.—acc. *sich*, gen. *sîn* masc. and neuter, *ir(e)* fem., dat. *im(e)*, masc. and neuter, *ir(e)* fem.; pl.—acc. *sich*, gen. *ir(e)*, dat. *in*.

Further reading

PAUL, H., *Mittelhochdeutsche Grammatik*, 20th edn., ed. H. Moser and I. Schröbler (Niemeyer, Tübingen, 1969), 166–82.

THE VERB IN MIDDLE HIGH GERMAN

Strong verbs in Middle High German

The personal endings of the strong verbs in MHG were changed by the merger of the unstressed OHG vowels in -*e*. In the present indicative the third person sg. was reduced to -*et*, OHG *er nimit*, MHG *er nimet*, and the first person sg. to -*e*, OHG *ih nimu*, MHG *ich nime*. The ending -*s(t)* for the second person sg. present, which was already in use in late OHG, becomes more frequent in MHG, particularly in UG. The *t* will be bracketed in the paradigms to show that it is not yet universally used. In the second person sg. past tense indicative and throughout the whole of the subjunctive past tense, the OHG stem vowel, if it was a back vowel, i.e. *ă*, *ŏ*, or *ŭ*, was mutated, e.g. OHG *nāmi*, *buti*, *hulfi*; MHG *næme*, *büte*, *hülfe*. In MHG the subjunctive past pl. was distinct from the indicative past pl. only in its stem vowel. The following paradigms show the differences between OHG and MHG:

	Present		
Indicative		Subjunctive	
OHG	MHG	OHG	MHG
ih nimu	*ich nime*	*ih neme*	*ich neme*
du nimis	*du nimes(t)*	*du nemēs*	*du nemes(t)*
er nimit	*er nimet*	*er neme*	*er neme*
wir nemēn	*wir nemen*	*wir nemēn*	*wir nemen*
ir nemet	*ir nemet*	*ir nemēt*	*ir nemet*
sie nemant	*sie nement*	*sie nemēn*	*sie nemen*

Past

ih nam	*ich nam*	*ih nāmi*	*ich næme*
du nāmi	*du næme*	*du nāmīs*	*du næmes(t)*
er nam	*er nam*	*er nāmi*	*er næme*
wir nāmun	*wir nâmen*	*wir nāmin*	*wir næmen*
ir nāmut	*ir nâmet*	*ir nāmīt*	*ir næmet*
sie nāmun	*sie nâmen*	*sie nāmīn*	*sie næmen*

In MHG the vowel gradation classes have been mostly retained and underwent only minor changes. In Class II, OHG *biotan*, the *io* of the infinitive was replaced by the MHG diphthong *ie* and the first, second, and third persons sg. present had the stem vowel [yɪ], spelt *iu*, which was a regular development of the OHG diphthong *iu*. Some verbs of Class III, MHG *bresten, dreschen, vehten, vlehten, erleschen*, which in OHG had past tense pl. forms with a stem vowel *u*, became remodelled in MHG after Class IV verbs and have a long *â* as their stem vowel in MHG: *brâsten, drâschen, vâhten, vlâhten, erlâschen*. Class VII in OHG contained those verbs which originally formed their past tense by reduplication. Their stem vowel in the past tense was either *io* or *ie* in OHG, but in MHG the only stem vowel is *ie*. The other classes remained unchanged. The OHG vowel gradation classes are represented in MHG as follows:

	Infinitive	First person sg. pres.	sg. past	pl. past	past participle
Class Ia	*rîten*	*rîte*	*reit*	*riten*	*geriten*
Ib	*zîhen*	*zîhe*	*zêch*	*zigen*	*gezigen*
Class IIa	*biegen*	*biuge*	*bouc*	*bugen*	*gebogen*
IIb	*ziehen*	*ziuhe*	*zôch*	*zugen*	*gezogen*
Class IIIa	*binden*	*binde*	*bant*	*bunden*	*gebunden*
IIIb	*helfen*	*hilfe*	*half*	*hulfen*	*geholfen*
Class IV	*nemen*	*nime*	*nam*	*nâmen*	*genomen*
Class V	*geben*	*gibe*	*gap*	*gâben*	*gegeben*
Class VI	*varn*	*var(e)*	*vuor*	*vuoren*	*gevarn*
Class VIIa	*heizen*	*heize*	*hiez*	*hiezen*	*geheizen*
VIIb	*loufen*	*loufe*	*lief*	*liefen*	*geloufen*

Weak verbs in Middle High German

Through the reduction of the OHG unstressed vowels the endings of the indicative and the subjunctive present have become the same, except for the third person sg. and pl. The paradigms of the present tense are as follows:

Indicative		Subjunctive	
OHG	MHG	OHG	MHG
ih leggu	*ich lege*	*ih legge*	*ich lege*
du legis	*du leges(t)*	*du leggēs*	*du leges(t)*
er legit	*er leget*	*er legge*	*er lege*
wir leggēn	*wir legen*	*wir leggēn*	*wir legen*
ir legget	*ir leget*	*ir leggēt*	*ir leget*
sie leggent	*sie legent*	*sie leggēn*	*sie legen*

The geminate consonants in the OHG forms were gradually lost in MHG and the single consonants of the second and third person sg. indicative were generalized throughout the indicative and subjunctive.

All the infinitives of the weak verbs in MHG have the same ending, *-en*: OHG *leggen, salbōn, sagēn*, MHG *legen, salben, sagen*, and thus cannot be divided into three classes as in OHG. In OHG the first person sg. present indicative was different for each class: *ih leggu, salbōn, sagēn*, but in MHG the ending of Class I, *-u* (which was also the ending for the strong verbs), became reduced to *-e* and was transferred to the weak verbs of OHG Classes II and III, e.g. MHG *ich lege, salbe, sage*. On the basis of the past tense forms one can divide weak verbs in MHG synchronically into two classes. Class I weak verbs have a different stem vowel in the past tense from the present and the ending *-te* is added directly to the stem: *zeln—zalte; hœren—hôrte; küssen—kuste; wænen—wânde*. This alternation between a mutated vowel in the infinitive and present and an unmutated vowel in the past tense and past participle is known as *Rückumlaut* (for its origin, see p. 121). There are other alternations, e.g. between a velar stop and a voiceless velar fricative in the past tense: *decken—dahte; denken—dâhte; bringen—brâhte* (the letter *g* of the cluster *ng* was pronounced as a voiced velar stop in MHG, see p. 68). Historically Class I comprises those verbs of OHG weak verb Class I which had no medial *-i-* in the past tense, i.e. with original long stems. The verbs of MHG Class II do not change their vowel to form the past tense, *leben—lebete*, but usually add *-ete*. Historically this class comprises the verbs of OHG Classes II and III, and those verbs of OHG Class I which retained medial -*i*- in the past tense, i.e. those with an original short stem: OHG *salbōn—salbōta*; *sagēn—sagēta*; *nerren—nerita*; MHG *salben, salbete*; *sagen, sagete*; *nern, nerete*. Due to the merger of OHG unstressed vowels there is no difference between the indicative and the subjunctive of the weak verbs in the past tense, e.g. *ich hôrte, du hôrtes(t), er hôrte, wir hôrten, ir hôrtet, sie hôrten*. The *i* or *ī* of the OHG endings has not caused mutation, e.g. OHG *ih hōrtī, sie hōrtīn*. The absence of mutation in these forms has never been satisfactorily explained.

Irregular verbs

(a) Preterite-present verbs

There are few changes among these verbs. OHG *kunnan* has forms both with and without *i*-mutation in MHG, *künnen, kunnen*; similarly, OHG *durfan* and *mugan* both have forms with and without *i*-mutation in the infinitive and present pl. in MHG. The forms with *i*-mutation in the present probably come from the subjunctive. OHG *scolan* already had forms without *c* in Notker's writings and in MHG the main forms are: infinitive *suln*, present *ich sol, du solt, er sol, wir suln, ir sult, sie suln*, the form *süln* with mutation also occurs. OHG *muozan* has only a mutated form for the infinitive and the first and third person pl. present indicative in MHG, *müezen*. The remaining forms of the present are: *ich muoz, du muost, er muoz, ir müezet*. OHG *unnan* occurs with both mutated and unmutated forms in the infinitive and third person pl. present in the compound form *gunnen, günnen* (OHG *gi-unnan*). From the third person sg. present form *touc* a new infinitive *tougen* was formed in MHG. The first and third person pl. present is either *tügen*, with mutation, or *tugen*, without (these forms also occur as an infinitive in early MHG). The verb 'to dare' also has infinitive and first and third person pl. present forms with and without mutation, *türren, turren*. MHG has the simple forms without a prefix, *ich tar, du tarst, er tar*, cf. OHG *ih gitar*. The past tenses of all these verbs are formed like regular weak verbs, e.g. *kunde, konde, durfte, solte, muoste* (but early MHG *muose*), *gunde, gonde*. The verbs *mugen* and *tougen* change the *g* to the velar fricative [x], spelt *h* before the -*te* of the past *mohte* (the past tense form *mahte* also occurs), and *tohte*. The verb *turren* uses the stem ending in -*rs* to form the past tense, *torste*. This stem also appears in the second person sg. present form *tarst* but in the infinitive and other forms it has been assimilated to *-rr-*, *turren*. The subjunctive of all these verbs is formed by mutating the stem vowel of the past tense, e.g. *künde, dürfte, sölte, müese, müeste, günde, mähte, möhte, töhte, törste*. They are conjugated like weak verbs. The verb *wizzen*, OHG *wizzan*, has several past stems: *wisse, wesse, wiste, weste*, the latter two forms being more common in CG. The past participle is *gewest* or *gewist*, which has ousted the OHG past participle *giwizzan*, MHG *gewizzen*, which only survives in adjectival use. The other forms of these verbs have developed regularly from the OHG forms.

(b) The verb 'to be'

The forms for the first and second person pl. present, MHG *wir birn, ir birt* (for the OHG forms, see p. 124), died out in the thirteenth century and were replaced by *wir sint, ir sît*. The past tense shows a mutated vowel in the subjunctive, e.g. *wir wæren*, as against indicative *wir wâren*. The present subjunctive is the same as in OHG. From the MHG infinitive *wesen* a past participle *gewesen* was formed which was in competition with *gesîn*, from the other infinitive *sîn*, which was used in Alemannic, and *gewest*, which was used in East Franconian and CG. The imperative second person sg. is *wis*, later being replaced by *bis*, the second person sg. present indicative stem *du bis(t)*.

(c) Other irregular verbs

OHG *tuon, gēn*, and *stēn* did not undergo any major changes in MHG except in the first person sg. present indicative, OHG *tuon, gēn, stēn*, for which the subjunctive forms MHG *tuo, gê, stê* are also used. In the present indicative both forms *gên/gân* and *stên/stân* occur: Alemannic only has forms with *â*, and Bavarian usually has forms with *ê*. The other forms are regular developments from the OHG forms (see p. 126). The MHG verb *wellen* has *wil(e)* as its first and third person sg. present indicative like the preterite-present verbs. The OHG endings for these forms were *-u* and *-i* respectively, OHG *ih willu, er wili*. The second person sg. present indicative form was *du wil(e)* (OHG *wili*) or *du wilt* (by analogy with the preterite-present verbs, e.g. *du solt*). The past tense is the same for the indicative and subjunctive and shows no mutation, *wolte*. The contracted forms of the verb 'to have' are the same as in

OHG, except from OHG *habēta* the past tense indicative form *hâte* has arisen, from OHG *hebita* the form *hete*, and from *hapta* the form *hatte*. The past tense form *hœte*, with mutation by analogy with the subjunctive of the preterite-present verbs, is used both for indicative and subjunctive, as is *hete*, which was probably formed by analogy with *tete*.

Further reading

PAUL, H., *Mittelhochdeutsche Grammatik*, 20th edn., ed. H. Moser and I. Schröbler (Niemeyer, Tübingen, 1969), 184–219.

WOLF, N. R., 'Zur mittelhochdeutschen Verbflexion in synchronischer Sicht', *German Quarterly*, 44 (1971), 153–67.

NEW HIGH GERMAN AND THE DEVELOPMENT FROM MIDDLE HIGH GERMAN

NOUN INFLECTION IN NEW HIGH GERMAN

New High German has three basic classes of nouns, traditionally called strong, weak, and mixed. The strong and weak classes correspond to MHG Classes I and III respectively. The mixed class in NHG comprises chiefly fem. nouns from MHG Classes II and III, but also contains a smaller number of masc. and neuter nouns from MHG Classes I and III. The main characteristic of the mixed declension in NHG is that the nouns have the pl. ending -*en*. In the sg. the fem. nouns of this class are uninflected, NHG N/A *die Zunge*, G/D *der Zunge*, whereas the masc. and neuter nouns take -(*e*)*s* in the gen. *des Dornes*, *des Bettes*, and an optional -*e* in the dat. The fem. nouns from MHG Classes II and III have undergone changes in the emergence of this new class: the nouns of Class II have -*en* throughout the pl. and the nouns of Class III have lost the final -*n* of the oblique cases of the sg. In addition to the development of a new declensional class many nouns have changed classes, i.e. weak nouns have become strong, strong nouns have become weak, or pl. endings and, in some cases, the grammatical gender of nouns have changed. Nouns with -*e* in the nom. sg. most frequently changed classes and are to be found in all three classes in MHG: Class I, *hirte*, gen. *hirtes*; Class II, *gebe*, gen. *gebe*; Class III, *bote*, gen. *boten*.

Nouns whose nom. sg. ended in *-e* either underwent one of two developments, which then led to other changes, or the final *-e* was retained. The first development was that the final *-e* of the nom. sg. was lost. This is part of a general process of apocope, i.e. loss of final *-e* which is an irregular sound change (see p. 92). MHG Class I nouns whose nom. sg. ended in *-e* always lost the *-e* if they remained in Class I, e.g. MHG *sige*, NHG *der Sieg*, MHG *netze*, *rîche*, NHG *das Netz*, *das Reich*. The only exceptions are *der Käse*, *das Erbe*, and some collectives and abstracts with the prefix *Ge-*, *Gebirge*, *Getreide*, *Getue*, *Geblase*. In Class II apocope occurred in some nouns, e.g. MHG *huote*, NHG *die Hut*, but the majority of this class retained their final nom. sg. *-e*. Some masc. nouns of Class III lost their final *-e* in the nom. sg. and changed over to Class I, still retaining their masc. gender: MHG *blitze*, *schelme*, *kîme*, NHG *Blitz*, *Schelm*, *Keim*. In a few cases nouns which underwent this change developed new pl. forms with a mutated vowel, MHG *hane*, NHG *der Hahn*, *die Hähne*; MHG *swane*, NHG *der Schwan*, *die Schwäne*. Some masc. nouns, mostly those denoting animate beings, remained in Class III even though they had lost their final *-e*, *Herr*, *Graf*, as did the neuter *Herz*. In this class the loss of *-e* is irregular. It is most frequently lost after *-r*, MHG *tôre*, NHG *der Tor*, MHG *herre* (a form which survived into the eighteenth century), NHG *Herr*, after consonant clusters containing a final voiceless consonant *der Held*, *der Hirt* (there is a poetic and archaic form *Hirte*), or after the affricate [ts], *Spatz*, *Steinmetz*. The final *-e* has tended to be retained if the stem vowel was short, *Affe*, as against *Graf*. As late as the eighteenth century the nouns *der Christ*, MHG *kristen*, *der Sklave*, *der Mensch*, *Hirt*, *Graf*, occurred both with and without a final nom. sg. *-e*. The neuter nouns *Glück*, *Stück* and the collectives, e.g. *Gebirge*, also occurred with and without *-e*. Some fem. nouns, notably NHG *Ursache*, *Sprache*, *Geschichte*, *Eile*, occurred without *-e*. NHG *Tür* still has a South German variant in *-e*, *Türe*. In a few cases a semantic differentiation between a form with a final *-e* and one without has arisen, e.g. *der Bub* UG 'boy', and *der Bube* 'rogue; jack (in a pack of cards)'; in a few abstract nouns formed from verbs, e.g. *Gebell*, *Gebelle*; *Gebrüll*, *Gebrülle*, the form with *-e* has a pejorative connotation whereas the form without *-e* is neutral. Because of the loss of final *-e* a number of fem. nouns have become either masc. or neuter in NHG, MHG *strâle*, *witze* (fem.),

NHG *der Strahl, der Witz*; MHG *âventiure, mâze* (fem.), NHG *das Abenteuer, das Maß*, possibly influenced by MHG *daz mez* 'measure'.

The second development was the addition of a final *-n* after the *-e*, MHG *garte*, NHG *Garten*. This is an analogical change whereby the form of the oblique cases of the nouns of Class III has been levelled out in the whole paradigm. Thus MHG nom. sg. *garte*, acc. gen. dat. sg. *garten*, has been replaced by *Garten* in NHG. Subsequently a new gen. sg. *Gartens* was formed by analogy with the nouns of Class I, cf. *des Tages*. The nouns which underwent this development moved from Class III to Class I and some even developed pl. forms with mutated vowels, e.g. *der Garten, die Gärten*. For some nouns this process has not yet been completed, they have a gen. sg. in *-ens*, but they still have a nom. sg. form with or without an *-n*, e.g. *Glaube, Glauben*; *Friede, Frieden*; *Funke, Funken*; *Gedanke, Gedanken*; *Wille, Willen*. The gen. ending *-ens* has also come to be used with two weak nouns of Class III, *der Name, das Herz*, originally being more widespread among them in Early NHG, e.g. *des botens, des affens*, NHG *des Boten, des Affen*. The variants *der Drache*, weak noun, and *der Drachen*, strong noun, have become semantically differentiated, the former referring to the mythological 'dragon' and the latter to 'a quarrelsome woman' or a 'kite' (toy).

The retention of final *-e* has been most frequent in nouns of Class II, cf. NHG *die Erde, Gabe*, MHG *diu erde, diu gebe* (both *gebe* and *gâbe* existed in MHG but *gebe* has died out in NHG); but it has also taken place among masc. nouns of Class III, many of which denote animate beings, e.g. NHG *der Affe, der Bote*. The NHG weak noun *der Heide*, with final *-e*, has, however, resulted from the loss of a MHG final *-n, heiden*, and does not represent the retention of a MHG *-e*. A number of masc. and neuter nouns of MHG Class I did retain their nom. *-e*, but were interpreted instead as being fem. nouns; NHG *die Sitte, die Hirse* 'millet', were masc. in MHG, and NHG *die Rippe, die Wette* were neuter. A larger number of masc. nouns of MHG Class III retained their nom. *-e* and have become fem. in NHG: *Blume, Fahne, Niere, Schlange, Schnecke, Wade*. Of the four neuter nouns of Class III only one, *wange*, has retained its nom. *-e* and become fem. in NHG, *die Wange*. These new fem. nouns subsequently developed pl. endings in *-en*. Some of the nouns concerned in this change showed variation in grammatical gender even in MHG. Although MHG *ende* (Class I) and MHG *ouge* (Class III) have joined the mixed declension in NHG, they have retained their original neuter gender as well as their nom. *-e*. NHG *das Ende* has a new pl. in *-n* and NHG *das Auge* has a new strong sg. gen., *des Auges*, dat. *dem Auge*, cf. MHG *des ougen, dem ougen*. There are only a few examples of strong nouns in NHG whose nom. sg. ends in *-e*, *der Käse, das Erbe*, and collectives and abstracts with the prefix *Ge-*, *Gebirge, Geblase*, which have been mentioned before. In MHG *der Käse* and *das Gebirge* belonged to Class I whereas *das Erbe* fluctuated between Classes I and II and appeared as both neuter and fem. The final *-e* in NHG *Schläfe, Schürze, Gräte* was a pl. ending in MHG, cf. the sg. forms *sláf, schurz, grât* (NHG *Rückgrat*). The pl. forms of these masc. nouns and others were interpreted as singular fem. forms because of the final *-e*. Thus these nouns became fem. and subsequently formed new plurals in *-n*. NHG *die Stute*, pl. *Stuten*, represents a MHG pl. *stuote* without mutation, cf. sg. *stuot*.

NHG Class I and Class III nouns have retained the same pl. endings as in MHG but their distribution has changed. Neuter nouns which formed their pl. in MHG by adding *-er*, accompanied by mutation of the stem vowel where possible, were not very numerous (for a full list of OHG nouns with *-ir* pl., see p. 106); but in NHG this is the main pl. ending for the neuter nouns and it has even spread to a few masc. nouns, e.g. *Wald, Mann, Gott, Geist*. The ending *-e*, without mutation of the stem vowel, also began to be used with neuter nouns, especially in CG, but it has only been accepted in a limited number of words, many of which are, however, in frequent use: *Boote, Jahre, Spiele*. There are even two nouns which have stem vowel mutation, *das Floß* 'raft', *die Flöße*; *das Klöster, die Klöster* (the pl. ending *-e* does not occur after unstressed *-er, -en, -el* in NHG). It is, however, among the masc. nouns of Class I where the pl. ending *-e* accompanied by stem vowel mutation has spread most widely. The following are examples of Class I nouns which now have stem vowel mutation in the pl. although this was originally not the case: *Baum, Bock, Busch, Floh, Knopf, Stuhl, Sturm, Traum*. There are, however, still quite a number of masc. nouns in Class I which form their pl. by adding *-e* unaccompanied by stem vowel mutation; indeed masc. nouns of Class I seem almost equally divided between those which mutate their stems vowel in the pl. and those which do not. The pl. ending -*en* of MHG Class III nouns has become the main pl. ending for nouns of the NHG mixed class. Those fem. nouns of MHG Class II which in MHG had no pl. ending apart from -*n* in the dat., e.g. *gebe*, dat. pl. *geben*, have -*n* throughout the pl. in NHG, *die Gaben*. The ending -*en* has also spread to many fem. nouns which in NHG formed their pl. by adding -*e* accompanied by stem vowel mutation where possible, e.g. MHG *tæte*, *pflihte*, NHG *Taten*, *Pflichten*. Some fem. nouns of MHG Class II still exist which add -*e* with stem vowel mutation where possible, e.g. *Hand*, *Hände* (where vowel mutation has arisen by analogy), or *Kraft*, *Kräfte* (originally an *i* stem). These latter nouns are regarded as strong in NHG and they have levelled out the nom. and acc. sg. forms in the gen. and dat., the latter having stem vowel mutation in MHG, gen. dat. *krefte*, NHG *der Kraft*.

A new pl. ending -*s* has come into use in NHG, originally with French loan-words, *das Hotel*, *die Hotels*; *der Chef*, *die Chefs*. In French the pl. -*s* had ceased to be pronounced in the fourteenth century and its pronunciation as [s] in NHG is due probably to both LG influence where a pl. -*s* still existed and spelling pronunciation. More recently it has come into NHG with English loan-words, *der Streik*, *die Streiks*, and is used with many loan-words of all grammatical genders from many different languages especially when they ended in a vowel: *der Torpedo*, *die Torpedos*; *die Kamera*, *die Kameras*; *das Sofa*, *die Sofas*. The -*s* pl. is also used with words of LG origin, e.g. *das Wrack*, *die Wracks*, some colloquial words, e.g. *das Mädel*, *die Mädels*; *der Kerl*, *die Kerls*, and in addition with words formed from initial letters, e.g. *der PKW*, *die PKWs*. The -*s* pl. is also used when a word from another part of speech is used as a pl. noun, e.g. *die Wenns*, *die Jas*, *die Hochs*, *die Tiefs*. The words with an -*s* pl. do not have the ending -*n* in the dat. pl. One word, *der Junge*, has a colloquial pl. in -*s*, *Jungens* or *Jungs*. The -*s* pl. is still a marginal pl. ending in the NHG nominal system, being limited in its distribution.

A possible trend in the extension of pl. forms in the development from MHG to NHG has been towards a closer correlation between pl. endings and grammatical gender. Thus the pl. ending for most fem. nouns is -*en*, for neuter nouns the ending -*er* accompanied by stem vowel mutation where possible, and for the masc. nouns the ending -*e*, either on its own or accompanied by stem vowel mutation. Other pl. endings do occur with nouns of all three genders but -*en*, -*er*, and -*e* are the most typical. The development towards a full correlation of pl. ending and grammatical gender is still far from complete.

Although NHG still retains a threefold gender distinction among nouns, masculine, femine, and neuter, some nouns have a different gender in NHG from MHG. In the cases mentioned hitherto any change in gender has been seen to have resulted from the form of the noun, but there are cases where there seems to be no formal reason for a change in grammatical gender. A number of neuter nouns of MHG Class I have become masc.: *Honig*, *Speer*, while some masc. nouns of the same class have become neuter: *Segel*, *Zeug*. These changes in grammatical gender must have been preceded by a period of uncertainty as to the correct grammatical gender of many nouns; this led in some cases to the fluctuating forms of what was originally one word becoming semantically differentiated by grammatical gender in NHG: *der See* 'lake', *die See* 'sea'; *der Flur* 'hall', *die Flur* 'meadow'. Even in the standard language today there are words with fluctuating grammatical gender: *der* or *das Dotter* 'yolk'; *der* or *das Knäuel* 'ball (of wool)'; *die* or *der Klunker* 'clod (of dirt)'.

Most of the changes in noun inflection between MHG and NHG can be seen to be part of a tendency to reduce the importance of case distinctions and to make the number distinction singular: plural all-important. NHG fem. nouns of the mixed declensions like *Zunge* have only two forms: sg. *Zunge*, pl. *Zungen*. Any changes in case have to be shown in the article or adjective, e.g. nom. acc. *die Zunge*, gen. dat. *der Zunge*. Nouns like *Tag* and *Wort* do have a gen. sg. form, *Tages*, *Wortes*, but, as is often pointed out, the gen. is in the process of being replaced by alternative constructions, e.g. *von* plus the dat. case (cf. Lockwood, *Historical German Syntax*, pp. 18 ff.). The final -*e* of the dat. sg., *Tage*, *Worte*, is now optional and usually a sign of archaic and stylized language, except for a few set phrases such as *zu Hause*, *im Falle*. Only the nouns of Class III, the weak nouns, show any real distinction of case, and that is simply between a nom. or basic case and an oblique case, e.g. *Junge*: *Jungen*, the latter form also being the pl. form. Those nouns whose pl. does not end in -*s* or -*n* have a separate form for the dat. pl., e.g. Class I *Tagen*, *Gästen*, *Häusern*, Class II *Kräften*.

Further reading

BACH, H., *Laut- und Formenlehre der Sprache Luthers* (Levin & Munksgaard, Copenhagen, 1934), 69–76 (a brief outline of noun inflexion
in Luther's writings).

Duden Grammatik, 2nd edn. (Dudenverlag, Mannheim, 1966), 134–207
(a description of the modern standard language).

HOTZENKÖCHERLE, R., 'Entwicklungsgeschichtliche Grundzüge des
Neuhochdeutschen', *Wirkendes Wort*, 12 (1962), 321–31 (outlines
some tendencies in noun inflexion and in other areas of grammar).

MOLZ, H., 'Die Substantivflexion seit mhd. Zeit', *Beiträge zur Geschichte der deutschen Sprache und Literatur*, 27 (1902), 209–342;
31 (1906), 277–392 (a detailed traditional account).

NERIUS, D., *Untersuchungen zur Herausbildung einer nationalen Norm
der deutschen Literatursprache im 18. Jahrhundert*, Zweiter Teil:
*Zur sprachlichen Realisierung der nationalen Norm. Darstellung am
Beispiel des Geschlechts der Substantive* (Niemeyer, Halle, 1967),
81–137.

OHMANN, E., 'Die Pluralformen auf -*s* in der deutschen Substantivflexion', *Zeitschrift für deutsches Altertum*, 91 (1962), 228–36.

PAUL, H., *Deutsche Grammatik*, vol. ii (1916–20; repr. Niemeyer, Halle,
1959), 1–118.

SEMENJUK, N. N., 'Zustand und Evolution der grammatischen Normen
des Deutschen in der 1. Hälfte des 18. Jahrhunderts', in *Studien zur
Geschichte der deutschen Sprache*, ed. G. Feudel (Akademie, Berlin,
1972), 89–97 (deals with variation in noun inflexion).

WERNER, O., 'Das deutsche Pluralsystem: Strukturelle Diachronie',
Jahrbuch des Instituts für deutsche Sprache, 5 (1968), 92–128.

ADJECTIVE AND ADVERB IN NEW HIGH GERMAN

The clear distinction in form in MHG between adjective and
adverb in predicative position is no longer present in NHG, e.g.
sie ist schön (adj.), *sie singt schön* (adv.) Adjectives which ended in a
consonant added -*e* to form an adverb, *eben—ebene*, *hôch—hôhe*,
lanc—lange. Adverbs which already ended in -*e* became adjectives
by stem vowel mutation where possible: adverbs: *ange*, *harte*,
sanfte, *veste*, *spâte*, *swâre*, *suoze*; adjectives: *enge*, *herte*, *senfte*, *veste*,
spæte, *swære*, *süeze*. In NHG the ending -*e* has been lost after
MHG voiceless consonants and nasals: MHG *süeze*, *schœne*,

NHG *süß*, *schön*, but has been retained after voiced consonants: NHG *trübe*, *feige*, *träge*, *blöde*, *böse*, *leise*. It has usually been the adjectival form, with mutation of the stem vowel where possible, which has become the only form of the adjective/adverb in NHG, e.g. *spät* for MHG *spâte* and *spæte*. Only in the case of NHG *hart* and *sanft* has the form with no mutation supplanted the form with mutation. Where both forms are still in existence they usually differ in meaning: e.g. *schön* 'beautiful' and *schon* 'already'; *fest* 'firm' and *fast* 'almost'. The NHG adverb *lange* with a temporal meaning, *er war lange weg*, has become differentiated from the adjective/adverb *lang*, *er war lang*. Other adjectives, especially those which ended in *-ec*, formed their adverbial forms in MHG by adding the suffix *-lîche* or *-lîchen*, e.g. *sælec*, *sæleclîche*; *êwec*, *êweclîchen*. When the distinction between adjective and adverb was lost the adverbial forms with *-lîche(n)* were replaced by the simple adjective form NHG *selig*, *ewig*. However, this did not apply to adjectives formed from nouns, e.g. NHG *königlich*, MHG *küneclîche*, which has retained the suffix *-lich*. With the passing of the adverb as a separate part of speech, comparison of the adverb has also disappeared, except in a few cases where there was comparison by suppletion, that is using a different stem, and even here some of the stems have been replaced by others in NHG, e.g. the comparative and superlative forms for NHG *wohl* are the same as those for *gut*, e.g. *besser*, *am besten*; the comparative and superlative forms *minder*, *mindest* have a new positive form, *wenig*, instead of MHG *lützel* which has now died out. Now new comparative and superlative forms *weniger*, *wenigst* have almost ousted *minder*, *mindest*. Some adjectives in NHG have a comparative and superlative without mutation: adjectives with *au* as their stem vowel: *faul*, *grau*; derivative adjectives such as *langsam*, *eßbar*; and monosyllabic adjectives: *bunt*, *flach*, *froh*, *stolz*, *voll*, even though their stem vowel could be theoretically mutated. This is a continuation of the situation which existed in MHG.

In attributive position the following changes in the distribution of the adjective endings have taken place. In the strong declension the MHG ending *-iu* has disappeared. In the nom. and acc. neuter pl. it has been replaced by the corresponding masc. and fem. form, *-e*, resulting in the loss of a distinction according to gender in the pl., and in the nom. fem. sg. it has been replaced by the acc. fem. sg. form, also ending in *-e*. These changes seem to have taken place in CG and spread from there into the standard language. The masc. and neuter gen. sg., MHG *-es*, has been replaced by *-en*, but the *-es* lingered on into the eighteenth century, *gutes Muts* (Goethe) for *guten Muts*. In NHG the masc. and neuter gen. sg. of both the weak and the strong adjective declension are the same. Because of the merger of MHG *s* and *z* in final position the nom. and acc. sg. became *-es*. The seven MHG endings: *-er, -en, -es, -ez, -em, -iu, -e* have been reduced to five in NHG: *-er, -en, -es, -em, -e*, as can be seen from the paradigm of the NHG strong adjective declension:

| | Singular | | | Plural |
	Masculine	Feminine	Neuter	All genders
N	*blinder*	*blinde*	*blindes*	*blinde*
A	*blinden*	*blinde*	*blindes*	*blinde*
G	*blinden*	*blinder*	*blinden*	*blinder*
D	*blindem*	*blinder*	*blindem*	*blinden*

In the weak adjective declension in NHG there has been no change in the number of endings, there are still only two: *-e* and *-en*, but the distribution has changed in the fem. acc. sg., MHG *blinden*, which now has the ending *-e*, *blinde*. Otherwise the declension is the same as in MHG. (For the details of the changes in the syntactic use of the strong and weak adjective declension, Lockwood, *Historical German Syntax*, pp. 37 ff. should be consulted.)

The numerals have undergone several changes from MHG to NHG. The cardinal numerals 'two' and 'three' are no longer inflected, the masc. and fem. nom. and acc. form in MHG, *drî*, with regular diphthongization of long *î* to *ei* (see pp. 69 f.) has become the NHG form for 'three', *drei*, and the MHG nom. and acc. neuter form *zwei* is the usual MHG form for 'two'. The nom. and acc. masc. in MHG *zwêne* and fem. *zwô* were regularly used up to the end of the eighteenth century. The form *zwo* still exists in NHG but is chiefly used to distinguish between *zwei* and *drei* in oral communication, e.g. over the telephone.

For the numeral 'one' the form *eins* is always used, which is the neuter nom. and acc., MHG *einez*, with the loss of the unstressed vowel. The genitive forms *zweier, dreier* are used in formal written style, *das Leben zweier Menschen, die Aussagen dreier zuerlässiger*

Zeugen, and in the words *zweierlei, dreierlei*. The dat. forms appear in the set expressions, *zu zweien, zu dreien*, but these are now mostly replaced by *zu zweit, zu dritt*. MHG *zwelf* has been replaced by *zwölf*, a sporadic change of rounding which has happened in a number of words (see pp. 88 f.), and MHG *eilf, zweinzec* have had their diphthong *ei* replaced by *e* and *a* respectively, NHG *elf, zwanzig*. The MHG long forms for 'seventeen' and 'seventy', *sibenzehen, sibenzic*, have been replaced by the short forms, *siebzehn* and *siebzig*. Among the ordinal numbers the MHG form *ander* 'second' has been replaced by the new formation *zweite* (there is also *zwote* formed from *zwo*). In MHG the suffix *-te* was used only after voiceless consonants while *-de* was used after stems ending in *-r* and *-n* to form ordinal numbers but in NHG the only suffix is *-te*: MHG *vierde, vierzehende, ahte*, NHG *vierte, vierzehnte, achte*. The ending *-te* has been levelled out in all ordinals in NHG.

Further reading

BRINKMANN, H., 'Das deutsche Adjectiv in synchronischer und dia-chronischer Sicht', *Wirkendes Wort*, 14 (1964), 94–104.
Duden Grammatik, 2nd edn. (Dudenverlag, Mannheim, 1966), 207–45.
PAUL, H., *Deutsche Grammatik*, vol. ii (1916–20; repr. Niemeyer, Halle, 1959), 119–25 and 139–42.

PRONOUNS IN NEW HIGH GERMAN

The development in the pronouns from MHG to NHG is due to sound change, the replacement of one form by another, and the lengthening of forms by the addition of suffixes. In the personal pronouns the nom., acc., and gen. of the third person sg. neuter became the same through sound change, the merger of MHG *s* and *z* in final position, MHG *ez, es*, NHG *es* (see pp. 80 f.). The vowels in MHG *in, im(e)* and *ir(e)* have been lengthened, partly because of the general lengthening of short vowels before final *r, n*, and *m*, or perhaps as part of the general lengthening of short vowels in open syllables in the alternative forms *ime, ire*. In NHG the acc. sg. masc. and the dat. pl. became differentiated, the acc. sg. masc. is *ihn*, MHG *in*, and the dat. pl. is *ihnen*, MHG *in*. The suffix *-en*

may come from the weak adjective inflexion. The first occurrence of
the form *ihnen*, as *inen*, occurs in Notker's writings but it does not
become the regular form until the sixteenth century.

The greatest changes have been brought about by the replacement of one form by another, leading to the abandonment of case
distinctions. The nom. sg. fem. third person sg., MHG *siu*, has
been replaced by the acc. sg. fem. form, MHG *sie*, to give NHG
sie [ziː]. The acc. : dat. distinction in the second person pl. has
been lost, the acc., MHG *iuch*, NHG *euch*, has displaced the MHG
dat. form *iu*. In the nom. acc. pl. form of the third person there was
a distinction in gender between masc. and fem. on the one hand,
MHG *sie*, and neuter on the other, MHG *siu*, but in NHG these
two forms have merged in *sie* [ziː] so that in NHG there is no
longer any distinction in gender in the pl. of the personal pronouns of the third person. The paradigms for the personal pronouns are as follows:

	sg.	pl.	sg.	pl.		sg.		pl.
					Masc.	Fem.	Neuter	
N	*ich*	*wir*	*du*	*ihr*	*er*	*sie*	*es*	*sie*
A	*mich*	*uns*	*dich*	*euch*	*ihn*	*sie*	*es*	*sie*
G	*meiner*	*unser*	*deiner*	*euer*	*seiner*	*ihrer*	*seiner*	*ihrer*
D	*mir*	*uns*	*dir*	*euch*	*ihm*	*ihr*	*ihm*	*ihnen*

There are archaic remnants of short forms for the gen., e.g. *mein*,
dein, as in *Vergißmeinnicht*. Even the longer gen. forms, with *-er*
by analogy with the gen. sg. fem. and gen. pl. strong adjectival
ending *-er*, are generally limited to formal style. They are chiefly
used after verbs which govern the gen., *erbarme dich meiner*. (For
the development of the pronouns of address, see Lockwood,
Historical German Syntax, pp. 61 ff.)

Changes of form have taken place in the MHG demonstrative
pronoun *dise*. The MHG *dirre* forms have been replaced by the
NHG *dies-* plus the appropriate ending; this has made the stem
uniform throughout the paradigm. All the forms ending in *-iu*
in MHG have been replaced by forms with *-e* in NHG, i.e. in the
nom. acc. pl. neuter and the nom. sg. fem. The forms with *-e* were
CG forms. This change resulted in the distinction in gender in
the nom. acc. pl. between the masc. and fem. with one form, and
the neuter with another form, being lost. The nom. acc. sg. neuter,

MHG *ditz(e)*, has been replaced by the NHG stem *dies-* plus the strong adjectival ending *-es*. The complete paradigm in NHG is:

sg.	Masculine	Feminine	Neuter	pl.	All genders
N	*dieser*	*diese*	*dieses*		*diese*
A	*diesen*	*diese*	*dieses*		*diese*
G	*dieses*	*dieser*	*dieses*		*dieser*
D	*diesem*	*dieser*	*diesem*		*diesen*

The definite article, *der*, has undergone the following changes. The MHG forms with *diu*, i.e. the nom. acc. pl. neuter and nom. sg. fem., have been replaced by the form *die*, the acc. sg. fem. and masc. fem. nom. acc. pl. form. This change has meant that there is no longer any distinction in gender in the pl. of the definite article in NHG. The nom. acc. sg. neuter, MHG *daz*, has become *das* in NHG. One of the features of the history of the definite article in NHG in its use as a relative pronoun is the development of the extended forms for the gen. sg. masc. *dessen*, for the gen. sg. fem. and pl. all genders, *deren* (these are also used attributively as demonstrative adjectives), and for the dat. pl. *denen*. Another extended form is *derer*, gen. pl. of the demonstrative pronoun. The suffix *-en* possibly comes from the weak adjective declension or the MHG negative particle *en-* in sentences such *des enist* (*dessen ist*), and the suffix *-er* from the strong adjective declension. The paradigm of the definite article in NHG is as follows:

sg.	Masculine	Feminine	Neuter	pl.	All genders
N	*der*	*die*	*das*		*die*
A	*den*	*die*	*das*		*die*
G	*des*	*der*	*des*		*der*
D	*dem*	*der*	*dem*		*den*

The indefinite article *ein* is declined like a strong adjective in NHG. In MHG and Early NHG there was only the form *ein* for all genders in the nom. sg., cf. Luther: *Ein feste Burg ist unser Gott*, but in NHG the fem. has the form *eine*.

Of the MHG interrogative pronouns, *swer*, *swaz*, and *weder* (except for relics in *entweder*, *weder . . . noch*) have died out. Of the MHG indefinite pronouns, *sum*, *iht* have died out and *nechein*, *dechein* have been replaced by *kein* which declines like either a strong or a weak adjective. The dat. sg. third person of the reflexive pronoun, MHG *im(e)*, has been replaced in NHG by the acc. form *sich*.

Further reading

Duden Grammatik, 2nd edn. (Dudenverlag, Mannheim, 1966), 245–87.
PAUL, H., *Deutsche Grammatik*, vol. ii (1916–20; repr. Niemeyer, Halle, 1959), 126–38.

VERB INFLECTION IN NEW HIGH GERMAN

NHG still retains the MHG division of verbs into strong and weak but within these two classes many changes have come about, as a result of either sound change or the replacement of one form by another. The strong verb vowel gradation classes have been obscured by sound changes and analogy. Although some attempts have been made to divide them into classes on purely synchronic grounds, it seems better to regard them as a closed set of irregular verbs.

Strong verbs in New High German

The most noticeable change among the strong verbs is that whereas in MHG the sg. and pl. in the past tense each had a different stem vowel, except in Classes VI and VII, in NHG all strong verbs have only one stem vowel in both the sg. and pl. of the past tense. The alternation of stem vowel was unnecessary since one vowel differing from the present stem vowel was quite sufficient to show that the verb was in the past tense. The NHG representatives of MHG Classes I, IV, and V show that the vowel of the pl. has been introduced into the sg.: Class I MHG *reit, riten*, NHG *ritt, ritten*; Class IV MHG *nam, nâmen*, NHG *nahm, nahmen*; MHG *gap, gâben*, NHG *gab* [gaɪp], *gaben*. In the case of the NHG representatives of MHG Class III: MHG *half, hulfen*, NHG *half, halfen*; MHG *bant, bunden*, NHG *band, banden*, the vowel of the sg. has been introduced into the pl. The NHG representatives of

MHG Class II verbs seem to show in the past tense the vowel of neither the MHG sg. nor pl. but that of the past participle which has been lengthened, MHG *gebogen*, NHG [gəbɔɪɡən]. This long *ō* is the same vowel as in the sg. past tense of MHG strong verbs of sub-class IIb, whose stems ended in MHG -*h* or an alveolar, e.g. *ziehen, zôch; bieten, bôt*. MHG Class IIa, *bouc, bugen, gebogen*, is represented in NHG by *bog, bogen, gebogen*, all of which have a long stem vowel. The sg. pl. stem vowel distinction in MHG *wart, wurden* was retained until recent times, but spelt *ward, wurden*; but it is now archaic.

Normally in NHG the stem vowel of the past tense subjunctive is formed by mutating the stem vowel of the indicative past tense where possible and adding the personal endings of the subjunctive, and these, with the exception of the third person sg., which is -*e*, are the same as the present indicative endings, e.g. *er bot, ritt*, indicative, *er böte, ritte*, subjunctive. With verbs of Class III the stem vowel of the subjunctive is *ü* with verbs whose stems end in a liquid or a nasal plus a stop or fricative: indicative, *er half, starb, verstand*, subjunctive, *er hülfe, stürbe, verstünde*. Those verbs whose stem ended in a double nasal have *ö* as their stem vowel in the subjunctive, *er begann*, indicative, *er begönne*, subjunctive. The forms with *u* are the original forms containing the MHG past pl. stem vowel. Before *nn*, as sporadically in other words, MHG *u* was lowered to *o*, and *ü* to *ö* (see p. 89). In most verbs of this class a new past tense subjunctive has been formed: *band—bände*, by mutation of the past tense sg. stem vowel. The forms with *ü* and *ö* still exist, but are usually regarded as formal and literary.

The majority of strong verbs which show mutation of the stem vowel in the second and third person sg. present in MHG do so in NHG as well. The only exceptions are: *rufen, ruft*, which also had unmutated forms in MHG, *kommen, kommt*, which had mutated forms as late as the eighteenth century, and the verbs *hauen, schaffen*, and *schnauben* which were conjugated weak as well as strong. The replacement of one form by another has taken place in the present tense of those verbs which in MHG showed an alternation of *iu—ie, i—e* between the sg. and pl. The first alternation, which was characteristic of Class II verbs, has been levelled out in favour of *ie*, [iː], the vowel of the pl. present and the infinitive. This has also happened in the imperative second person sg. and third person sg. present, where there are some archaic forms showing NHG *eu*, the regular development of MHG *iu*, e.g. *zeuch*, imperative of *ziehen*, *kreucht*, third person sg. of *kriechen*.

MHG		NHG	
sg.	pl.	sg.	pl.
ich biuge	*wir biegen*	*ich biege*	*wir biegen*
du biuges(t)	*ir bieget*	*du biegst*	*ihr biegt*
er biuget	*sie biegent*	*er biegt*	*sie biegen*

The alternation *i—e* is still found in Class III where the verb stem ends in a liquid followed by a consonant and in Classes IV and V. In NHG the first person sg., which had *i* as the stem vowel in MHG, has been replaced by a form with *e* from the pl. present or infinitive.

MHG		NHG	
sg.	pl.	sg.	pl.
ich hilfe	*wir helfen*	*ich helfe*	*wir helfen*
du hilfes(t)	*ir helfet*	*du hilfst*	*ihr helft*
er hilfet	*sie helfent*	*er hilft*	*sie helfen*

Classes VI and VII had the same stem vowel in both the sg. and pl. of the past tense in MHG and they may have provided the model for the elimination of the stem vowel difference between sg. and pl. in the past tense.

Grammatical change has largely been eliminated in NHG. This happened in various ways: e.g. the verbs died out, for instance *twahen* 'to wash', *rîsen* 'to rise', or they have become weak, e.g. *niesen, nieste, geniest*. However, the most important development has been the levelling-out of one consonant throughout the whole paradigm. In NHG *gedeihen, gediehen*, same form for the past plural and past participle (the old past participle, *gediegen*, has been retained as a separate adjective meaning 'solid, genuine, sterling'); *leihen, liehen, geliehen*; *genesen, genasen, genesen*; *lesen, lasen, gelesen*, the consonant of the infinitive and the present was levelled out into the other forms, whereas in NHG *frieren, froren, gefroren*; *verlieren, verloren*, same form for the past plural and past participle; *schlagen, schlugen, geschlagen*; *heben, hub, gehoben*; *fangen, fingen, gefangen*; *hangen, hingen, gehangen*, the consonant of the past plural and past participle has been levelled out into the other forms. In NHG *werden, wurden, geworden*; *finden, fanden, ge-*

funden the levelling-out of the *d* had largely taken place by Early NHG. (The OHG forms of all these verbs can be found on p. 119.) MHG *kiesen, kôs, kuren, gekoren* also levelled out the *r* of the past plural and past participle in Early NHG, but all the forms except the past participle have now died out. In NHG there are only four verbs which show grammatical change: *ziehen, zogen, gezogen*; *schneiden, schnitten, geschnitten*; *leiden, litten, gelitten*; and *sieden, sotten, gesotten*, the latter now mainly conjugated like a weak verb. There are also relics of grammatical change in the alternation *s—r* in word formation, e.g. *frieren, Frost*; *verlieren, Verlust*.

The personal endings of the strong verbs have remained virtually the same as those in MHG apart from the regular loss, or syncope, of MHG unstressed *-e-* before the endings *-st* and *-t* (except where the stem ends in a dental stop): MHG *du nimes(t)*, *er nimet*, NHG *du nimmst, er nimmt*, but MHG *du redes(t), er redet*, NHG *du redest, er redet*. If the stem of the strong verb ends in a dental stop and the stem vowel changes in the second and third person sg. present, no *-et* is added: *braten, er brät*; *treten, er tritt* (the second *t* is purely orthographic and does not affect the pronunciation). This loss of *-e-* even occurred with verbs whose stems ended in *d* or *t* in Early NHG, e.g. *er redt, er schneidt*. Subsequently an *-e-* was introduced in all weak verbs whose stem ended in *d* or *t* and in those strong verbs which did not undergo any stem vowel change in the sg. present, e.g. *er schneidet, er bindet*. The only other forms to change are the third person pl. present, MHG *nement*, and the second person sg. past tense, MHG *næme*. In NHG *nement* has been replaced by *nehmen*, which is either the third person pl. present subjunctive or the first person pl. present indicative (in NHG *sie sind* the original [t] has been retained). The second person sg. past tense *næme* has been replaced by *nahmst* in MHG with *-st* from the present tense which appeared as early as the twelfth century in the form *næmest*; then in Early NHG the vowel of the past tense pl. was introduced into the second person sg. past tense. As a result of these changes the subjunctive in NHG is only formally separate from the indicative in the second and third person sg. present, e.g. indicative *du hilfst, er hilft*, subjunctive *du helf(e)st, er helfe*. Those verbs whose stem vowels cannot change in the second and third person sg. present only differ in form from the indicative in the third person sg. subjunctive, e.g. indicative *er reitet, er bindet*, subjunctive *er reite*, *er binde*. In the past tense the subjunctive and indicative are distinct in every person in those verbs whose stem vowels can mutate, but in those verbs whose stem vowels cannot mutate, the distinction between the indicative and the subjunctive exists only in the third person sg., e.g. indicative *er ritt, er ging*, subjunctive *er ritte, er ginge*.

Many verbs which in MHG were strong have become weak in NHG: *grînen, nîden, rîhen, bellen, rechen, ziemen, bannen, schalten, walten*. This may be due to the fact that the infinitive of both strong and weak verbs was the same in MHG. As in NHG one could not tell from the infinitive alone whether a particular verb was weak or strong. The following paradigm shows the past tense, indicative, and subjunctive in MHG and NHG:

Indicative

MHG		NHG	
sg.	pl.	sg.	pl.
ich nam	*wir nâmen*	*ich nahm*	*wir nahmen*
du næme	*ir nâmet*	*du nahmst*	*ihr nahmt*
er nam	*sie nâmen*	*er nahm*	*sie nahmen*

Subjunctive

sg.	pl.	sg.	pl.
ich næme	*wir næmen*	*ich nähme*	*wir nähmen*
du næmes(t)	*ir næmet*	*du nähm(e)st*	*ihr nähm(e)t*
er næme	*sie næmen*	*er nähme*	*sie nähmen*

Both the present and past participles could be inflected in MHG in predicative position but this is no longer possible in NHG. The infinitive could also be inflected in the gen. and dat. case in MHG: *sehen, sehennes, sehenne*, but again this is not so in NHG. Originally the prefix *ge-*, used to form the past participle in NHG, had a perfective meaning and could be used throughout all forms of a verb in all tenses, but in NHG this prefix is used only with the past participle except when the verb ends in *-ieren, telephonieren*, past participle *telephoniert*, or when the verb has an inseparable prefix, e.g. *bezahlt, vergessen*, as against *abgegeben, aufgemacht*. Until the nineteenth century the past participles of some strong verbs with perfective meanings were often used without *ge-*, e.g. *Er ist auf Erden kommen arm* (Luther); *Was ich sucht', hab' ich funden* ... (W. Müller, 1794—1827). In the second person sg.

imperative form of all strong verbs except those which change their stem vowel from *e* to *i*, a final *-e* was added by analogy with the weak verbs: *trage, biete*, cf. *lies, nimm*. The final *-e* is, however, usually dropped in colloquial speech. The only exception to this is *siehe* 'behold', which is regarded as different from *sieh* 'look'.

Weak verbs in New High German

The two MHG classes of weak verbs have merged in a single class in NHG. MHG Class I weak verbs levelled out the vowel of the infinitive and present to the past tense and past participle: MHG *hœren, hôrte, gehôrt*, NHG *hören, hörte, gehört*, and in MHG Class II weak verbs the past tense ending *-ete* and the past participle ending *-et* became reduced to *-te* and *-t*, the ending of MHG Class I, except when the verb stem ended in *d* or *t*: MHG *lebete, gelebet*; NHG *lebte, gelebt*; *redete, geredet*; *rettete, gerettet*. There are a small number of verbs which still have *Rückumlaut* (see p. 121) in NHG: *rennen, nennen, kennen, brennen*, having *a* as their stem vowel in the past tense and past participle, e.g. *rannte, gerannt*. They also developed new past subjunctive forms in Early NHG by mutating the vowel of the past tense, e.g. *rennte*. The verbs *denken* and *bringen* change both their stem final consonant as well as their stem vowel to form the past tense and past participle, *dachte, gedacht, brachte, gebracht*. The NHG *decken* has levelled out the stem *deck-* in the past tense and participle, *deckte, gedeckt*, cf. MHG *dahte, gedaht*, probably to avoid a clash with MHG *dâhte* after its vowel was shortened. The verbs *denken* and *bringen* have formed new past subjunctive forms by mutating their past tense stem vowel, *dächte, brächte*. Apart from *denken, bringen*, and the *Rückumlaut* verbs like *rennen* NHG weak verbs have only one past tense paradigm which must serve for both the indicative and the subjunctive (*brauchen* has a subjunctive form *bräuchte*, widely used in speech and to be found in some authors, but not accepted by *Duden*). For this reason a construction using the form *würde* of the modal verb *werden* has come to be used as a paraphrase for the subjunctive. The only really strong subjunctive form is the past tense subjunctive of strong verbs and even this has lost its past tense meaning and has simply come to be used as a sign that the sentence or clause is in the subjunctive mood. The direct result of the partial coalescence of the indicative and subjunctive in NHG has been that the category of tense in sentences where the subjunctive is used has become unimportant (cf. Lockwood, *Historical German Syntax*, pp. 127 ff.). Most of the changes in the inflexions of the verbs are part of a general tendency to eliminate the categories of person and number, and to restrict the use of the subjunctive. On the positive side, the category of tense has become important in the indicative. For the six personal endings in the present indicative in NHG there are only four distinct forms: *-e*, first person sg., *-(e)st*, second person sg., *-(e)t*, third person sg. and second person pl., *-en*, first and third person pl. The situation is the same in the past tense indicative: six personal endings but only four distinct forms, zero, i.e. the bare past tense stem, *nahm*, *sagte*, first and third person sg., *-st*, second person sg., *-t*, second person pl., *-en*, first and third pl.

Irregular verbs

(a) Preterite-present verbs

Those verbs whose second person sg. present indicative ending was *-t* in MHG, *darft*, *maht*, *solt*, had the ending *-st* transferred to them by analogy with the strong and weak verbs and other preterite-present verbs such as *kanst* (those verbs whose stem ends in [s] in NHG merely add *-t*, *mußt*, *weißt*). Most changes among these verbs amount to idiosyncratic changes in individual forms. NHG *wissen* has a past tense with *u* as the stem vowel in NHG, *wußte*, which first appeared in the fifteenth century. The vowel probably became rounded after the initial *w*, MHG *wiste*. The subjunctive form is *wüßte* and the past participle *gewußt*. MHG *künnen*, *mügen*, *dürfen* had infinitive and present pl. forms with and without stem vowel mutation, but in NHG only the forms with stem vowel mutation exist in these categories. This change was by analogy with the subjunctive forms and also with the weak MHG *Rückumlaut* verbs, e.g. *hœren*, *hôrte*, which levelled out the mutated vowel of the infinitive and present in NHG. MHG *müezen* had no unmutated vowel in the infinitive but in NHG the stem vowel has not merely been monophthongized but also shortened (see p. 72). In NHG *sollen* is the only preterite-present verb with an unmutated back stem vowel. The vowel of the sg., MHG *er sol*, has been generalized to the pl., MHG *wir suln*, NHG *wir sollen*. In *künnen* and the past tense *kunde* the stem vowel has been lowered before a nasal (see p. 90). The stem vowel has also been lowered, and lengthened, in NHG *mögen*. In NHG the MHG verb *türren* has died out; the impersonal verb MHG *tougen* has become weak, NHG *taugen*, *taugte*, as has MHG *günnen*, OHG *gi-unnan*, with a lowering of *ü* before a nasal, NHG *gönnen, gönnte*. The vowel of the infinitive has been generalized throughout all the forms. The subjunctive is formed in NHG as in MHG, by mutating the stem vowel of the past tense, except for NHG *sollen* which does not undergo mutation but has the same vowel as the indicative, *sollte*. The present subjunctive mostly occurs in the third person sg. and ends in -*e*, *könne, möge*, etc.

(b) The verb 'to be'

Of the various stems which were used to form the parts of the verb 'to be' in OHG and MHG, the following have become standard in NHG: the infinitive *sein* has ousted *wesen*, the latter surviving only as a noun, *das Wesen*. In the past tense the alternation between *s* and *r*, MHG *ich was, wir wâren*, has been levelled out in NHG, *ich war, wir waren*, but the past participle *gewesen* has retained the *s*. The second person sg. past tense, MHG *wære*, has been replaced by *warst* in NHG. In MHG both *gewesen* and *gewest*, and in Alemannic dialects *gesîn*, are recorded as past participles of the verb 'to be', but in NHG only *gewesen* is recognized as the standard form. The imperative forms for the second person sg., MHG *wis, bis*, have been replaced by the form *sei* from the subjunctive. The MHG present participle *wesende* has been replaced by the form *seiend*, but the former remains in such forms as *anwesend, abwesend*.

(c) Other irregular verbs

The verb *tun*, MHG *tuon*, has levelled out the vowel of the past tense pl. into the sg.: MHG *ich tete, wir tâten*; NHG *ich tat, wir taten*, and the final -*e* of the sg. form has been dropped by analogy with the strong verbs. The final -*e* of the first person sg. present, NHG *ich tue*, comes from the regular weak and strong verbs, cf. *ich sage, ich helfe*. MHG *gên* and *stên* have developed dissyllabic forms in the infinitive and first person sg. and first and third person pl. in NHG: *gehen, stehen*; *ich gehe, ich stehe*; *wir gehen, wir stehen*; *sie gehen, sie stehen*. The stem vowels of the MHG past indicative, e.g. *ich gienc, ich stuont*; *wir giengen, wir stuonden*, were monophthongized and shortened in Early NHG: *ich ging, ich stund*; *wir gingen, wir stunden*. From the latter part of the seventeenth century the forms *stund* and *stunden* were replaced by the NHG forms *stand, standen*, probably containing the stem vowel of the past participle; the forms *ging, gingen* are the NHG forms. The MHG second person sg. imperative forms, *ganc, stant*, have been replaced in NHG by *gehe, stehe*. In NHG there is no longer any distinction between the contracted forms of the verb 'to have', MHG *hân*, and the full form *haben*. The full forms are used in the infinitive, *haben*, the first person sg. and pl., *ich habe, wir haben*, the second person pl., *ihr habt*, and the third person pl., *sie haben*. The contracted forms are found in the second and third person sg., *du hast, er hat*, with a shortening of MHG long *â*. In the past tense the short form *hatte*, from OHG *habēta*, is the standard indicative form in NHG. It has replaced MHG *hete*, which is still used in NHG, but as the subjunctive, *hätte*, probably to enable a distinction to be made between the past indicative and subjunctive. The past participle is a full form, *gehabt*, although in Early NHG the contracted form *gehat* also existed in CG. The forms with *o* in NHG *wollen* are due to a rounding of *e* to *o* after *w*. The past participle *gewollt* was not formed until NHG. The second person sg. present indicative, MHG *du wilt*, has the ending *-st* in NHG, *du willst*, by analogy with the strong, weak, and preterite-present verbs. The third person pl. present indicative in MHG, *wellent*, is *wollen* in NHG, the same form as the subjunctive. The past tense indicative and subjunctive are the same, *ich wollte*, etc.

Further reading

BACH, H., *Laut- und Formenlehre der Sprache Luthers* (Levin & Munksgaard, Copenhagen, 1934), 86–116.

Duden Grammatik, 2nd edn. (Dudenverlag, Mannheim, 1966), 68–134.

HALLE, M., 'The German Conjugation', *Word*, 9 (1953), 45–53.

McLINTOCK, D. R., 'Die umgelauteten Praeterito-Praesentia und der Synkretismus im deutschen Verbalsystem', *Beiträge zur Geschichte und Literatur der deutschen Sprache*, 83 (Tübingen, 1961), 271–7.

MAIER, G., 'Das *ge-* Partizip im Nhd.', *Zeitschrift für deutsche Wortforschung*, 1 (1901), 281–318.

NEWMAN, J., 'Levelling in the German Verb Paradigm', *Acta Linguistica Hafniensia*, 15 (1974), 91–100.

INDEX OF WORDS

legen, past tense in NHG 76; conj. in MHG 139
leggen, conj. in OHG 139
legō (Latin), present tense 114
leicht 92
leiden 22; parts in NHG 157
leihen, parts in NHG 156
leihwan (Gothic) 32
leípō (Greek), principal parts 116
leise 149
leiten 22
lember, Lämmer 85; pl. forms in MHG 129 f.
lempir (Bavarian OHG) 50
lernēn 121
lesan 118; parts in OHG 119
leschen, löschen 88
lesen 69, 74, 79; past tense in NHG 80; parts in NHG 156
lētan (Gothic) 46
leu, lau 78
lewe 88
Licht 22, 72, 77. 83
līdan, parts in OHG 119
lidum (OLG) 34
lieben 71 f., 78
lied 64
lieht 72, 77, 83
liep, lieb(es) 8
liet 67
lifa (ON) 45
ligan (Gothic) 32
liggen 118
līhan 32, 117; parts in OHG 120
lîhte 92
linēn 51
liod 64
liogan 117; present tense in OHG 54
liogente 54
list 130
līthan (OLG) 34
little xiv, 46
liute 64, 67
loben xiv, 16
Loch 18
Löffel 88
loge 82
logos (Greek) 100
lohhir, löcher 57
Lohn, lōn, lôn 52, 87
loub 106
löuber 67
loufan, parts in OHG 119; *loufit* 57

loufen 57; parts in MHG 138; *löufet* 57; 64
looks xiv
Los, losen 81
löwe, Löwe xiv, 78, 88
Luke 71
lúō (Greek), optative forms 115
luog 106
lupus (Latin) 101
lutschen xiv
lützel, comparison in MHG 133
luzzil, comparison in OHG 110; 46

machen xv
machōn, mahhōn 47, 121
Macht 34
mächtig 73
mad 14, 17
Mädel(s) 146
mádhyas (Sanskrit) 30
mâhe 88
mähtic 73
mahtīg 57
máiza (Gothic) 5, 34
maken xv
makon (OLG) 47
malan 119
man 113, 136
mâne 26, 88, 92
manec 69, 76
Mann xiv, 96, 98, 108, 145
manne 69, 76
mânôt 88
manus (Latin) 100
Mantel xiv, 21
Maß 144
māter (Latin) 30
matris (Latin) 100
mausern 81
mâze 144
medius (Latin) 28, 30, 32, 41
Meer 83
mégas (Greek) 30, 32
mein xiii, xiv, 8, 16, 25, 70
meirr (ON) 5
men 96
mensa (Latin), sg. forms 95, 97, 100, 102
Mensch 143
mēro 5, 34
messe, Messe 69, 74, 79, 80
mêre 73
metá (Greek) 30